Naturally Intelligent Systems

Naturally Intelligent Systems

Maureen Caudill and Charles Butler

A Bradford Book
The MIT Press
Cambridge, Massachusetts
London, England

Second printing, 1991

This book was set in Palatino and Avant Garde using Ready, Set, Go!™ 4.5 by Letraset® USA, Paramus, NJ.
Ready, Set, Go! is a trademark of Manhattan Graphics Corporation.

Library of Congress Cataloging-in-Publication Data

Caudill, Maureen.
   Naturally intelligent systems / Maureen Caudill and Charles Butler.
      p. cm.
   "A Bradford Book."
   ISBN 0-262-03156-6
   1. Neural computers. I. Butler, Charles. II. Title.
QA76.5.C387   1989
006.3—dc20   89-13218
                                                                         CIP

Contents

Acknowledgments

We would like to thank those who assisted us in bringing this book to print. We received a number of suggestions and comments from people; if we failed to follow them properly, the responsibility is ours. Substantial detailed comments from Claude Cruz and Pinchus Laufer were especially helpful. Similarly, the people of MIT Press/ Bradford Books, and in particular Joanna Poole, have been more than helpful with suggestions, advice, and emotional support. It is difficult to imagine a more pleasant and professional staff to work with. We would like also to thank Tom Niemann, who conceived and drew the cartoons found in this book.

Maureen would also like to express special appreciation to Harriet Caudill, who so clearly exemplifies exactly why it is people so often thank their mothers. She provided support, encouragement, and not a little copy-editing and proofreading assistance as needed. Charles is grateful to Mary Odell, his wife, for her patience and encouragement; she sort of thought he could do it all along.

Finally, we would like to thank our readers. This book has been more than two years in the making and has been written and rewritten several times. Many of you have been waiting for it for many months. Thank you for your patience; we hope you find the wait worthwhile.

Part I

Each goodly thing is hardest to begin.
—Spenser

I'll tell you why we need "natural intelligence":
We're short of the human variety!

To you a robot is a robot.... But you haven't worked with them.... They're a cleaner, better breed than we are.
— Isaac Asimov

1 Natural Intelligence

The worlds of science and science fiction have often become one and the same. *From the Earth to the Moon* (Jules Verne, 1865) has become reality, as have laser beams, miraculous medical advances, genetic engineering, and other scientific marvels. In few other places has this technical wizardry been more evident than in the development of computers. Yet with all its marvelous capability and power, the computer has remained little more than a super-fast, super-sophisticated adding machine, performing wondrous feats more by its ability to run very fast than by any level of understanding of the problem at hand. We do not yet have machines that *think*.

Researchers have long been looking for a way to make an artificial system that has at least some ability to think. Science fiction depicts such systems frequently, ranging from the mechanistic droids of *Star Wars* to the humanlike Commander Data, android of *Star Trek: The Next Generation*. But such systems belong far in the future; we cannot come close to building them today. Although they are not yet reality, however, some researchers are taking the first steps toward building truly intelligent devices. The current experimental systems have many of the characteristics of biological computers—brains in other words—and are beginning to be built to perform a variety of tasks that are difficult or impossible to do with conventional computers. Because of their structural similarity to biological intelligent systems we call them "naturally intelligent systems."

This book is about these new brainlike devices, which are just beginning to come out of the laboratory into the world of applications. Called neural networks, or neurocomputers, they are designed to mimic the architecture of the brain. They are massively parallel in nature, just as the brain is, but not in the sense of traditional parallel computer designs. Moreover, they are not the artificial intelligence computer systems that have received so much publicity in past years. Neural networks are not programmed with a computer language the way conventional computers are but are literally trained to behave in the way we want them to.

How do these systems work if they are not programmed? What can they do, and what can they not do? What kinds of applications can we expect them to perform today, and what lies ahead? These are the questions this book addresses. We will review the basic neural network architectures, showing how they work and how they can be used as well as their limitations and problems. Throughout we take occasional forays into the world of applications, explaining how these systems are being used today to solve problems in such varied fields as speech understanding, robotics, and autonomous vehicle control. Finally, we give an honest appraisal of where we think these systems will go in the near future.

Neural networks are exciting systems, and they have the potential to be so revolutionary that it is easy to hype them far beyond their current capabilities. The fact of the matter is that this technology is still in its infancy, so we will be as honest about the current state of the art as we can be. We will present the complete picture, warts and all, so that you can make up your own mind about the field's promise and potential. Let's begin by looking at what a neural network is.

Neural Networks in a Nutshell

Suppose Sam the engineer wants to divide one seven-digit number by another. He will undoubtedly reach for his hand calculator, or, if he expects to do similar operations often, he will write a small program for his personal computer. If one of these instruments isn't available, he might grudgingly resort to pencil and paper. He would almost certainly not be tempted to try the division in his head. Unless he were an idiot savant, one of those rare persons able to do seemingly impossible feats of mathematics or memorization, he simply couldn't do it without external aid.

But suppose Sam wanted to find a familiar face in a crowded room. He wouldn't need a computer; he could easily do it himself. Yet the most advanced digital computer would find this task almost impossible.

We can learn two things from Sam's case: (1) digital computers and brains are handy to have, and (2) digital computers and brains do fundamentally different things. Most of the operations a digital computer does well boil down to adding, moving, and comparing data. Most of the operations the brain does well can be characterized as pattern processing. This generalization may seem surprising at first, but, in fact, in activities as diverse as understanding speech, recognizing a face, and controlling an automobile in traffic, the brain is really just recognizing and acting on constantly changing patterns of input stimuli.

For a long time people have tried to make a computer that treats information as patterns in the same way that the brain does. For many years they met with only limited success because the job proved to be more difficult and frustrating than they expected. A great deal of progress has been made over the past two decades, however, and a new growth industry, neural networks, has developed.

A good starting definition of a neural network is that it is a type of information processing system whose architecture is inspired by the structure of biological neural systems. (By architecture, we mean the way the components are connected together. We treat structure and architecture as synonyms in this book.) In particular, neural networks attempt to mimic the functions of the central nervous system and some of the sensory organs attached to it. If we are successful at replicating some of the major cognitive and sensorimotor functions of the brain, we know right off the kinds of things we expect neural networks to do well: the same kinds of things that animals do well. We had better not expect neural networks to be better than humans, or flies, or even ants at many endeavors for a while, however. Neurophysiologists, those scientists who study the makeup and function of the brain and other parts of the nervous system, estimate that humans have about ten billion brain cells or neurons. A fly's brain has about a million. Since the largest neurocomputers are able to mimic the action of only a few million neurons, we might say that they possess "fly power."

Think about what a fly can do, however. First, it flies. It interprets the complex images formed by its compound eye system in order to find or avoid particular shapes and objects. It recognizes the

presence of minute concentrations of organic molecules in the sur-
rounding air as it searches for food or a mate. It performs exacting
and complicated motor actions with its antennas and appendages as
it sips its food or washes its face. And it even knows how to
approach a ceiling at an astonishing velocity (for its size), come to a
sudden halt, and land upside down. Have you ever seen a fly muff a
landing? Not bad for a million neurons.

The fly's brain has a highly structured organization that provides these sophisticated capabilities. Although we compared current neurocomputers to a fly a moment ago, they aren't really up to a
fly's brain; they have far fewer interconnections among their artificial neurons than a fly has.

The brains of humans are incredibly more complex than those of
flies. The motor skills of a trained athlete, musician, or dancer, the
abstract intellectual achievements of philosophers or mathemati-
cians, and the creative genius of a skilled artist or writer attest to the
complexity and versatility of the human brain. But simple acts like
recognizing a familiar human face, riding a bicycle, following a moving object with our eyes, and even combing our hair are also amaz-
ing in their own right.

If animals and people are so good at such tasks, why do we need
artificial neural networks? To begin answering this question, let's go
back to Sam and think again about our need for traditional digital
computers. Although we invented Sam and his grudging attitude
toward a pencil-and-paper solution to his division problem, there is
little doubt that most people would share his response to the prospect of dividing one long number into another. There are a lot of
other tasks, like Sam's, that people find onerous and that digital computers can do instead. More important, the simplest digital computer
can perform these calculations millions or even billions of times
faster than the best-trained person. Other tasks are simple enough
and do not require blinding speed but must be done over and over
all day, such as sensing traffic conditions at an intersection and
changing the duty cycle of traffic signals to maintain an efficient traffic flow pattern. Even for this simple application, keeping track of
the different sensor inputs at a large intersection and responding
with the proper action could tax the ability of a well-trained and
patient human.

Neurocomputers offer a similar advantage. Eventually they will
be able to perform many pattern processing tasks that humans, or
even digital computers, are able to perform, but they will do them
more economically, reliably, and rapidly. Because they mimic the

operation of natural neural systems, they will also be able to carry out tasks that traditional digital computers can do only with difficulty, if at all. Moreover, there are jobs that need humanlike judgment and learning ability but are too dangerous for a human to do, jobs like cleaning up nuclear waste or assembling future space stations. Neurocomputers will (probably) not complain about being given these dangerous assignments, and they will be cheaper to train and to use.

There is a more subtle reason why we expect neurocomputers to become indispensable. Any successful new technology creates its own set of applications that did not exist at the time it was conceived. For instance, at the time the telephone, automobile, and microprocessor were introduced, few could predict that these technologies would become essential to the ways we live and work. Yet these and many other less obvious bits of technology have become necessities for our everyday existence. We think a similar self-generating process will follow the introduction of the neurocomputer. Neural networks will create their own niche.

Characteristics of Neural Networks

What are some of the characteristics of neural networks that make them potentially so useful? For now, we are just going to make a list; we will take up each characteristic in more detail later in the book. Note that we are listing the characteristics of ideal neural networks. We will point out distinctions between the ideal and the real as we examine different ways to implement neural networks. (Several new terms introduced in this list are explained in detail in the chapters that follow.)

1. A neural network is composed of a number of very simple processing elements that communicate through a rich set of interconnections with variable weights or strengths. In this book we call these simple processing elements "neurodes."

2. Memories are stored or represented in a neural network in the pattern of variable interconnection weights among the neurodes. Information is processed by a spreading, constantly changing pattern of activity distributed across many neurodes.

3. A neural network is taught or trained rather than programmed. It is even possible to construct systems capable of independent or autonomous learning; some neural networks are capable of learning by trial and error.

4. Instead of having a separate memory and controller, plus a stored external program that dictates the operation of the system as in a digital computer, the operation of a neural network is implicitly controlled by three properties: the transfer function of the neurodes, the details of the structure of the connections among the neurodes, and the learning law the system follows.

5. A neural network naturally acts as an associative memory. That is, it inherently associates items it is taught, physically grouping similar items together in its structure. A neural network operated as a memory is content addressable; it can retrieve stored information from incomplete, noisy, or partially incorrect input cues.

6. A neural network is able to generalize; it can learn the characteristics of a general category of objects based on a series of specific examples from that category.

7. It is highly fault tolerant, or "fail soft." This characteristic is sometimes also called "graceful degradation." A neural network keeps working even after a significant fraction of its neurodes and interconnections have become defective. Its performance degrades slowly and smoothly as neurodes and interconnections fail.

8. A neural network innately acts as a processor for time-dependent spatial patterns, or spatiotemporal patterns.

9. A neural network can be self-organizing. Some neural networks can be made to generalize from data patterns used in training without being provided with specific instructions on exactly what to learn. This effect is best appreciated through an example, which we will present in a later chapter.

Comparing a Neural Network to a Digital Computer

The secret of the performance of a neural network lies in its physical structure or architecture. To appreciate the revolutionary nature of the neural network as a processor architecture, it will be useful to compare it to a conventional serial digital processor, or uniprocessor. (We will look at the relationship of neural networks to parallel processors and parallel digital computers after describing the architecture of a neural system.)

A typical digital microcomputer is quite simple in principle. The microprocessor, acting on instructions from the software program stored in its memory, dictates what operation is to be done at a given time, sends and receives information to and from the memory, and performs the elemental bit-level operations out of which the more complex computations and logic operations are constructed. As well as holding the stored program that guides the steps of the microprocessor, the internal memory is used to store initial data that the program needs, along with intermediate and final results of computations before they are transferred to some form of permanent memory. Key to this operation is the fact that the information being processed has been broken into individual and discrete numeric chunks. These chunks are numbers, perhaps binary or octal or hexadecimal, which encode the data to be processed. The input/output (I/O) interface units —there are usually several—allow the system to communicate with the outside world. Magnetic disks, video terminals, and other peripherals are attached to the system through these units.

The computer has internal pathways over which the parts of the system communicate. These buses are essentially cables composed of a number of parallel conductors over which digital signals representing memory locations and control instructions are transmitted from the processor to other parts of the system and over which data are shared among the processor, memory, and I/O units. Somewhere in the system, often part of the processor itself, there is a clock. This clock paces the operation of the central system, making sure that every part stays synchronized with every other part. This lockstep operation is the essence of digital computers.

For our purposes, the important observations are these: (1) the system operates on discrete chunks of data; it is digital; (2) a memory system records the data to be processed, a sequence of specific instructions on how to process the data, and the answers that result, it is serial; and (3) the system operates by a continuous cycle of fetch-

The Irony of von Neumann's Architecture

There is a bittersweet story circulating within the neural network community connected with the name of John von Neumann. The real hope of von Neumann and his coworkers, the story goes, was to construct parallel processors capable of manipulating large blocks of information at the same time. When it became apparent to him that his dream could not be realized using the technology of his day, he suggested key changes to the serial architecture developed for ENIAC in the mid-1940s by Presper Eckert and John Mauchly at the University of Pennsylvania: (1) to utilize the binary number system instead of the decimal system used in the ENIAC and (2) to store the program in the memory of the machine instead of supplying it from the outside or making it part of the circuitry of the machine. The result of these suggestions was the EDVAC, the first modern digital computer.

There is no doubt about von Neumann's contribution to the EDVAC. A brief investigation we made, however, has failed to verify that von Neumann was actively working on parallel machine design when he suggested the architectural changes that brought him his reputation as father of the modern serial computer. It appears that he was well aware of the neural model introduced by Warren McCulloch and Walter Pitts in the early 1940s. It seems likely that some have mistakenly attributed von Neumann's work in the late 1950s on learning automata to an earlier time. If the circulating story is correct, however, it is an exquisite irony that parallel processors and neural architectures, which he is said to have pioneered, are continually compared to the "von Neumann approach" to computing.

ing an instruction from memory (along with any necessary data items), executing that instruction, and storing the result of the instruction, if any, back into memory. A computer with these design characteristics is often described as having a von Neumann architecture.

Neural networks conform to none of these observations. They are neither digital nor serial; instead they are analog (continuous valued) and parallel. Neural networks do not contain data and algorithmic instructions in a separate memory system; instead they store data throughout the network in the pattern of weights, interconnections and states of the neurodes. Finally neural networks do not follow the fetch-execute-store process of the von Neumann digital computer; instead they globally respond to input pattern stimuli. The operation of a neural network thus differs markedly from that of a digital computer.

Safe upon the solid rock the ugly houses stand;
Come and see my shining palace built upon the sand.
— Edna St. Vincent Millay

2 Building Blocks of Neural Networks

We come now to the structure and operation of neural networks. To prepare the way, let us first present a simple overview of the building blocks of biological neural systems. We have sketched a generic biological neural cell, or neuron, in figure 2.1 and labeled the important parts.

A neuron accepts input from a large number of similar neurons, processes these inputs, and sends copies of its single output to yet other neurons over a network of interconnections called "axons." The axons send out many branches called "axon collaterals." Each collateral ends at the input of another neuron in a special connection called a "synapse," shown in the figure as broadened areas on the axon collaterals. The parts of a neuron to which these synapses usually connect are called "dendrites." Many, but not all, synapses are adaptive or plastic; that is, they can increase or decrease in strength under the proper conditions. As a result, they can have differing strengths or synaptic weights. Synapses also come in two forms: they can have an excitatory (positive) or an inhibitory (negative) effect on the activity of their associated neuron. Last, synapses are unidirectional; they pass signals in only one direction.

The structure of an artificial neural network mimics this very simplified view of biological neural architecture. An artificial neural network has only three building blocks: neurodes (an artificial model of the biological neuron), interconnects (the paths or links between

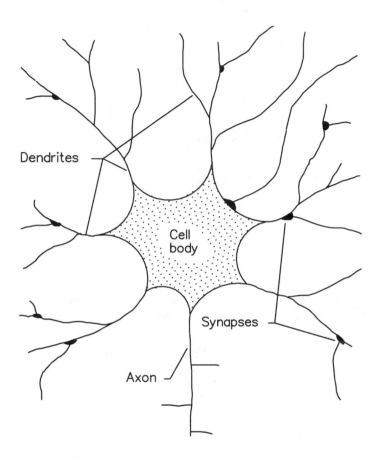

Figure 2.1 A typical biological neuron.

neurodes), and synapses (the junction where an interconnect meets a neurode). These correspond to the neurons, axons, and synapses of biological systems.

A neurode accepts input from a large number of other neurodes, processes these inputs, and sends copies of its single output to yet other neurodes over a network of interconnects. Each such output interconnect ends at the input of the recipient neurode in a special junction or termination we call a synapse in analogy to biological systems. Like biological synapses, artificial synapses are unidirectional. They may be plastic or fixed and can have varying weights or

Why *Neurode?*

There is as yet no consensus concerning the terminology used in the neural network field, and our use of the words *neurode*, *interconnect*, and *synapse* to designate the principal components of an artificial neural network is a carefully considered compromise. On the one hand, we think that avoiding biological terminology when referring to artificial neural systems is a virtue. The use of a distinct set of terms indicates that the corresponding components are not equivalent and reduces confusion when both artificial and biological networks are being discussed. On the other hand, the practice of using biological terminology is widespread. Thus, although we are uncomfortable with using the term *synapse* in connection with artificial neural systems, we find no other existing term suitable and have not been able to invent one that we think is better.

Such is not the case for the biological term *neuron*. Although this word is preferred by some, *processing element* is also widely used. Because the latter is awkward, however, we have coined the term *neurode*. We like the word because its root conveys that it corresponds to the biological neuron, and its suffix signifies that it is an artificial system element.

strengths. And they can be either excitatory (positive) or inhibitory (negative). When we connect hundreds or millions of these simple components together, they resemble a complicated web or net. It is this resemblance that gives neural networks their name.

The Anatomy of a Neurode

Let's see how a neurode operates and follow that by looking at how patterns of neurode activity are transmitted from place to place within a network. Each neurode receives a large number of individual input signals that together constitute an input pattern. This input pattern causes the neurode to reach some level of activity. If the activity is strong enough, the neurode, like its biological analog, generates a single output signal that is transmitted over the neurode's interconnects to other neurodes or to the outside world. For all intents and purposes, the neurode computes a mapping, or a function that associates a given level of input stimulus to a particular level of output activity. This overall mapping is usually called the transfer function for the neurode.

The computation of a transfer function is a three-step process. First, the neurode must figure out its total incoming stimulation from all sources. Next it must decide the level of activity that total incoming stimulation corresponds to. Finally, it must generate the appropriate output signal for the resulting level of activity and transmit it along its output interconnect. The transfer function appears in many guises in the literature; this three-step process is sometimes implicitly merged into a two- or even a single-step procedure. Buried beneath all the variations, however, is the same basic procedure of computing input-activation-output. For the moment we will separate these three steps so we can see each clearly; later we will assume the three-step process is implicit and will simplify it as appropriate to the discussion.

First, let's consider the way a neurode can compute its net input, or stimulation. For now, we assume that all input signals are of the same type and that every neurode performs a simple weighted sum of the many input signals brought to it by the interconnects. The weighting factors are the synapse weights. We can compute the weighted sum by multiplying each input signal by the synaptic weight associated with that interconnect and then algebraically adding the result. This particular computational technique is by no means the only one we could use, and we will run into neural network architectures that require modification of this simple scheme. We could, for instance, provide several kinds of special-purpose direct inputs to each neurode. Additionally we could put a threshold on each input signal, requiring input signals to be at least the size of the threshold before contributing to the weighted sum. We could also use a more complex combining strategy, such as multiplying all inputs together or delaying some inputs before acting on them. In fact, biological neurons display a large repertoire of input-combining treatments. But the linear algebraic sum assumption we have made is by far the simplest and most common in artificial systems and serves well as an introduction to neural network design principles.

Next, we must see how the neurode computes its activation level for a given input level. Note, by the way, that at this stage all knowledge of which specific input signals are strong and which are weak has been lost. The details of input patterns are no longer available, and only the net effect is recorded. It is the net amount of input arriving at the neurode that determines the activation level. (Of course, this net input stimulation level is directly determined by the correspondence between input signals and weights, but a large signal arriving through a weak synapse may have precisely the same effect as a weak signal arriving through a strong synapse.) In various implementations of artificial neural networks, activity or activation refers to such things as DC voltage level, pulse repetition rate, or some other physical quantity used to measure the level of excitation of the neurode. We have so far introduced no specific form for a neurode, however, and activation is just an abstraction in this chapter. A large number of choices exist for this operation, and designers are usually free to choose the one that works best for their application. The exact form chosen generally depends on design decisions made on other levels. It is often, although not always, of the form of an S-shaped (sigmoid) curve, with asymptotic limits usually at 0 and +1.0. Except for the very simplest networks we discuss in part II, the activation function is a nonlinear one; it does not correspond to a straight line plot. For a number of reasons we will discuss later in the book, including compatibility with biological systems, this is generally the best choice.

Finally, neurodes must translate this internal activity level into an output signal. Quite commonly, the output signal is merely the activation level, although it is often modified by a threshold value; that is, the neurode's output does not begin to rise until the activation exceeds some minimum value. As with the activation function, the designer adopts the output function that best achieves the desired design goals. The key notion here is that whatever the output value, that same value is transmitted along all output interconnects to all receiving neurodes. The output value is not split or apportioned among all possible receivers; every receiving neurode sees the same signal from this transmitting neurode.

The Network in Action

We cannot just throw neurodes and interconnects together in a random way and sit back, expecting something magical to happen. Neural nets work only if they have a suitable underlying structure. Designers have often found that the most appropriate arrangement

Art Imitating Nature

If we were truly to imitate nature in designing a neurode, what would its characteristics be? Well, for one thing, it would be a pulsed device. A typical neuron emits voltage spikes at rates between about one and a few hundred pulses per second, depending on its activity level. Thus, it could not exhibit negative output since the concept of a negative spike rate is meaningless. Moreover, its neurode transfer function would invariably be nonlinear; the activity of a neuron saturates for large summed input values. Also the output of our true-to-nature neurode would show thresholding; the output spike rate of a neuron does not begin to rise until its internal activity level exceeds some threshold value. Finally, biological synapses are actually electrochemical in nature rather than strictly electronic. Neurons use special chemicals called neurotransmitters to aid the transmission of information across the synaptic junction. The net effect of these transmissions can be either to excite the receiving neuron or to inhibit its activity.

In artificial neural networks, pulsed operation has seldom been used for neurodes, and designs that violate one or more of the other characteristics are common. As someone has said, if we always had to imitate nature, airplanes would have feathers and cars would have legs.

is that of interconnected layers of neurodes, much as is found in the cortex and other parts of the brain. Although there are uses for networks containing only one layer of neurodes, or even a single neurode, most applications require networks that contain two, three, or more layers of neurodes. In later chapters we will look at some fundamental reasons why this is so and will introduce several network designs based on a hierarchical layer structure. For now, however, let's look in a general way at how a pattern of neurode activity gets transmitted and transformed as it moves from one layer to another.

In chapter 1 we noted that a neural network processes information as a spreading pattern of activity distributed across many neurodes and that it stores learned information as patterns of synapse weights. These two intimately related concepts are at the heart of neural network operation. Let us look at them carefully.

We can most easily see how activation patterns get transmitted between layers of a network if we consider a concrete example. Assume the two-layer network shown in figure 2.2. In the figure, each of the neurodes in the input layer is connected to each of the neurodes in the second layer. Such an arrangement is called a "fully connected" network layer. For this case, none of the neurodes is connected to other neurodes within their own layers. The input pattern, or input vector, contains five elements, each presented to a single neurode in the input layer by a direct connection.

Because there are three neurodes in the second layer of the network, each input-layer neurode has three output connections—one for each second-layer neurode. Each second-layer neurode, in turn, has five inputs—one from each of the five input-layer neurodes. Thus, eight neurodes have 5 x 3, or 15, interlayer connections, or interconnects. Each interconnect ends in a synapse, so there are also

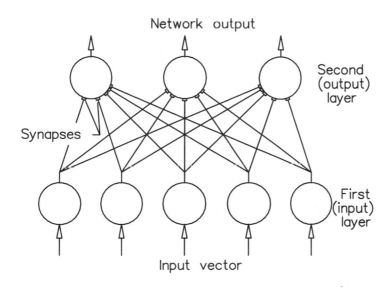

Figure 2.2 A network of two fully connected layers.

15 synapses in our example network. Later in the book, we will see several networks that have connections in both the forward and reverse directions. In this network, however, there are only forward synapses. (Remember that synapses are not bidirectional.) As a result, in order to send a signal back to the first layer from the second, the network would need a completely new set of interconnects. If our present network were fully connected in both directions, for instance, it would require an additional set of 15 interconnections and associated synapses.

So that we can clearly see the effects of input summation and thresholding, let's also assume that the input pattern presented to the network is analog; that is, the individual elements of the input pattern can take on any of a continuous range of values. (This, by the way, is in contrast to the discrete values that digital computers manipulate so well. Digital systems must first translate the analog input to distinct numbers in, say, the binary number system, before processing can be performed.) A particular input pattern always excites the same unique activity pattern in the input layer, but that activity pattern is generally not identical to the input pattern because of the neurode's nonlinear transfer function. If the activity of an input neurode exceeds the required threshold value, the neurode produces an output that is distributed to the three second-layer neurodes. If the activity does not exceed the threshold value, no output is sent to the next layer of neurodes. At each of these second-layer neurodes, the signal is multiplied by the weight of the relevant synapse and presented to the neurode for summing. For instance, a synapse might multiply the incoming, or presynaptic, signal by some number between 0 and 1.0 to produce the weighted, or postsynaptic, signal that is summed.

Now the input summation process is repeated at the second layer. Each of the three second-layer neurodes adds the five postsynaptic signals presented to it and takes on an appropriate activity level. This time there is no possibility that the activity pattern will even be similar to the input pattern since there are only three neurodes in the second layer. Finally, each second-layer neurode having an activity above its threshold value produces an output. The input signal has been transformed, or processed, by the network.

The critical factor determining the nature of the activity patterns that a given input pattern generates at each layer is the value of the synapse weights. How do the synapses attain these weights? How are they modified? Learning in a neural network consists of changing the values of these weights (rather than changing the way input signals are processed, for example). If the network is to be capable of learning, there must exist some means of altering synapse weights and some rule to dictate by how much and in which direction those weights will be changed. Such rules are called "learning laws." Later in the book we will have a great deal more to say about learning laws; indeed, they are among the most important implements in a designer's tool box.

So far, we have surveyed the operation of artificial neural networks and the building blocks out of which they are made. Before we leave these introductory chapters, we will clarify two topics that seem to bother many people: the relationship of neural networks to artificial intelligence and to parallel processing.

Implementation:
The Artificial Retina

Caltech's Carver Mead has long been one of the leading advocates of imitating nature in designing neural networks. He and his associates have successfully implemented several biologically inspired neural designs in state-of-the-art microelectronic hardware. One of the earliest of these designs was the silicon retina.

The human retina is a complex structure containing many different types of cells, blood vessels, and other structural features. In essence, however, it is analogous to a sheet of interconnected resistors and amplifiers that detect either the stationary image formed on them by a lens or motion in that image. Many cells of the retina respond only to motion. Even those that do not respond only to motion cease to respond at all after a short time if a stationary image is focused on them. This can be demonstrated by a simple experiment. Stand near a well-lit but featureless surface, such as a wall painted some light, uniform color, and stare at it without consciously moving your eyes. After a short time, you will find that the image of the uniform wall begins to be replaced by a perceived blackness. You have frustrated the action of the small oscillatory motions constantly performed by the eye. This small, unconscious motion, which keeps even stationary images in motion on the retina, is called "dithering." When you stare at the wall, dithering still occurs. The uniformity of the surface, however, causes the intensity of the light falling on the retina to stay constant despite dithering. The cells soon saturate, and the image fades into blackness.

The reason for this property seems to be that it gives the eye several advantages it would not have if it detected only steady, stationary images. Among these advantages are the fact that many of the objects we need to pay immediate attention to are in motion. But there are more subtle advantages, such as the ability to tune out the presence of the blood vessels that overlay the retina, to obtain better spatial resolution than would otherwise be possible, and to detect the edges of objects with more accuracy.

Cells in the top layer of the retina, the photoreceptors, provide an output proportional to the logarithm of the intensity of the light falling on them. Among other things, this logarithmic response provides the retina with the ability to detect images over a wide range of illuminations. The next layer of cells acts like a planar network of interconnected resistors, with a photoreceptor's output connected to each junction. A signal injected by a photoreceptor at one of these junctions spatially spreads out with a finite velocity and at the same time diminishes in magnitude. The net effect is that the sheet temporally and spatially averages the output of the photoreceptors.

Also connected to the output of each photoreceptor is a second type of cell whose response is proportional to the difference between the instantaneous output of the photoreceptor and the averaged output of those photoreceptors lying within a short distance. This average is taken by the resistive layer. The resulting difference signal is large at the boundary between an illuminated and an unilluminated area and allows the eye to detect accurately the edges of smooth images, an ability that is very useful in discerning the shapes of objects. Additionally, because the difference is greatest when the image intensity is changing rapidly with time or moving rapidly across the retina, the differencing cells implement a very sensitive motion detector.

Mead built his silicon retina using analog microelectronic fabrication techniques. Each electronic component in the silicon retina corresponds to a structure found in a biological retina. While designing the silicon retina, he found that at least one feature of silicon microelectronic circuits that is troublesome in most microcircuits was a windfall in his chip. A so-called parasitic transistor, an unavoidable by-product of the integrated-circuit fabrication process that causes instability in many circuit designs, could be used as a highly sensitive photoreceptor. An important part of his circuit was provided free and was already wired into the right spot.

The resulting chip is as sensitive as the cone cells of the eye. It contains about 100,000 transistors, although due to a peculiarity of silicon fabrication technology, many of these are needed only to make the resistors of the resistive network. Even with this many components, the chip is relatively compact, uses little power, and can probably be scaled up considerably in size. A 48 x 48 array of photoreceptors takes only 0.25 square centimeters and requires only 0.0001 watt of power to run. Because it is built in fast electronic hardware and utilizes no computer simulations or other software, the chip works in real time.

The chip Mead built has direct commercial and military applications, but it is even more meaningful as a demonstration of the good sense we often show when we copy nature.

Comparisons are odious.
— Shakespeare

3 Neural Networks and Other Systems

At first glance neural networks seem to be closely allied to artificial intelligence and parallel processing. After all, doesn't AI already solve the same problems? And doesn't parallel processing offer the same advantages that neural networks do? In fact, aren't neural networks just an entry in the family tree of parallel computers? The quick answers to these questions are "no," "no," and "no." If you want more careful answers, read on.

Neural Networks and Artificial Intelligence

Artificial intelligence attempts to generate heuristics, or rules of thumb, to guide the search for solutions to problems of control, recognition, and object manipulation. These heuristics assume that such problems can be solved by applying sequences of formal rules for symbol manipulation. This is called "symbolic processing," and digital computers do it well. A number of high-level programming languages like Lisp and Prolog have been developed to make this job simpler, and AI has been successful in areas that would require a human to use symbolic or purely cognitive skills.

Neural networks attempt to solve the same kinds of problems but at a much lower level—that of the structure of the machine itself.

Symbolic processing, when it occurs at all in the neural approach, is a result of the low-level structure of the physical system as it is regrouped into higher levels of network organization. Neural networks by their nature deal with sensory tasks (processing visual stimuli, for example), motor tasks (controlling arm movements), or the intelligent decision making by which sensory tasks drive motor tasks (deciding on a trajectory for a specific arm movement).

The distinction between the AI and neural network approaches can be restated in terms of the way the two disciplines view knowledge or information. AI attempts to capture intelligent behavior without regard to the underlying mechanisms producing the behavior. This approach involves describing behaviors, usually with rules and symbols. In contrast, neural networks do not describe behaviors; they imitate them.

AI techniques have proved to be effective in forming some kinds of expert systems. Designers of expert systems typically assume that the actions and knowledge of a human expert in some field can be embodied in a set of facts and in an accompanying hierarchy of explicitly stated rules involving symbolic manipulation of those facts and lower-level rules. Expert systems for diagnosis of lung diseases, placement of heavy equipment in military transport aircraft for optimum weight distribution, and design of computer systems to meet complex customer requirements often equal or exceed the success rate and cost-effectiveness of human experts.

Despite its success in these areas, however, AI has consistently failed at those tasks that are not completely solved in humans or animals at the cognitive level: scene and speech recognition, motor control and object manipulation, and association. These are the very problems for which neural networks seem to be ideally suited. Moreover, it is not clear that AI even has the expert system market cornered. Researchers are showing that human experts often do not function at a cognitive level. They operate from an intuitive understanding of the structure of the task they are performing—from a learned internal model of the process they are involved in—rather than from a set of facts or cognitive rules about the process. This type of model building is more reminiscent of intuition than of symbolic processing and is the natural domain of neural networks.

Thus, neural networks and artificial intelligence take quite different approaches to problem solving. Even so, it is possible that the present sharp distinction between the fields will eventually disappear and the two will be viewed as complementary parts of the same discipline. An indication that this may already be happening is that many persons who consider themselves AI specialists are now designing neural networks to attack some of the same problems for which they were formerly writing Lisp programs.

Under any circumstance, there are unquestionably complementary uses for both disciplines. We can envision a large hybrid system in the not-too-distant future composed of a combination of neural, AI, and digital systems. It might have a number of neural networks at the low end to combine the outputs of several types of sensors, to reduce the amount of information that later stages of the system must handle, and other so-called low-level tasks. It could have larger neural networks at intermediate and higher processing levels for integrating visual, auditory, and other sensory information and for adding contextual information. These, in turn, might be coupled at the high end with an AI expert system and a large database. The system very likely would contain a digital computer for rapid numerical computations and for other algorithmic and symbolic tasks. Finally, additional neural networks might act as adaptive human/machine interfaces and as executive schedulers or controllers for the entire system.

Neural Networks and Parallel Computers

As we ever-so-subtly intimated earlier, outside of the fact that the many neurodes in a neural network form a massively parallel structure, we think there is little connection between artificial neural systems and present-day parallel computers. We see only two points of similarity: (1) both operate in parallel, performing many operations at the same time, and (2) parallel computers may be an effective vehicle for implementing a neural network if appropriate software tools are available. Not everyone agrees with our position, however, and to let you form your own opinion, we will briefly review the family of architectures associated with parallel processing.

There are several architectural and operational differences that we could use to distinguish among the large number of parallel computers on the market or under development. The three distinguishing features most useful for our purposes, though, are the total number of processors in the system, whether each processing node has a small amount of memory capacity or all processors share one large memory unit, and the way in which the processing nodes are interconnected. We refer to processing nodes rather than just to processors because there may be memory chips, coprocessors, and other integrated circuits associated with each processor in a parallel architecture.

Parallel computers with a small number of processing nodes often use buses similar to those found in serial computers. These computers usually contain fewer than a dozen or so processors and often run separate programs at each node. The processors are usually standard uniprocessors, and one large memory unit is usually shared among the processing nodes. The buses serve as the routes over which data, instructions, and results are transmitted between memory units, between processors, between memories and processors, and to the I/O units communicating with the outside world.

A second type of architecture does not use permanently connected buses. Instead a fast electronic switch is used to connect up to several hundred processing nodes together. In this scheme, each node has its own memory unit, and the switch routes data and other information among nodes.

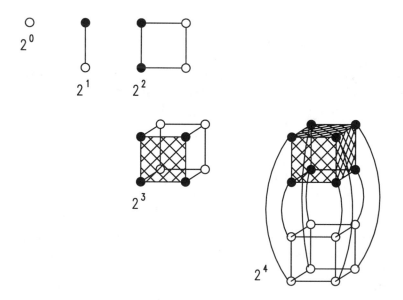

Figure 3.1 Hypercubes of dimension 0, 1, 2, 3, and 4.

We still have seen nothing so far that would remind us of a neural architecture; however, we now come to the specific parallel architecture known as the hypercube. It is the latter that is most often associated—we would say confused—with neural network architecture.

What is a hypercube? Let's make one in our minds, aided by figure 3.1. Starting with a single point, a hypercube of zero dimensionality, we construct a one-dimensional hypercube, two points connected by a line, by translating the point sideways while keeping our original point. By translating the line sideways, we make a two-dimensional, or planar, hypercube; and by translating that planar one "into" the page, we obtain a three-dimensional hypercube, an ordinary cube.

Now we would like to translate our three-dimensional cube "sideways" once more to make a four-dimensional hypercube, but we've run out of space—literally. Here, we must stop to consider what has happened. With each translation operation, we have increased the number of vertices, or intersections, by a power of two, and we have increased the number of neighbors each vertex is connected to by one. Each vertex in each hypercube is connected to n nearest neighbors, where n is the dimensionality, or order, of the hypercube. We have labeled the hypercubes in the figure with the proper power of two.

Let's define a hypercube by these characteristics and press on in faith, for we will no longer be able to visualize our hypercubes easily in terms of simple geometrical objects. Although a three-dimensional surface is the object of highest dimensionality that we can conveniently depict on a two-dimensional surface, we can still represent a four-dimensional hypercube in several ways. We show one way in figure 3.1. It is true to the test: there are 16 vertices (equal to the fourth power of two), and each vertex is connected to its 4 topologically nearest neighbors, although "nearest" is no longer easy to represent geometrically. We can imagine yet higher-order hypercubes by considering translations of the pair of geometrical cubes sideways to form a figure resembling a square, and so on.

The value of an nth-order hypercube in multiprocessing is that we can reach any vertex from any other in at most n steps. If the vertices are processing nodes, we have an efficient way of routing binary information among nodes with permanent connections without using a complex external switching arrangement. In real hypercube-based computing systems, messages containing small amounts of information are passed from one node to the next. Instructions for

We Knew It All Along:
Southern California Is Only
1/16th Inch Thick

When the United States launched *Explorer I* in January 1958, anxious officials wanted to be able to announce America's successful entry into the space age at the earliest possible time. The first opportunity to obtain definitive orbital information occurred as *Explorer* passed over southern California, nearly at the end of its first orbit. The satellite would be well into its second orbit by the time the data could be collected by tracking stations, sent to a central site by teletype, entered by hand into one of the army's mainframe computers, and the important orbital parameters calculated. It became the responsibility of a team of scientists at the Caltech Jet Propulsion Laboratory (JPL) to determine the orbit of the satellite as quickly as possible after it passed over the California coast. To do this job, the scientists recruited teams of volunteers at military bases, universities, industrial laboratories, and amateur radio clubs in southern and central California and helped them set up a network of simple tracking stations.

The JPL scientists knew that they could determine most of the needed information by comparing precalculated plots of the tracking information to plots of the actual data received as the new satellite passed near the station. How to obtain the height of the satellite as it passed over southern California remained a problem, however. Calculating the height in real time using the computers and data entry methods of the day was out of the question. The JPL team finally hit upon a clever scheme. They made a three-dimensional aluminum scale model of southern California. It was a thin shell, 4 feet in diameter, with a small hole drilled at the location of each tracking station. They placed the shell on a stand and passed weighted lengths of fishing line through each hole. The upper ends of the cords they secured to a small brass ring that could slide up and down a steel rod kept vertical to the spherical surface by a small wheeled stand. Thus, the steel rod and its stand could move freely on the surface of the sphere. As the distance of closest approach of the satellite to each receiving station in southern California was determined from the precalculated plots, it was translated into a length of the fishing line and a small clip attached on the line at the proper place. Once the closest-approach distances had been set for every station, the scientists found the height of the brass ring and the location of the assembly on the model that brought all of the lines taut at the same time while allowing the clips to stay in contact with the aluminum surface. The height of the satellite above the surface of the earth was read directly from a scale etched into the steel rod, and the location of the path on the ground was read from the longitude and latitude lines etched into the model's surface. With this aluminum analog computer, the JPL tracking team quickly solved a complicated set of coupled differential equations without ever writing a line on paper or entering a number into a digital computer.

Another kind of analog computer was in use that night. Sitting cross-legged on a table at one end of the tracking room was the lone figure of the late Richard Feynman. As information from each station arrived, the Caltech professor quietly consulted a 20-inch bamboo slide rule and jotted notes on a piece of paper. Shortly after the JPL team triumphantly announced the altitude and other parameters of *Explorer's* orbit, Feynman laid his slide rule down, smiled impishly, and said to those standing nearby, "Yes, that's about right."

any operations that a node is to perform on the data before sending it on its way are contained in the message. A host serial computer, running under controlling software, composes the messages. A human programmer composes the controlling software.

Sixteen-dimensional hypercube systems having 65,536 1-bit processors are commercially available. Hypercube machines with large numbers of processing nodes can simulate many of the actions of simple neural networks more naturally and rapidly than serial machines. But such a machine runs under the control of an external program; its individual processing units each have a small amount—typically 2 to 4 kilobits—of storage or memory, even if only to route received messages to the next processor; and it is invariably digital and clocked.

None of these important attributes of a hypercube architecture is shared by a true neural network. Neural networks do not run under the control of an external program, they have no separate memory, and they are analog and asynchronous. There is, however, an even more fundamental difference between neural networks and any kind of traditional computer, serial or parallel: neural networks do not compute. A neural network responds or behaves more than it computes.

Do Neurodes Have Internal Memory?

At least one of the differences between neurodes and the processing units of a hypercube machine can be questioned. It is argued by some that a neurode, even one in an ideal neural network, has a considerable amount of internal memory and thus is a form of hypercube architecture.

First, the presence of a certain amount of "memory" is indicated by the fact that a neurode must hold a particular activity level over a period of time. The amount of memory this implies can be expressed by the equivalent amount of digital random access memory (RAM) required to represent the numerical value of the neurode activity. Using this measure, activity levels can be specified using only a few binary bits—a tiny amount of memory. If our network architecture demands that we consider changes in the activation level of the neurode or of the neurode dynamics, then more memory is required.

If we assume that synapses are integral parts of their associated neurode, however, then the neurode must "remember" the strength and algebraic sign for each of perhaps thousands of synapses. Since this can amount to several kilobits using the RAM analogy, this one distinction between parallel architectures and neural networks seemingly disappears. This similarity, though, is a practical one arising from the fact that most operational neural networks are currently simulated or emulated using digital computers. The synapse of an ideal neural network, such as that of a network realized in electronic or optical hardware, is usually a physical connection and takes no memory to store.

Thus, the question of whether neurodes have memory is largely semantic; the answer depends on whether the questioner is thinking only of present-day neurocomputers and simulations or has a broader view.

Relationship to Analog Computers

Ultimately neural networks will not be in competition with AI in the application arena, and they are not in competition with serial computers in the numerical computing arena. We are equally certain that neural networks ultimately will not be in competition with parallel digital computers. There are application areas for which each of these classes of machines is ideally suited, and we believe that the nature of these areas will become increasingly clear in the next few years.

If neural networks belong on any existing branch of the computing family tree, it is on that of analog computers. Neural networks can be considered a type of massively parallel analog computer. Analog computers were used extensively before the era of the digital computer and are still in use today for specialized applications. Such computers can be mechanical, electronic, or even chemical. The slide rule is a mechanical analog computer, for instance. A modern electronic analog computer might contain several amplifiers and other electronic components that are custom interconnected in some configuration to solve a particular engineering or other problem approximately. Usually the problem is one that has proved impossible or too costly to be solved by a digital computer. For instance, the final output voltage of an analog system might be numerically equivalent to the solution of a set of nonlinear differential equations under particular constraints or initial conditions. Or the time history of the output of a properly connected analog computer might reproduce, in analogy, the time history of the concentration of one chemical species in a complex chemical reaction.

Analog computers do not offer the high accuracy, convenience of programming, or versatility of digital computers. They are seldom of parallel design, and they do not contain the large numbers of processing units or the interconnect structure needed to simulate neural architectures. Still, they are useful for emulation of small neural networks, and at least one research system has been in operation for many years, analyzing characteristics of spoken language and music.

In the remainder of this book, we will look in detail at the principal kinds of neural network architectures, at the ways in which neural networks are actually implemented in hardware and software, and at some of their most promising application areas.

Part II

My memory was never loaded with anything but blank cartridges.
—Mark Twain

*He's experimenting with a neuron booster. It enhances
positive attitudes and rounds off flaky eccentricities.*

Most of the learning in use is of no great use.
—Benjamin Franklin

4 Associative Memories

A memory system is any device that can store information and recall
it on demand. Anything with this capability, from paper and pencil
to a silicon chip, can be considered a memory system.

An associative memory is a memory system that stores information by associating, or correlating, it with other information in the
memory. For example, a thesaurus is an associative memory. We
look up a word such as *go,* and find many others associated with it.
Entries in a thesaurus are organized so that words appear near other
words with similar meanings. We can think of still other examples.
Many memory improvement schemes rely on the technique of association for their effectiveness. Students of these systems are taught to
correlate some highly memorable item with what they actually want
to remember. When they later want to recall something, they can easily do so by recalling the item they associated with it. Just as a student in a memory course might pair Mr. Duckworthy's name with
the image of a self-important duck in a three-piece suit, an associative memory associates new information with other patterns that are
similar in some way.

Associative memories lie at the center of neural network
research efforts. Most neural network architectures can be used as
associative memories, and this capability is in fact one of the reasons
neural networks are of such interest. It is difficult to implement an
effective associative memory with a digital computer. If we can

create a neural network that operates as an efficient and capable associative memory, then someday we may be able to use these systems for applications as diverse as intelligent databases and truly autonomous robots.

To understand why associative memories are so useful, we need to look at their unique features.

Features of Associative Memories

It should be evident from these examples that associative memories come in a variety of forms. There are, however, characteristics that are common to nearly all such systems. Most can recall information based on incomplete or garbled inputs; most store data in a distributed fashion; most display some degree of content addressability; and most are strongly robust. By robust we mean that the performance of the memory does not degrade appreciably if some of its neurodes or interconnects are lost or if it is presented with inaccurate input stimuli. Finally, associative memories can generalize; that is, they can detect similarities between new patterns and previously stored patterns. Let's explore each of these features.

Imagine the following conversation between two friends:

"Do you remember the guy at work?" asks Sue.

"Which one?" George responds.

"You know, the one with the black hair," she replies.

"Do you mean the man with the funny purple glasses?"

"No, I mean the guy who always wore green and orange plaid pants."

"Oh, you mean Joe Flamespitter! Didn't he have the very worst temper of anyone you ever met?"

In this conversation George recalls Joe Flamespitter based on the combination of facts that the person in question (1) worked with Sue and George, (2) had black hair, (3) did not have funny purple glasses, and (4) consistently wore green and orange plaid pants.

We can guess that Sue and George know many more facts about Joe Flamespitter than the ones they gave; however, George was able to recall Joe's name and temper based only on these few items. This is an example of the ability of a natural associative memory—the brain—to recall information based on a sparse set of input data.

Let's look at another example. Suppose we walk down the street and meet a friend who has new eyeglasses and a new hairstyle. Her

To Hash or Not to Hash

Computerized databases often use hashing schemes to determine the storage location of a data item. Typically the data values that make up all or a portion of a particular item are used as an input to a specialized function called the "hashing function." For example, a bank might use a depositor's last name and social security number as the input to its hashing function. The hashing function is different for each database and is one of the features that makes each database program unique. This function usually has the property that identical data inputs will produce identical numerical outputs, but most nonidentical data inputs will produce different numerical outputs. The function's value, or output, determines the storage address for the input data within the database. If the storage location already has data stored there, the database has a set of rules that tell it how to find a second-best storage location. This scheme has the advantage that a given piece of information is stored in an easily reproducible location so that it can be retrieved without having to search through the entire database.

current visual image does not match the pattern stored in our brains; we have never seen her in glasses or with this hairdo. Yet we would normally have little difficulty greeting her by name. A good associative memory system, whether neurological or computational, should be able to retrieve information even when the input stimulus is incomplete, approximate, or garbled.

Most associative memories are also distributed memories. Traditionally, computers have placed individual facts in specific storage pigeonholes, called "addresses," in memory. The facts can be retrieved electronically from the appropriate address. In a distributed memory, on the other hand, there is no single location within the memory that contains each item of information. Instead the

Our Declining Brains

We can compare the robustness of neural networks to the robustness of our brains. Several thousand of the brain's neurons die every day. Neurons do not reproduce, so each day the total number of neurons in our brain is reduced. Why do we not find our mental capacities steadily decreasing (the assertions of teenagers notwithstanding)? The fact is, that with 10 billion to 100 billion neurons in our brains at birth, the natural loss over a life span of even 100 years represents perhaps 1 to 3 percent of our total brain circuitry. Many neural network architectures have sufficient redundancy built into them to absorb this same kind of attrition with little or no reduction in effectiveness over their service life. In addition, although neurons normally cannot reproduce themselves, they can and do extend their axons to make new connections, thus allowing the remaining neurons to cover for those that die. Now, what was that about old dogs and new tricks?

responsibility for storing each item is shared by a number of elements in the memory.

Content addressability is another characteristic of associative memories. A content addressable memory (CAM) accesses stored data by the data's value. A primitive form of content addressability can be found in database systems that assign storage locations based on the contents of the data to be stored. In such schemes, an entry's value is hashed, or processed by a special function that generates a database address as its output. The entry is stored in that location. We retrieve data by hashing the desired values through the function and collecting all entries at some designated memory location.

In associative memories, the content addressability characteristic is usually much more sophisticated. Often the input stimulus used to recall a data pattern is the pattern itself rather than a hashed version of the pattern. This makes more sense when we remember that the input may be a garbled or incomplete version of the original pattern.

Finally, associative memories are often extremely robust. This robustness is evident in both the memory's ability to give the correct response to incorrect stimuli and in its general insensitivity to errors in small sections of the memory. These assertions need some elaboration. Inputs to a neural network associative memory can be thought of as activity patterns. What matters to such a memory is not any one part of an input pattern but rather the overall pattern. Associative memories respond to the gross features of a stimulus and are generally not sidetracked by small differences or minor details. It is the overall input activity pattern, its Gestalt in psychological terms, that gives rise to the output activity pattern of an associative memory.

The second kind of robustness we mentioned—the lack of sensitivity to loss of a few neurodes or interconnects—arises from the fact that information is stored in a distributed fashion. Because there is no single neurode or interconnect within the memory that contains any one item of information, the functionality of the network may not be seriously affected by anything less than the loss of major sections of the network.

Associative memories also can generalize from the specific to the general. If a child has already seen a maple tree, an oak tree, a pine tree, and a willow tree, each in context, she will have constructed a general model of "treeness." If she then sees a picture of a redwood tree in its proper context, she will have little difficulty in deciding that this too is a tree. Similarly, once an associative memory has stored a number of specific patterns belonging to a particular category, it will generally be able to recognize an unfamiliar but similar pattern as belonging to the same category. The associative memory generalizes from specific examples to broader categories.

These, then, are the features typical of associative memory systems. It should be easy to see why they are the subject of such intense interest. The potential applications of associative memories in databases or expert systems provide powerful economic incentives for their development. Moreover, it seems that some kind of associative memory will be required to build any truly "intelligent" system.

From the earliest days of artificial intelligence and neural network research to the present time, those attempting to make intelligent systems have found the undertaking truly formidable. One challenging aspect of the problem is the difficulty of achieving quick and reliable recall of input information that almost, but not quite, matches stored information. Recognizing the friend's face with her new glasses and hairdo is a good example of this capability. It should be evident that the ability of associative memories to perform this feat makes them prime candidates for inclusion in large intelligent systems developed in the future.

Now that we know what associative memories are, let's take a look at the kinds of neural networks that can be used in this way.

Classes of Neural Network Associative Memories

Associative memories can be classified in several ways. One is by the kinds of data patterns that are stored. This kind of classification scheme leads to labels such as "autoassociative memory" and "heteroassociative memory." An autoassociative memory is one where each data item is associated with itself. In this case, a data pattern is recalled by providing part of a data item or a garbled version of the whole item. A heteroassociative memory is one in which two different data items, say A and B, are associated with each other. A can be used to recall B, and B can be used to recall A. Both of these systems have applications.

Consider the case of a system used to "clean up" stereotyped pictures. We might, for example, want to give the network garbled or incomplete versions of the letters of the alphabet and receive back complete, legible versions. To do this, we would store "clean" examples of the letters A, B, and so on. Afterward, when we input a noisy or garbled F, for instance, we would get back the original, legible F pattern. As long as there is not so much garbling of the input patterns that the wrong associations are made, an autoassociative memory will clean up input patterns presented to it and return correct versions.

In another case, we might want to use pictures of the letters of the alphabet as input patterns but might want to get back some other pattern, perhaps the ASCII code for each letter. When we input the picture of an A, we would get back the binary pattern 01000001. This is an example of a heteroassociative memory; the inputs and outputs are different. The associative memory is really acting as a translator or lookup table in this case, translating between the picture representation of the letters and their equivalent binary codes.

For all practical purposes, we can consider the autoassociative memory a special case of the heteroassociative memory. If we generally associate A with some data item in a heteroassociative memory, then associating A with itself is just the special case in which some data item happens to be A.

Another way of classifying associative memories is by how they handle inexact data matches. Suppose that we have somehow stored colors in our associative memory. We have stored, say, the colors red, blue, and green and have associated them with the numbers 1, 2, and 3, respectively. What happens if our input to the associative memory is magenta? Is it supposed to output the number 1.5? Or perhaps it should output either 1 or 2, depending on the exact hue of magenta. Which is correct? The answer depends on the kind of associative memory we are using. If it is an accretive associative memory, it will output the closer of 1 or 2. If it is an interpolative associative memory, it will output 1.5 (or some other number between 1 and 2 depending on the exact color of magenta). Both accretive and interpolative associative memories have their uses; the application determines which should be used.

Of course, both of the classification methods can be used. It is quite reasonable to talk of an accretive heteroassociative memory or an interpolative heteroassociative memory. The terms may sound imposing, but the ideas they represent are simple.

Over and above these somewhat generic descriptive terms are the specific models used to implement the memory. As we have already seen, neural networks are not the only systems that can act as associative memories. From this point on, however, we will be talking only about neural network implementations. Now that we understand something of what an associative memory is and know some of its features, we are in a place to see how we might store information in an associative memory and later retrieve it.

Using an Associative Memory

What are the processes by which we store and retrieve information in an associative memory? The details of the procedure depend on the particular type of network we are using, but we can understand the overall process without reference to any particular system. Suppose we have a group of patterns to store in an associative memory. We call such a selection a "training set." For now, we won't concern ourselves with how the patterns in the training set were put in a suitable form for presentation to the network, and we will assume that the network is large enough to hold all the patterns we wish to present to it.

Suppose we want to be able to retrieve the actual pattern we placed into the network; that is, we want to make an autoassociative memory. To store the training set, we present each pattern to the input of the system and simultaneously stimulate the output neu-rodes with the same pattern. That's all there is to it in principle. When we have stored the pattern, we can input a garbled or incom-plete version of one of the training patterns or a similar but unfamil-iar pattern from a second data set, and the memory will obediently produce an output consisting of the stored pattern most nearly matching it. The set of patterns used to stimulate this output and confirm that things are stored correctly is called the test set.

Now suppose we want to do this with a heteroassociative mem-ory. What is different? When we store data in a heteroassociative memory, we must have a training pattern pair rather than a training pattern. This pair consists of the input pattern and the desired output pattern to be associated with it. The collection of such pattern pairs is the training set. To store the pattern pairs in the training set, we present each input pattern to the system and simultaneously stimu-late the output neurodes with the second member of the training set, the desired output pattern. To recall the stored information, we pro-ceed much as before, providing a garbled or incomplete version of one of the training patterns or a similar but unfamiliar pattern from a second set of patterns. This time, however, the system outputs not the original pattern but the second member of the training pair, the asso-ciated pattern. As before, the collection of patterns we use to confirm that storage is correct is called the test set. Unlike the training set, it need not consist of pattern pairs. Although presented for associative memories, the storage and recall procedures we have just discussed are indicative of the general procedures used to train neural net-works. A set of training patterns is used to store information, and a separate but similar set of test patterns is used to confirm that the training patterns are correctly stored. We must exercise care in con-structing the training and test sets for associative networks. The two sets must be similar but not identical, and both normally must be characteristic of the patterns the network will encounter during its intended use. There often are other constraints, such as the order in which items are presented. Some types of networks are even more demanding in the construction of their training and test sets, and we will revisit this topic several times as we progress.

Neural Network Models

It is difficult to classify the varieties of neural network architec-tures that are useful as associative memories. Nearly every network

Hopfield Networks

Crossbar systems are among the most studied neural network systems. Two factors contribute to this popularity: they are relatively simple to understand and to build or model, and they are closely associated with the name of John Hopfield of Caltech. Hopfield was already well respected in the fields of solid state physics and biophysics when he began publishing and speaking on the subject of neural networks. His initial series of articles beginning in 1982 found an enthusiastic audience that was already familiar with the quality of his work and the mathematical methods he employed. His work and personal enthusiasm are often cited as major factors in the resurgence of interest in neural network research in recent years. Although he was not the first to work with crossbar networks, he is so commonly associated with them that they are often called "Hopfield networks" in the literature.

model we will talk about has either an associative memory component or the ability to act as an associative memory. In spite of this, there are architectures that are considered primarily associative memories. These can be placed into three broad classifications: crossbar networks, adaptive filter networks, and competitive filter networks. We will define each of these in this chapter and then take a close look at one or two networks of each type in the following three chapters.

A crossbar network has one or two layers of neurodes arranged so that each input line can connect to any output line through a variable-weight interconnect. If there are two layers, they are usually called the "input layer" and the "output layer," for obvious reasons. Although crossbar networks are not yet widely employed in practical applications, they show promise for such operations as restoration of degraded or distorted patterns in certain types of telecommunications systems.

An adaptive filter network can be thought of as a collection of neurodes, each of which tests the input pattern to see if it is in one specific category assigned to that neurode. The name of this network comes from the facts that the individual neurodes act as little filters that screen the input data and that these neurodes can be made to alter their screening criteria adaptively over time. The name also betrays the origin of these systems in digital signal processing applications.

As an example of such a network's use, we might have a system that correlates red inputs with the binary output pattern "10" and green inputs with the binary output pattern "01." We can build a simple network to accomplish this by using two adaptive filter neurodes. The first neurode sorts each input pattern into the classes "red" and "not red"; the second sorts each input pattern into the classes "green" and "not green." When the first neurode sees a red input, it generates an output of 1; otherwise it outputs 0. The second neurode does the same for the green classification. Taken together, the outputs of the two neurodes reproduce the required output patterns.

The neurodes in adaptive filter networks act as independent data sorters, or feature detectors, each looking for some specific characteristic of the input pattern. We can imagine huge arrays of such filters that scan for such specifics as "warm-blooded," "furry," and "bears live young" and that then generate a biological classification. In fact, like nearly everything else in real life, it's not quite that easy. Even so, adaptive filter networks have been successfully used for applications ranging from predicting the weather to balancing a broomstick on end.

The third model of associative memories uses competition among the neurodes in order to sort patterns. In this type of network, an input pattern is sorted into one of many categories in a manner similar to that of an adaptive filter network. The difference is that the neurodes compete with each other for the privilege of being the one to classify the pattern. In the competitive model, each neurode does not sort the pattern for its particular category independent of all others; rather, the neurodes try to overwhelm the output from all of the other neurodes and cause the network to classify the unknown pattern as the one that neurode represents. The most successful neurode in this competition determines which category the pattern is placed in by the network. These networks have other intriguing characteristics. They inherently perform statistical modeling of the input patterns presented to them, and they self-organize into functioning networks without the benefit of outside assistance.

These, then, are the principal neural network models usually identified as associative memories. We will look at examples of each of these in the following chapters, considering the construction of each system and its problems and limitations. We will begin by looking at what is probably the easiest neural network to understand, the crossbar associative memory.

Education is the same, but capacities differ.
— Sadi

5 Crossbar Associative Memories

Crossbar memories include some of the most studied and best understood neural networks, among them popular research designs like the Hopfield network, the Brain State in a Box network, and the bidirectional associative memory, otherwise known as the BAM. As different as they often appear at first glance, however, all networks in this classification are variations on the same theme and share similar advantages and limitations.

Crossbar networks take their name from their architecture, which is identical to the manual crossbar switching system used in early telephone systems. In those systems, any telephone in a town could be linked to any other by making a single connection on a large switchboard located in the central office. A simple crossbar associative network is shown in figure 5.1. Any input line can communicate with any output line through connections—synapses—located at their intersection points.

One feature makes crossbar networks popular with researchers: they can be represented by a table in which the rows and columns denote the values of the synapse weights connecting the input and output lines. Mathematically such a table is called a "matrix." Matrices are attractive to those interested in examining the theory of neural networks because the properties of matrices are well understood. As a result, it is possible to describe conveniently and succinctly the storage and recall processes, to prove theorems about associative networks, and to predict the way associative networks will behave under various conditions. These things are often more difficult to do for network architectures that cannot be represented as matrices. In addition, matrices are often already familiar to workers in the fields of mathematics, psychology, physics, and engineering, so many newcomers to neural network research already have the primary mathematical skills they need to investigate associative memories.

Another feature of crossbar networks that prompted some early workers to study them is their high degree of interconnection, or "connectivity." It seemed obvious to some that a fully interconnected system had more computational power and was more versatile than one having less connectivity. To many, however, the proposition is no longer as attractive as it once was. The reason for this change of heart is twofold: nature seldom uses fully interconnected architec-

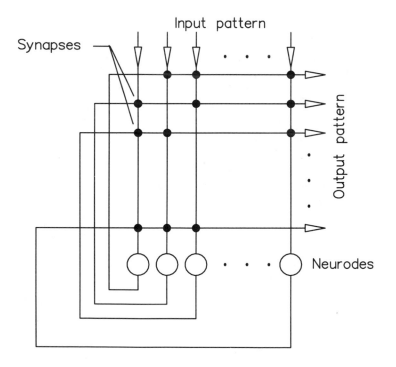

Figure 5.1 A typical crossbar network.

tures, and powerful, versatile artificial networks now exist that are far from fully interconnected.

Although their basic design is simple, crossbar networks offer surprisingly good insights into the general properties of neural networks.

Energy Surface Representation

Probably the most useful construct in the study of crossbar networks is the energy surface. The concept provides a useful physical analogy to the way a crossbar network stores information. Imagine that we have a supply of some soft plastic substance, say modeling clay, that we can dent by pressing it firmly with a finger. Let's suppose we want to associate the size and weight of several spheres made from different materials like lead, cotton, and wood. We spread the modeling clay in a rectangle on a large table so that it is an even 3 inches thick all over. We then label two adjacent sides of the rectangle with the ranges of the numbers we want to use. Along the side nearest us, we tape a scale with numbers ranging from zero to the maximum diameter we expect to encounter; along the side to our left, we tape another scale with numbers ranging from zero to some maximum expected weight.

For each sphere, we press our finger into the clay at the spot corresponding to the measured values of the diameter and weight, leaving a conical dent. As a reminder, we can place a slip of paper containing the name of the material at the bottom of each dent. When we are all done, the clay may look something like figure 5.2. For our illustration, we have assumed that there is not a lot of overlap of the dents.

This is a slightly simplified model of the way an associative memory stores information. When we have made dents for all samples, we find that spheres that are similar in size and weight are associated. In neural network terms, memories of similar spheres are stored near each other. Given a new sphere of unknown makeup, we can easily find which of our example materials it most closely resembles in these two combined properties. If we place a marble on the surface of the clay at the spot corresponding to the size and weight of the unknown sphere, it will roll to the bottom of the nearest dent. Readers familiar with introductory physics recognize that the ball minimizes its potential energy by moving to the lowest accessible position on the surface; it seeks the nearest potential energy minimum.

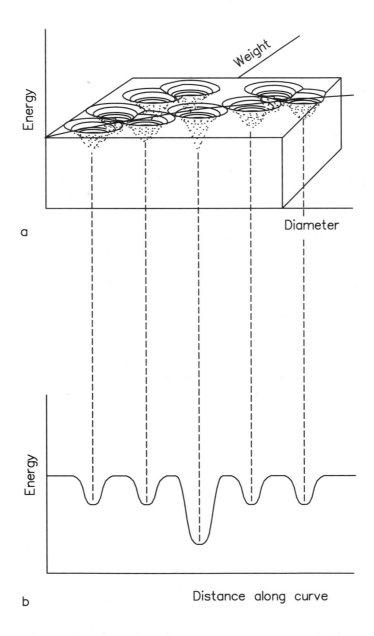

Figure 5.2 The basins of attraction around energy wells (a) showing the energy surface in 3D and (b) from a side view.

If we look a little more closely at the characteristics of the clay surface, we see that there are two kinds of spots on it. If we release a marble at a place where the surface is level, it does not move. If we release the marble on a slope, it moves into the nearest dent that is downhill from it, as if the dent attracted the ball. By placing the marble at many different places around a dent, we can map out the region of influence of that dent, its "basin of attraction."

Crossbar networks have their own "energy surfaces" that are comparable to the clay surface of our example. Mathematically the crossbar's energy is analogous to the potential energy of the ball on the clay surface, but in the network, each energy value corresponds to a state of the network, that is, to a unique set of synapse weights and neurode activations. Researchers working with crossbar networks often talk about "sculpting the energy surface." They mean that they store patterns in the weight matrix so that appropriate "dents" are created in the energy surface. Just as with our clay surface, these dents have basins of attraction. Any input pattern that causes the state of the system to fall within the basin of attraction of a dent will also cause the system to recall the memory associated with that dent.

John Hopfield of Caltech has shown that these energy surfaces are mathematically equivalent to those of some of the familiar systems of physics, in particular, systems known as spin glasses. Because of this equivalence, insights and results obtained during years of research on these physical systems can immediately be applied to crossbar networks. This is one more reason physical scientists have been especially attracted to crossbar associative memories and have spent a great deal of time analyzing them.

Matrix Representation of Crossbar Networks

The storage and recall operations of crossbar associative networks can be described mathematically using matrices. To store a memory, the vector representing the input pattern is multiplied by the vector we want to associate it with. The result of this operation is a matrix, or a two-dimensional rectangular (or square) collection of numerical elements. When we have associated every input vector with an output vector, we have a collection of matrices representing individual "memories." To obtain the complete memory matrix of our crossbar network, we add these individual matrices together. Recall operations are performed by multiplying the input vector pattern by the

Have You Heard the One About

The similarity of the crossbar network to physical systems has inspired researchers to apply neural networks to some physical problems. One famous use of the crossbar network is to solve the Traveling Salesman Problem, often abbreviated TSP in the literature. This problem asks how a salesman should choose a route among, say ten cities, so that all cities are visited, no cities are visited more than once, and yet the shortest possible route is taken. The problem is notoriously difficult to solve by traditional computing techniques. The neural network solution involves forming a matrix in which the rows and columns represent individual cities and the entries in the matrix represent the "cost" of traveling between each pair of cities. Often these costs are just a measure of the distances between the cities. The resulting network is then allowed to converge to an appropriate path. The problem with this approach is that the network is used only as a means to manipulate a large matrix quickly and efficiently. The solution to the problem is already present, hidden in the costs or distances between cities that were calculated in advance in order to set up the crossbar matrix. Unfortunately, this method is quick and efficient only as long as we use real electronic hardware to implement the crossbar network. As we will see in chapter 16, such hardware is currently limited mostly to experimental systems.

memory matrix and then thresholding the resulting vector to obtain the final output vector. (The details of the matrix addition and multiplication are unimportant here. It is enough to know that they are entirely analogous to the same operations in arithmetic and standard algebra.)

We have presented two ways of viewing the operation of a crossbar associative memory. In the energy-surface view, each added memory pattern sculpts its unique signature onto the energy surface of the network, and a stable recall condition is reached because the network settles into the energy state nearest the energy corresponding to the supplied input vector. In the matrix view, memories are incorporated into the system by carrying out a prescribed matrix operation, and recall is effected by performing an inverse set of operations on that matrix. Each of these views is equally valid, but one may be more useful than another when thinking of different aspects of crossbar network operation.

There is yet a third way to view the operation of a crossbar associative memory. We can equally well understand that a crossbar network settles on the correct memory because of a competitive process among the neurodes. This is the feedback-competition view. To understand this view, let's look at crossbar networks once again, this time from the standpoint of what happens to the electrical signal representing an input pattern as it passes through the system.

Feedback Competition Representation

In everyday speech, the term *feedback* is usually used in a context in which the recipient of a piece of information reacts to the giver of that information. This happens when members of an audience respond to a lecturer, for instance. The technical use of the term is not much different. In our case, feedback consists of sending a fraction of each neurode's output signal back to the input of all the other neurodes for recycling.

The crossbar architecture inherently provides this feedback or recycling function. Notice in figure 5.1 that each output line has a chance to couple its output to all of the input lines, including, in principle, its own. The fraction of the output of one neurode that is fed back to the input of another is determined by the weight of the synapse between them. Without feedback, an external binary input signal would produce just a matching output. With feedback, however, things are much different. The output of a neurode now depends not only on the value of the external input signal placed on its input line but also on the internal input signals derived simultaneously from the outputs of all of the neurodes. Thus, feedback has introduced an internal signal that competes with the input signal to arrive at the proper output pattern.

If we place a signal representing a stored pattern on the input lines of an analog crossbar associative memory, a series of actions and reactions rapidly occur that result in a stable output. To see how this happens, let's think through one or two cycles of operation of a binary crossbar network.

You Can't Do Just One Thing

It is not entirely proper to talk of cycles of operation for strongly interacting, parallel, analog systems like cross-bar associative memories. In reality, everything happens at once, and everything affects everything else, so we are stuck with a continuously changing mayhem that defies easy analysis. Still, we can usually trace a causal sequence of operation as we have done here. Such a procedure is common in analysis of complex systems in fields as diverse as electronics, ecology, and economics.

First we must define the characteristics of our crossbar network. Let's assume a simple additive input function. This means that the net input to each neurode is its external input signal plus the sum of inputs from all other neurodes, as filtered through the appropriate synapses. This is the usual type of input function used for crossbar networks. Because of feedback from the other neurodes, the net input to a neurode can be negative or zero even if its external input is positive. Let's also assume that the activity function of the neurodes is a sigmoid function such as that introduced in chapter 2 with minimum and maximum activities of 0 and +1, respectively. For an output function, let's imagine that the output is −1 unless the internal activity of the neurode has exceeded some threshold value, say, 0.5.

Before an input signal is applied, the neurodes of the network are in random states of activation; some outputs are +1 and others are −1. When an external input is applied, neurodes receiving a +1 signal begin to become active, and those receiving a −1 signal begin to turn off. Let's follow the action of a particular neurode that is receiving a +1 external input and that had an output of −1 before the external signal was applied. As soon as the internal activity of this neurode exceeds 0.5, its output starts to change from −1 toward +1. Notice the word *toward*. We know that its output is fed back to the input of all the other neurodes through the connecting synapses. Thus, as its output starts to swing upward, the input of every other neurode is changed from what it would have been, and all bets are off as to whether our neurode will reach the output state dictated by its external input alone.

Identical things are going on with all the other neurodes. They are trying to reach the output demanded by their external input and affecting the inputs of all the other neurodes in the process. The net effect is a competition that ends with every neurode having affected every other neurode and the entire system having reached a state in which all the neurodes are as "comfortable" as they can be within the constraints placed on them by their mutual interconnections. The particular state of comfort reached depends on the input pattern and the values of the synapses; in other words, it depends jointly on the input pattern and the nature of the memories stored in the synapses.

An Illustrative Example

We will describe a system originally developed by Bart Kosko of the University of Southern California that takes the idea of feedback beyond what we have seen so far. Instead of feeding signals back from one neurode to another, the bidirectional associative memory, or BAM, feeds signals back from an entire layer of neurodes to another layer of neurodes. In fact, it bounces these feedback signals back and forth until the neurodes in the two layers reach a state of comfort not unlike that described above. This is our first glimpse of two new concepts, multilayer networks and resonance (we will see both again in later chapters).

The BAM is designed to store pairs of number patterns that are encoded as an ordered sequence. These numbers can mean anything at all, depending on the encoding, and they can be real numbers, integers, or even binary digits. Let's make a BAM and have it give one member of a number pair if we input the other member. (If you are not interested in the details of BAM operation right now, skip to the next section.)

Before we begin, we must look at the BAM's physical structure. Our BAM will have two layers of neurodes: layer Λ and layer B, as shown in figure 5.3. Each neurode in layer A and layer B has one input from the outside world. We can tap into the output of each neurode in either layer if we want to determine the current output pattern of that layer. The output of each neurode in layer A connects to the input of each neurode in layer B, and the output of each neurode in layer B connects to the input of each neurode in layer A; thus the layers are fully connected, just as they are in any other crossbar associative memory. The connection strengths between layers A and B are symmetric. In other words, if the connection strength between the output of neurode 1 in layer A and the input of neurode 3 in layer B is 0.7, then the connection strength between the output of neurode 3 in layer B and the input of neurode 1 in layer A is also 0.7.

In a BAM, the number of neurodes in layer A does not have to be the same as the number of neurodes in layer B; hence, the BAM is inherently a heteroassociative memory. We can create an autoassociative BAM, however, by making the two layers equal in size and by always associating a number with itself.

Assume that we have calculated the storage matrix of our BAM by following the procedure outlined earlier. How do we recall a stored memory? First, we present an input pattern to one of the two layers, say A. This pattern generates an output signal from each of the neurodes in layer A. These output signals act as inputs—are fed back—to the neurodes in layer B. Layer B then generates an output signal from each of its neurodes, which in turn is fed back to the neurodes in layer A.

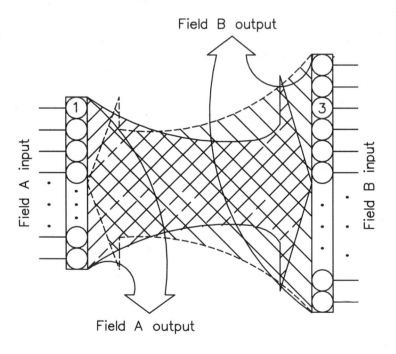

Field B output

Field A input

Field B input

Field A output

Figure 5.3 The BAM represented as two fields of fully connected neurodes.

Layer A now has two inputs: the external pattern and the input from layer B. Thus, each neurode in layer A experiences a stimulus that is the sum of its external input and the input from layer B. These latter signals are filtered through the synapses in the feedback path from B to A. Since the weight of these synapses may be inhibitory or excitatory, the net stimulus to a neurode may be positive, negative, or zero. The BAM is a binary network, so a positive net stimulus generates a +1 output, a negative net stimulus generates a 0 output (or a −1 if the network is bipolarized), and a zero net stimulus does not change the neurode's output from its previous value. Some of the neurodes in layer A may change their output state as a result of receiving feedback from layer B.

The new output pattern is now fed back to layer B, which goes through the same process that just occurred in layer A. The activity keeps bouncing back and forth between layer A and layer B until they achieve resonance, that is, a condition in which no further changes occur in the outputs of either layer A or B.

When this condition has been reached, we then tap into the outputs from layer B and—amazingly enough—find that the pattern represented by B's output is exactly the number pattern stored in association with the original input pattern.

Our decision to describe operation of a BAM in feedback terms is entirely arbitrary. We could just as well have described the recall operation using only matrix concepts, with no allusion to feedback. In these terms, we start by following the same procedure presented for recalling a stored pattern from a crossbar associative memory: we multiply the storage matrix by the input vector we wish to associate with a stored pattern. This operation produces an output vector or pattern that we use as a trial input for a second iteration of the recall process. In other words, we multiply this trial vector by the memory matrix. If this multiplication reproduces the trial vector, the BAM is "resonating" and we are through; this vector is the final answer. If the multiplication does not reproduce the trial vector, we must repeat the operation until it does—until resonance occurs. This usually happens quickly in BAMs.

The Problems with Crossbar Networks

Why don't all computers use crossbar associative memories? To answer this question, we will look at some of the shortcomings of these networks, using the BAM network as an example.

The first problem is efficiency. Let's say we want to store three pairs of binary numbers, with one member of each pair having three bits and the other having six. For instance, a typical pair might be (010) and (101001). Since each pair contains nine bits, we must store 27 bits of information in our BAM. To store those three pairs of binary numbers, we have to use a 6×3 matrix containing 18 integer numbers. If we implement this system in a standard computer, we might assign one 16-bit word in RAM memory to hold each element in the BAM's memory matrix. We would then end up using 18×16, or 288 bits, to store our 27 bits of information.

At worst, if we were doing this with a conventional computer memory instead of a BAM, we would assign each of our six binary numbers to one 16-bit word in RAM memory. Even in this worst-case scenario, we would use only 96 bits of RAM to store our numbers, one-third as many as with the BAM. This flaw is not an isolated case. BAMs and other crossbar networks are not very space efficient in the storage of information.

There is even a more difficult problem regarding efficiency hidden here. The total number of individual computations we must perform to store and recall a vector pair is much larger in a BAM than the number required to store and recall a pair of numbers in the RAM memory of a computer. In the BAM storage process, we associate one pattern, A, with another, B. Later, if we enter A, we obtain B, and if we enter B, we obtain A. To recall A or B, remember that we must multiply a matrix and a vector. That operation is computationally complex in its own right. Depending upon whether we want to recall A given B, or B given A, however, we additionally may have to carry out another operation, called transposition, on the matrix before performing the actual recall. Furthermore, we must then threshold the elements of the resulting vector to complete the recall sequence. For a matrix of size $(m \times n)$, this involves $m \times n$ total multiplication operations and $n(m-1)$ addition operations just to do the matrix multiplication. For the example, in which we store and retrieve three number pairs, we require 18 multiplications and 12 addition operations. This is much more complex and time-consuming than storing or retrieving a number from the memory of a computer. Digital computers utilize efficient, specialized hardware to perform storage and recall operations.

The most serious problem with crossbar networks is their capacity. For a matrix of m rows and n columns, the theory of associative memories tells us that the maximum number of pattern pairs we can expect to store is the smaller of m and n. For our (6×3) matrix exam-

---

When Less Is More

The idea of deliberately using very large matrices in order to increase the orthogonality of the stored data patterns, and thus improve the reliability of recall, is called "sparse coding." The data patterns stored in such sparsely coded systems have many more 0s than 1s. The total amount of data stored is very small for the required space, but it can be recalled more accurately and reliably. Of course, availability of this technique increases the demand for neural networks capable of representing huge matrices.

The term *sparse coding* has also—with at least a touch of seriousness—been applied to the level of productivity achieved by programming groups on Friday afternoons.

---

ple, we would saturate the capacity of the matrix with our three number pairs. If we actually performed the matrix operations and constructed a storage matrix using three binary number pairs, we would find that adding even one more pattern pair would cause at least one of the four pairs to be incorrectly recalled. If we moved to larger matrices to store more patterns, we would find that larger matrices do worse, relatively, than smaller ones. It is not uncommon for large crossbar networks to have storage capacity efficiencies of 10 to 15 percent or lower. Thus, a (100 × 100) matrix might be able to store only 10 or 15 pairs instead of the supposed maximum of 100 pairs. As a result, we might have to use matrices with 1000 or 2000 rows and columns to store 100 pattern pairs.

Another complicating factor is the problem of storing patterns that are very similar to each other. Crossbar associative memories produce the fewest recall problems when the patterns stored are orthogonal. In essence, two patterns are orthogonal if they do not overlap, that is, if they are completely distinct. Orthogonal three-dimensional vectors, for instance, are all perpendicular to each other in space; they do not overlap.

Of course, real-world problems are rarely orthogonal. Most of the time, we cannot be sure that the data patterns we must store are sufficiently different from each other to enable a crossbar to record them reliably. There is a clever scheme, however, that capitalizes on the storage inefficiency of crossbar networks in order to partially overcome the orthogonality problem. Remember that even at maximum theoretical efficiency, we are forced to use a matrix size of at least 10 rows if we want to store 10 patterns. But in 10 binary digits, we have the potential choice of two to the tenth power, or 1024, binary numbers. Since we need to store only 10 numbers, we can often choose a coding scheme that results in these ten numbers being nearly or completely orthogonal and thus obtain the best possible recall performance from our associative memory.

There is yet another problem associated with storage and recall by crossbar associative memories. We can best discuss this problem using the energy surface analogy. When we "sculpt the energy surface" by placing the energy dents or wells where we want to create memories, we invariably and unavoidably end up adding extra energy wells we don't want. It is as though we have to walk across our clay surface to get to the place where we want to make a dent, and the process of walking across the clay leaves dents where we don't want them or smooths out dents where we have stored data. These extra energy wells, called "spurious minima" by researchers, cause crossbars in general, and BAMs in particular, sometimes to generate output patterns that have nothing whatever to do with any of the input patterns stored. When this happens, the imaginary marble placed on the surface has rolled into one of those extra energy wells rather than into one of the wells we deliberately produced. In the terminology of the computer world, it's "good stuff in, garbage out."

These deficiencies are related and are part of the fabric of crossbar associative memories. They cannot be sidestepped without giving up one or more desirable properties associated with the architecture. Associative memory designs such as the Attentive Associative Memory introduced by Ravi Athale are able, for instance, to store virtually as many memories as the system has neurodes. In order to do this, however, these networks give up distributed memory storage. In that area, they possess the characteristics of standard RAM memory. You will recall that the ability to distribute each stored memory over the entire system is an important characteristic of the designs we discussed. Among other things, it grants fail softness to an associative memory. Thus, the more capacity the modified crossbar design has, the less distributed the memories and the less robust to loss of individual neurodes the system becomes.

Then Why Study the Crossbar?

You might think that with all these problems the crossbar would have been abandoned by now. In fact, it is not often used for applications at the moment, precisely because of the problems outlined. But suppose there were a way to do matrix and vector multiplications in a constant amount of time, no matter how large our matrix? Suppose we could do this cheaply with matrices that have millions or billions of elements on a side? Would the BAM and other crossbar systems be more useful then? Of course they would! If we could use large enough matrices, we could almost guarantee that the data patterns stored would have little overlap. If we could manipulate these huge matrices quickly and easily, we could afford to settle for low storage density. What technology would allow us to do this? The answer might be optical computers. If we can take advantage of some of the special characteristics of light, eventually we may be able to deal with enormous matrices as simply as we currently add binary numbers. If and when optical computers become a practical alternative, or even a supplement, to electronic computers, the day of the crossbar associative memory may finally be at hand.

The palest ink is better than the most retentive memory.
— Chinese proverb

6 Adaptive Filter Associative Memories

Adaptive filter systems were born in the 1950s and early 1960s as an outgrowth of digital signal processing studies. The classic example of an adaptive filter network is Bernard Widrow and M. E. Hoff's adaptive linear element, or *adaline*, first presented in 1960. The idea behind an adaptive signal filter is simply to make a system that can adjust the way it filters noise from a signal. The filter ideally will adapt to the types of noise presented to it and learn to filter the signal, removing the noise and thus enhancing the signal. It should come as no surprise to discover that the adaline has found applications in high-speed modems and in echo cancellation on telephone lines.

The adaline is of great importance in our study of neural networks because it is the first network we will look at that learns through an iterative procedure. Such learning procedures are more typical of neural networks than the kind of single-pass algorithm we discovered in the crossbar networks. The adaline's iterative learning procedure is more similar to some types of animal learning than the crossbar because new patterns are not instantly stored; instead they must be presented a number of times before learning is complete. The adaline also introduces a learning law that is one of the most important in the field of neural networks, the delta rule.

Chapter 6

Introducing the Adaline

One of the oldest neural networks, the adaline has been around for more than a quarter-century. In its simplest form, this network consists of a single neurode along with its associated input interconnects and synapses. That single neurode can learn to sort complex input patterns into two classes. For example, we might have it look at pictures of shapes and classify them as "circle" and "not circle." By combining many of these units, we might then have them accept an input pattern and generate a more complex output pattern. This arrangement is called the "madaline" (multilayered adaline).

The adaline neurode is almost identical to the one presented in chapter 2. It forms a weighted sum of all inputs, applies a threshold, and in this case outputs a +1 or −1 signal as appropriate. It has one input and one modifiable synapse for every element in the expected input pattern. In addition, it has an extra input. We use this extra "mentor" input in the training process to tell the neurode what it is supposed to output for the current input pattern. We leave the weight of the mentor input at a constant value of 1.0. It does not contribute to the summed input unless the adaline is being taught, but when it is in use, we want the mentor signal to overwhelm the combined effect of all other inputs.

We train the adaline by using a learning law called the "delta rule" to adjust the weights on the input-pattern signal lines. First, we define a group of input patterns that we will use to train the adaline. This training set must be carefully chosen to be typical of the patterns the adaline will see after training is complete. Next we define a test set of input patterns that we will use to test the adaline. The input patterns must be similar but not identical to the training set. If we test the system on the same patterns used to train it, it is as though we gave the questions on a test to a student before an exam; the network's response becomes a simple lookup of memorized answers and is of little use in determining what it can do with what we taught it.

We can now train the adaline by presenting the training set to the neurode, one pattern at a time. Every time we present an input pattern, we also provide a +1.0 or −1.0 signal on the mentor input to tell the neurode the correct output value for this input pattern. The neurode responds to the input pattern and generates an output signal, which we compare to the correct output value. If the adaline has the correct output value, we do not change the weights. If the adaline has the incorrect output value, we adjust the weights. Both of

What's in a Name?

The learning law used by the adaline is referred to by several names. Depending on who is doing the referencing and the circumstances, it can be called the delta rule, the Widrow-Hoff learning rule, or the least mean squared rule (LMS rule). The *delta rule* is the most commonly used term today, so that is what we use in this book. It refers to the fact that the original weight vector of the adaline is modified during training by adding a delta, or difference, vector to the original to get the resulting new weight vector. The Widrow-Hoff learning rule is a well-deserved nod to Bernie Widrow and Ted Hoff of Stanford, who created this learning algorithm. The LMS rule is Widrow and Hoff's name for their weight change law. In some ways it is the most descriptive, as we will see below. Finally, LMS is merely an acronym for least mean squared. Don't be surprised when you see all of these terms in the literature, but don't be confused either. They all mean the same thing.

these instructions are embodied in the delta rule. This rule says that we change the weight vector in proportion to the "distance" from where it is to where it ought to be. We determine this distance, or error value, by subtracting the network's actual output response from the response we wanted it to produce. We then multiply this error value by a learning constant and the size and direction of the input pattern vector to compute each specific weight change.

Let's look at each item in the rule. We will talk more later about the learning constant. For now, assume that it is a number less than 1. The length of a vector is the square root of the sum of the squares of the vector's components; thus, the denominator, which is the square of the length of the weight vector, is the sum of the squares of the individual interconnect weights. It is a pure number, or in vector terms, a scalar. To obtain the output error, we subtract the actual value of the neurode's output from the desired value we imposed on the neurode by means of the mentor line. This error is also a scalar.

Components and Multidimensional Spaces

In this book, we will often refer to the components of a vector. A vector is a line segment that points in a particular direction. The length of the line is a measure of the magnitude or size of the quantity the vector represents. For convenience, we often choose to draw vectors as pointing outward from the intersection (origin) of a set of mutually perpendicular axes. To introduce the subject, let's use a two-dimensional vector pointing outward from the intersection of the x and y axes. There is a simple way to visualize the components of this vector. Imagine that it can cast a shadow and that we shine a flashlight beam parallel to the y axis so that the vector casts a shadow onto the x axis. This shadow is the x component of the vector. Said another way, the x and y components of our vector are the distances we must travel parallel to each axis if we wish to get to the tip of the vector from the origin.

The result of the first two multiplications and the division, then, is a scalar. The final multiplication does two things. First, it multiplies this result by the length of the input vector. From the definition we used above, this length is the square root of the sum of the squares of the components of the input vector. Second, it makes the final result a vector pointing in the direction of the input vector. Thus, the delta rule is a vector rule.

Note that the rule does not require us to multiply two vectors together as we did when building the memory matrix of a crossbar network. Here we compute a scalar quantity, and then multiply it by a vector, quite a different operation.

There is another way to view the computational process represented by the delta rule. Instead of directly computing the length of the weight vector, we can equally well compute each component separately. We still obtain a vector, since knowing the value of each component of a vector is tantamount to knowing the length and direction of the vector itself. If this is not clear, the box "Components and Multidimensional Spaces" may help. In the component view, the

The components of a vector are scalars; they have no direction. We can, however, think of a "component vector" that is the result of multiplying the value of a particular component by a little vector one unit long that points along the axis associated with that component. If we lay all of the component vectors of a particular vector end to end in head-to-tail fashion, we obtain the original vector. That is the main reason we deal with components: we can decompose any vector into its scalar components, perform algebraic operations on them singly, and then reconstruct the resulting vector.

This is all well and good in, say, three dimensions, where vectors have only three elements, but a weight vector consisting of all of the weights on a neurode may contain hundreds or thousands of elements. For such vectors, we imagine a space with many axes, all perpendicular to each other. Although we cannot easily visualize such a multidimensional hyperspace, we can still conceive of vectors in that space and of carrying out operations on them or their components.

rule becomes: *To determine the amount to change the weight of each interconnect, multiply the adaline's output error by the value of the corresponding element of the input vector and by a learning constant, and divide by the square of the length of the weight vector.*

Carrying out algebraic operations on vectors ultimately comes down to dealing with their components. With this in mind, the second statement of the rule can be considered to be a recipe for carrying out the vector operation described in the first statement. Both ultimately lead to the same result. The total weight change is thus proportional to the size of the "mistake" the neurode made in its output when that training pattern was presented to it and is inversely proportionally to the length of the input vector. Finally, the change in the weight, when treated as a vector, is parallel to the input vector.

In summary, the purpose of the delta rule is to guide us in updating the interconnect weights during training. For each pattern in the training set, we determine the output error. We then use this error to compute a delta vector that is jointly proportional to both the output error and the size of the input vector and in the same direction. Finally, we add this delta vector to the current weight vector term by term to obtain the updated value. When we have done this, we are ready to present the next training pattern.

Surely this learning law was not plucked out of thin air? Where did it come from? Remember that we said the most descriptive name for the law is the one Widrow and Hoff originally gave it: the least mean squared rule, or LMS rule. The delta rule attempts to ensure that the standard, statistical least mean squared error is achieved in the network. The error is the aggregate error in the weights of the neurode based on a theoretical ideal ensemble value for the weights.

Geometry of the Delta Rule

We can think of this learning law geometrically. It can be shown mathematically that the statistical mean squared error is a quadratic function of the weight vector. This means that when we plot the mean squared error corresponding to all possible values of the

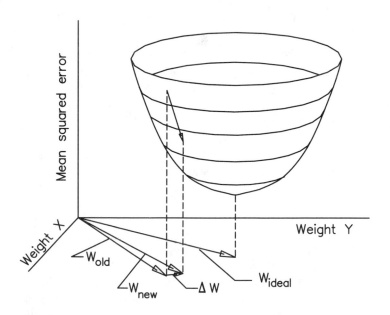

Figure 6.1 The delta rule moves the weight vector so that it follows the steepest descent of the hyperparaboloid.

weight vector, we obtain a parabola. We obtain a hyperparaboloid in general, since we usually do this in n-dimensional hyperspace. For illustration, though, a two-dimensional example will do. One feature of parabolas is that they have a bottom. In other words, there is one point where the bowl bottoms out into a minimum value. This point represents the minimum mean squared error—the least mean squared error, in fact. The weight vector that corresponds to this minimum error is our ideal weight vector.

The delta rule changes the weight vector so that its corresponding mean squared error value moves from wherever it is on the surface of this parabola toward the bottom of the bowl. It does this by moving along the negative gradient of the parabola, which is the most direct route to the bottom of the bowl. This process is illustrated in figure 6.1. If you are familiar with vector analysis, you will recall that the gradient always points along the direction of the steepest rise of a curve, and the negative gradient is the steepest descent of the curve at any given point. That means that this learning rule always takes the most efficient route from the current position of the weight vector to the "ideal" position, based on the current input pattern. The delta rule not only minimizes the mean squared error, it does so in the most efficient fashion possible—quite an achievement for such a simple rule.

Choosing the Learning Constant

What about the learning constant? How do we know what value to use? Should it be 100,000 or 0.000001 or 1? We will try to justify what reasonable values might be.

Let's use a little common sense to narrow this value down. The first thing we can see is that it must be positive. If it is negative, the direction of the delta vector is away from the ideal weight vector at the bottom of the bowl; we would be making the response worse, not better. Mathematically, the learning constant must be less than 2.0 or the network cannot be stabilized. What would a value between 1.0 and 2.0 do to the network? To answer this, we can think of the operation of the network as a whole. Suppose we have adjusted the weight vector so that it is almost at the ideal position at the bottom of the bowl—not perfect but fairly close to where we want the weight vector to be after training. When we calculate the new weight vector, we will find that as long as the learning constant is less than 1.0, the delta vector will tend to change the weight vector in the correct direction. But if the learning constant is, say, 1.5, we will overshoot the ideal position and end up somewhere on the other side of the bottom of the bowl. Thus, we always want to keep the learning constant less than 1.0.

The job of this constant is to set the speed of convergence of the weight vector to the ideal value at the bottom of the parabola. You might think that the way to make this system work best is always to set the learning constant to 1.0 to make the weight vector go toward the ideal position at the fastest possible rate. This is not necessarily an efficient training strategy, however. Certainly if our weight vector is far away from its correct position, we want to change it in fairly large steps; otherwise training can be unnecessarily prolonged. Choosing a large value for the learning constant, perhaps 0.8 or 0.9, allows the neurode to learn distinctions quickly between grossly different input patterns. But when we get close to the correct position on the error parabola, even small differences between similar training samples, when combined with a large learning constant, cause the weight vector to jump around excessively and be very slow to find the correct settling point. As a result, we want the constant to be much smaller—perhaps 0.1 or less—as the system nears the end of its training.

What Can the Adaline Do?

You might think that a network as simple as the adaline would have few if any applications in the real world. In fact, this is not the case. As simple as the adaline is, it has proved itself in a remarkable variety of applications. For example, it has been effective in a number of noise suppression applications, and is surprisingly reliable at a simple weather prediction task.

In the weather prediction application, a single adaline was provided with atmospheric pressure and time rate of change of atmospheric pressure from locations over a large area of the Pacific Ocean north and west of the San Francisco Bay Area. Its job was to decide if there would be rain in the Bay Area at a selected time in the future. Once trained, the adaline did at least as well as the local weather service in predicting whether it would rain 12, 24, and 36 hours in the future. Remarkably, these predictions were made using only a single neurode and its interconnects, and not a highly complex network. Comparing this lone adaline to the supercomputers in use today for weather forecasting gives new meaning to the environmentalist's adage that sometimes less is more.

Bernard Widrow, the coinventor of the adaline, distinguishes between neurodes with thresholded output of +1 or –1, as discussed above, and those that have an analog output and whose inputs are a time sequence derived from a tapped delay line. These latter, he contends, are not truly neural networks but are "merely" adaptive filters. In fact, there is little to distinguish them from the "pure" adaline, other than the temporal nature of their inputs and their analog outputs, and we draw no such fine distinctions between the two. Both use the delta rule for adapting their output to their experience with input data patterns, and both can justifiably be considered neural networks.

Networks using the delta rule have enjoyed greater commercial success than those using any other learning rule, partly because the rule has been around for nearly three decades but also due to its effectiveness in solving commercially important problems. In addition, the least mean squared error is important in many areas of mathematics and engineering, and the adaline's ability to model this error is especially valuable. For example, adaptive filters have become quite important in the field of signal processing. In other areas of technology, high-speed modems use adaptive filters for signal equalization, and both standard long distance and satellite-based communication systems use them for adaptive echo cancellation. Adalines abound in noise cancellation applications in electronic instruments. In electrocardiographs, they can be used to cancel the mother's heartbeat signal when monitoring that of a fetus. Other applications include performance improvements in radar systems and channel equalization in telecommunications.

Limitations of the Adaline

The adaline, like many of its historical ancestors, has one major difficulty that limits its usefulness: it can successfully attack only linearly separable pattern classification problems. We can illustrate what this means for a case in which the adaline must classify two-dimensional patterns into two classes, say, "A" and "not A." The adaline will be truly successful in learning only those problems where all examples of "A" and "not A" can be separated by a single straight line. In *n*-dimensional space the term *straight line* must be replaced by *hyperplane*. For now, we need only understand that the adaline cannot learn to separate every possible collection of patterns correctly. Furthermore, its inherently analog nature can cause it to need read-

justment after every pattern it is taught to ensure that it still remembers all previously taught patterns.

Some of these problems can be at least partially overcome by
using an array of adalines, a madaline. A madaline has been shown
to provide translation and rotation invariance in recognition of simple images. That is, a madaline can often recognize a learned pattern
even if it is presented to the system in a part of its field of view or in
an orientation that is different from the one used in the training set.
Other problems with the adaline can be resolved, or at least
improved, by careful implementation of the delta rule or by moving

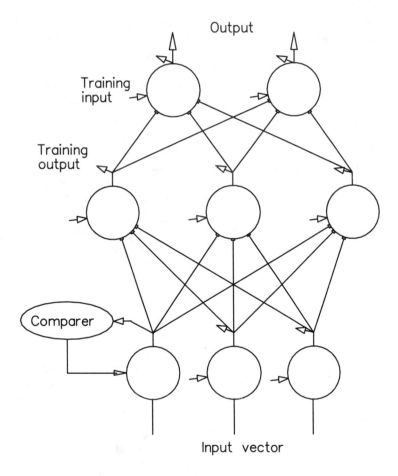

Figure 6.2 The architecture of the madaline.

away from the simple linear combiner to a higher-order polynomial combiner. Let's take a moment to explore these variations.

Training the Madaline

What new problems are we likely to encounter if we want to teach a madaline several input patterns? Let's suppose that we have a collection of adalines arranged in three layers, which we will call the input layer, the middle layer, and the output layer, as in figure 6.2. Using the usual delta rule, we train the network on an input pattern so that it responds correctly at the output layer. Now we want it to learn a second pattern; will it still recall the first when the second pattern's training is complete?

Maybe. We must check the first pattern after adding the second and readjust the weights in the network, if necessary, to ensure that the first pattern is retained. We then have to check the second pattern again to be sure it is still correctly recalled, and so on until no further changes are needed. If we add a third pattern, we must ensure that both the two previous patterns and the third are retained before continuing. This process can be frustrating and time consuming.

Bernard Widrow has suggested a way around this problem that seems to work quite well for the madaline. He calls his solution madaline rule II (MRII). In training a madaline using MRII, one of the key principles is that the training should disturb the fewest possible neurodes; it should minimally disturb the network. The procedure goes like this. We apply the first input pattern to the network and check the responses of the input-layer neurodes before the threshold is applied to each. Recall that the binary nature of the adaline's output means that an activity level that is even slightly positive generates a +1 output, and one that is even slightly negative generates a −1 output. We then identify the single neurode whose weighted input is closest to zero—the neurode that is closest to changing the sign of its output. We apply the delta rule to this neurode until its output sign reverses. We then propagate this modification in the input layer's output through the network to see if it reduces the number of output layer errors. If the number of output errors is reduced, we accept the change, permanently alter the neurode's weights to the new values, and proceed with training. If the number of output errors is not reduced with this change, we remove the weight changes from the delta rule and restore the network to its original state.

In either event, we next choose the input-layer neurode that has a weighted input second closest to zero and apply the delta rule tentatively until the neurode's output reverses. Again we propagate the resulting activity through the network to see if the output errors are reduced. If so, we accept the tentative weight changes in the input-layer neurode; otherwise we delete the changes and proceed to the next closest neurode. This continues until either all single neurodes that cause a reduction in output-layer errors have been trained, or the output error reduces to zero. If there are still output errors after we have checked all single input-layer neurodes, we move to pairs of neurodes, again changing only those pairs that effect a reduction in the output-layer error. Higher-order combinations (triplets, quadruplets, and so forth) can also be used, but single neurodes and possibly pairs are all that is required for many applications.

This procedure makes sense. Because the individual adalines are thresholded, one with a weighted input of 0.001 and one with a weighted input of 0.999 will each generate an output of 1.0. Why should we go to a lot of effort to modify the weights on the neurode with weighted input of 0.999 when we have another neurode with a weighted input of only 0.001 that might do the trick? As a result, we try the easiest case first, so that all we have to do is change its weighted input from 0.001 to, say, –0.001, compared to changing the other neurode's weighted input from 0.999 to –0.001. If this reduces the number of output errors, we know we're on the right track and make the change permanent; otherwise we try another neurode, perhaps one with a weighted input of –0.003, which we would want to modify to a weighted input of perhaps 0.001.

Once we complete training of the input layer, we follow the same procedure with the middle-layer neurodes. We again choose the single neurode with weighted input closest to zero and tentatively train it until its output reverses. If this reduces the number of output errors, we accept that value, and so on. Again, we first train single neurodes and go on to pairs only if necessary.

This procedure sounds quite complex and time-consuming, and in the worst case, it is. In a large fraction of cases, however, relatively few weight changes need be made to learn a particular pattern because weight modifications are always done on the neurode that has the easiest output to change. Thus, the smallest possible number of weights are altered as each new training pattern is presented. The procedure has another desirable feature: it permits minimal overlap between patterns when multiple patterns are stored in the network.

As a result, not only are individual patterns stored more easily, but more patterns can be stored.

The adaline's difficulty in solving nonlinearly separable problems has been successfully overcome in at least two ways. Although the delta rule is not associated with either of these methods, both use single neurodes, and at least one of them arose from the same group that created the adaline and madaline. To end our discussion of adaptive filters, we present two decidedly nonlinear adaptive filter associative memories: the higher-order network and the polynomial adaline. Each is able to solve nonlinearly separable problems.

Higher-Order Networks

Higher-order networks have been in use since the earliest days of serious neural network application. The adaline and madaline networks are first-order networks. Separate inputs are provided for each element in the input vector, and only the first power of each input vector element is used. Recall that the total input to an adaline or madaline neurode is a linear weighted sum of the elements of the input vector.

In a higher-order network, additional inputs are provided to each neurode to represent products among input vector elements. For a two-dimensional input with elements x and y, for instance, these combinations might be the powers x^2, y^2, x^3, y^3, as well as the cross terms xy, x^2y, xy^2, xy^3, x^2y^2, and so on. Because their physical structure inherently provides for higher-order correlations among the input vector elements, these networks can be taught to build complicated separating surfaces among categories. In fact, a single higher-order neurode can have the same ability to separate patterns that a many-layered first-order network does. Higher-order networks also typically learn complex discriminations much faster than multilayer networks, and their storage capacity is greater than that of a first-order network of comparable computational power.

A powerful gift comes free with higher-order networks: some problems that are difficult to solve with other types of networks become almost trivial when attacked with higher-order networks. For instance, the so-called n-bit parity problem can be solved with only a single higher-order input to a single neurode. The object of this problem is to be able to tell if a binary sequence has an even or an odd number of "true" bits. These two conditions correspond, respectively, to even and odd parity. To solve the problem, we make the input vector inverted (or negative-logic) bipolar, that is, we choose −1 to stand for "true" and +1 to stand for "false." (In normal positive logic, +1 stands for "true," and either 0 or −1 stands for "false," depending on whether we are using a binary or bipolar representation.) If we then make the single input to the higher-order neurode represent the product of every element in the n-bit input vector, the output is automatically (−1) for odd-parity inputs and (+1) for even-parity inputs.

An obvious disadvantage of higher-order networks lies in the number of input lines required to represent all possible powers and cross products of the elements of the input vector. As the size of the input vector or the degree of the highest-order term utilized grows, the number of possible combinations of input vector elements becomes very large. There are other problems. Standard training methods for higher-order networks often require storage, computation, and inversion of an $m \times m$ matrix, where m is the total number of inputs of all orders to the network. This number can be very large. Such training methods also often require storage of the entire training set before use. In addition, they usually are iterative; that is, they usually require several passes through the training set for adequate learning. These characteristics and the fact that standard training methods easily overfit the training data make standard higher-order networks difficult to use for some applications.

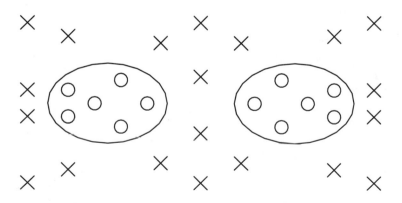

Figure 6.3 The padaline can even properly separate pattern examples in two disjoint regions.

The Padawhat??

The name Donald Specht used in his research papers for this modified adaline is polynomial discriminant method. We suggested a couple of simpler names to him, and of those, the name he preferred was *padaline*. We therefore use *padaline* to refer to his method in this book. The term is a contraction of *polynomial adaline* and refers to a modified adaline that uses a polynomial function rather than a line to separate pattern examples into categories.

The Polynomial Adaline

A second way of overcoming the difficulty the adaline has in solving nonlinearly separable problems is the polynomial adaline, which we call the "padaline." In the mid-1960s Donald F. Specht, a student of Widrow, modified the adaline by using a higher-order transfer function instead of a linear sum of inputs. This version of the adaline, which he called the polynomial discriminant method, effectively gives the adaline a transfer function that computes a polynomial expression for the separating boundary. Such an expression can represent complex boundary shapes.

This modification increases the mathematical complexity of software simulations of the adaline, although hardware representations become somewhat easier. Any increase in simulation complexity is more than offset for many applications, however, by the ability of the padaline to learn categories that cannot be separated by a straight line. For example, patterns that have disjoint regions, such as the one shown in figure 6.3, can be correctly learned with this technique. The modified network constructs a dividing region like that shown schematically in the figure to separate the two category examples. Multiple categories can be distinguished by a minor modification that is equivalent to the change from the adaline to the madaline.

A padaline has a remote relation to a higher-order network. The approach is functionally equivalent to determining the weights of a higher-order network. The coefficients of the computed discriminant function are not those weights, however. One of the major advantages of the padaline over a higher-order network is that the training sequence used with it is not iterative and requires the use of only one training vector at a time. Thus, no computationally complex operations need be performed on the training set as a whole, and each training vector can be discarded after use.

While the mathematical formulas that correspond to the padaline can appear intimidating at first inspection, the algorithm itself is not difficult to implement on a computer, especially in the two-category case, where we assign input patterns only to the classes "A" and "not A." The training technique for this situation consists of a single pass through the training set, during which coefficients are computed for a polynomial function that defines the separating surface between the categories. Unlike training methods required for most other higher-order networks, there is no need to store all of the patterns used to train the system; the padaline algorithm discards each training vector after it computes that pattern's contributions to the polynomial coefficients. These coefficients are then used to compute the value of the polynomial for each pattern in the unknown test set. If the resulting value of the polynomial is positive, then the category is "A"; if the resulting value is negative, the category is "not A." A zero polynomial value means that the unknown pattern lies directly on the separating surface. In principle, this technique is quite simple, but it requires a lot of computational power, especially for large-dimension patterns, multicategory decisions, or complex decision surfaces.

The adaline is a simple, highly useful neural network. Although it is easy to understand and implement, it has difficulty with nonlinearly separable problems, and old patterns can be lost if they are not relearned during the addition of new ones. These difficulties can and have been overcome to some extent but only at the expense of increased complexity in network form and training technique. In spite of these drawbacks, however, adalines remain one of the most useful and practical neural networks invented.

While useful and practical, the adaline and its cousins still have the restriction that they can be trained only when they are provided with the "right" answer. The problem with this is that we don't always know the right answer. Wouldn't it be nice if we had a network that did not depend on us to give it the correct response to an input pattern? These "self-organizing systems" exist, and the next chapter discusses one of the most important examples of this class of networks.

Application:
The Vectorcardiograph

The adaline was one of the earliest practical neural networks and is still used in several technically and economically important applications. There are many possible adaline applications we could choose to discuss, but we have selected one from the field of medicine as being typical.

One of the earliest potentially important applications for a madaline, indeed for any other neural network, was the vector-cardiograph abnormality detector, an expert system developed in 1963 by Donald Specht, a student of Widrow. In its most advanced form, this machine detected the presence of heart abnormalities more consistently than did trained cardiologists.

A standard clinical electrocardiograph (EKG) records electrical signals generated by the heart by means of leads placed at up to 12 locations on the patient's body. Separate, sequential recordings are usually made of the signal induced in each lead. A variation of the clinical EKG, the vectorcardiograph, records electric signals generated by the heart along three roughly perpendicular axes: front-back, head-foot, and right-left. The vectorcardiograph requires fewer leads than the clinical EKG. It also produces less redundant but potentially more useful information than the standard EKG because it records all three data channels simultaneously and thus preserves the time relationships among the three recorded traces. The form of the signal from a vectorcardiograph is nearly ideal for interpretation by a neural network.

Because Specht was working closely with physicians at the Palo Alto Stanford Medical Center's Cardiology Department, he had available a large number of vectorcardiographs taken from both normal and diseased hearts. As a first effort, he chose to utilize only the central section of the EKG signature known as the QRS complex. Because he intended to simulate the adaptive linear elements on a digital computer, Specht broke the analog data of the vectorcardiographs into response values at discrete time intervals. He found that he could adequately represent the waveform of each trace with 15 points taken at 5 millisecond intervals across the 75 millisecond time span that included the QRS complex. To this total of 45 points for the three traces, he added a forty-sixth point, the duration of the QRS complex. There are several equivalent ways of viewing this input. We can say that the input consisted of a 46-element vector, or we can say that the system considered 46 variables, or we can say that the input had 46 degrees of freedom.

There is yet another way to view this. The group of all inputs, including the training set, test set, and operating data, formed a set of points in a 46-dimensional space. The job of Specht's expert system was to define a hypersurface that completely separated the normal from the abnormal cardiographs. (A hypersurface in *n*-dimensional space is an extension of the concept of an ordinary surface in three-dimensional space. The prefix *hyper* simply indicates that the surface can exist in more than three dimensions.) We already know that a simple adaline with 46 inputs can place the input vectors on only one side or the other of a 45-dimensional hyperplane. If the points to be classified cannot be separated into two groups in this way, the system will fail. To allow the system to draw a curved surface around the points, that is, to apply more than one separation criterion, Specht used several adalines in parallel—a madaline—in his first system. Each adaline had 46 input synapses, and each element of the input vectors is applied in parallel to every adaline. He added a confidence-level unit to the madaline to count the number of +1 outputs from the adaline collection; this gave him a measure of the confidence the system has in the diagnosis.

In clinical practice, it is usually considered more important not to give a false positive test for a disease than not to give a false negative. The reasoning behind this rule is simple: there are usually several tests for a given disease, and if one does not identify it, another probably will. Thus, a false negative result in one test is likely to be offset by the positive results of other tests. On the other hand, it is upsetting to a patient to receive a positive diagnosis when there is no disease present, even if all other tests are negative. Specht realized that if each adaline within the madaline array tested for a different abnormality, the false-test rule would automatically be satisfied. When he constructed the new system and developed a training rule for it, he received a bonus: once an individual adaline was trained, it was not necessary to retrain it after each of the remaining adalines was trained or if other adaline elements were added at a later time. He also found that his system seldom required more than three adalines.

The new training procedure allowed him to train the adalines of the system sequentially instead of in parallel, as the usual mad-aline training procedure required. In his new sequential procedure, he trained the first adaline on the entire training set, using the usual LMS training rule, as if it were the only unit in the system. When the first adaline was able to identify all normal cases and some fraction of the abnormal ones, he then froze the weights on the first adaline and began training the second. The training set for the second adaline did not contain the abnormal cases that the first adaline recognized. When the second adaline could identify all normal cases and some fraction of the remaining abnormal ones, the weights of the second adaline were frozen. This process was continued until all of the abnormal cases could be identified by some adaline.

Specht trained the system using vectorcardiographs from 107 subjects. Of these, 50 had been judged normal and 57 abnormal by physicians using standard clinical EKGs and laboratory tests. When a test set of 60 new vectorcardiographs (27 normal and 33 abnormal) was used, trained clinicians were able to identify about 95 percent of the normals using only the QRS complex, but only 54 percent of the abnormals. The system, on the other hand, correctly identified 93 percent of the normals and 76 percent of the abnormals.

This performance did not represent the ultimate capability of the system. Specht proceeded to add a nonlinear capability to his system by training a single modified adaline using a variation of the standard adaline called the polynomial adaline, or padaline. In the analogy of our earlier hyperplane illustration, adding nonlinear capability to the adaline allows it to separate or even enclose a set of points in 46-dimensional space by using a curved surface instead of a flat hyperplane. This capability allowed the expert system to make a much better separation between the region of normal points and the regions containing points representing abnormal vectorcardiographs. For a system whose only job is to separate normal from abnormal vectorcardiographs, one nonlinear, adaptive padaline does the work of the several adaline units of the earlier system.

Because there was only one neurode, a sequential training procedure was not necessary for the nonlinear expert system. The padaline was trained on 249 cases, of which 192 were normal and 57 were judged clinically abnormal by the same criteria used earlier. When tested with 63 cases not in the training set, the network correctly diagnosed 97 percent of the normal and 90 percent of the abnormal cases. The corresponding success rate for trained clinicians using the QRS section of the vectorcardiographs of the same cases was 95 percent and 53 percent.

Specht later designed a network using several padalines in an arrangement analogous to the linear madaline. Its purpose was to separate abnormal cases into several categories more success- fully than the earlier system. No clinical trials of this unit were apparently conducted. To our knowledge, neither the linear mad- aline nor the padaline expert system has been constructed com- mercially. Despite this, the diagnostic capabilities of these relatively unsophisticated systems clearly demonstrate the pro- cessing power of even simple neural networks.

The only competition worthy a wise man
is with himself.
—Mrs. Anna Jameson

7 Competitive Filter Associative Memories

In the previous chapters we have seen two kinds of associative memories, each of which can learn the correct associations only when provided with the right response during training. There are times when such a training technique is adequate; however, there are also times when we need a system that can learn by itself. A neural network with such a capability is called a self-organizing system because during training the network changes the weights on its interconnects to learn appropriate associations, even though no right answers are provided. One of the simplest networks with this characteristic is the competitive filter associative memory, so called because the neurodes in the network compete for the privilege of learning.

Why is self-organization so important? In the early 1960s, researchers had naive notions about the prerequisites for constructing intelligent systems. Some expected that they could just randomly interconnect huge numbers of neurodes and then turn them on and feed them data to create automatically an intelligent mechanical brain. This is nonsense. As we now know, our brains, even the brains of lizards and snails, are highly organized and structured devices. Mere random interconnection of elements will not work. And yet one observation underlying those naive notions is certainly valid: our brains can learn without being given the correct answer to a situation.

Certainly we sometimes need a tutor during learning; this is one of the reasons we go to school. And learning from a teacher or a book is often a more efficient means of mastering cognitive tasks than simple discovery. But how did you learn to move your arm or hand? How did you learn to walk? How did you learn to focus your eyes and interpret visual stimuli to gain an understanding of the physical reality around you? This kind of learning clearly occurs in all of us, and yet there is no teacher to tell us how to do it. Such learning is not taught in any traditional sense. How does it happen?

Some of the most exciting research in neural networks addresses this question: how is it possible for a neural network (such as the brain) to learn spontaneously, without benefit of a tutor? In early days, many people postulated a little man living inside the brain, called a homunculus. The idea was that this little man acted as the decision maker/tutor/pilot for learning. The reason for this invention was simply that no one could envision a mechanism for learning that did not require some kind of tutor to be available. Of course, this explanation is not very helpful in the long run, because that means we still have to explain how the little man knows what to do. (Does the homunculus have a mini-homunculus resident in its brain for example? If not, how does the homunculus learn what to do?)

In any event, we clearly need a learning system that does not rely on predigested lessons with answers. Self-organization and self-organizing systems have thus taken on an important role in the search for biologically reasonable systems. Research into self-organization has generally been concentrated on two specific kinds of networks, one relatively simple and one highly complex. In this chapter we will address the simpler kind, which has been intensively developed and investigated by Teuvo Kohonen. This Kohonen network, as it is often called, is the competitive filter associative memory, and we use these terms, as well as the descriptive phrase *Kohonen feature map*, interchangeably in this book.

A Self-Organizing Architecture

The competitive filter network is exquisitely simple in concept yet has some remarkable properties. In its usual form, this network consists of three layers. The input layer consists only of fan-out neurodes, which distribute the input pattern to each neurode in the middle, competitive layer. The output layer similarly receives the complete pattern of activity generated in the middle-layer neurodes and processes it in some manner appropriate to each particular

---

Who's On First?

Stephen Grossberg of Boston University, Teuvo Kohonen of Helsinki Technological University in Finland, and others independently developed the concepts associated with competitive filter associative memories. Kohonen, however, is usually more closely associated with them because of his extensive theoretical and practical development of the subject. Consequently we illustrate competitive filter associative memories in this chapter with Kohonen's network architectures. Cases of parallel discovery of new concepts are legion in all fields of scientific endeavor, and the name associated with a particular system is nearly always that of the person who was most active in the wide application and development of the concept.

---

application. Both of these layers are garden-variety neurode layers, with little to distinguish them from other networks.

The interesting layer is the middle, competitive layer, and we will concentrate on its operation. Neurodes in this layer have connections to the input and output layers and also strong connections to other neurodes within the layer. We have not seen such intralayer connections before in this book. Since they are central to competitive learning, it is important that we understand their function before discussing how the network learns.

Lateral Inhibition

We have previously considered one way of introducing competition among the neurodes of a neural network. The crossbar associative network, when implemented in hardware, uses feedback competition to ensure that the correct neurodes become active. In that system, the output pattern is fed back to the input during network operation.

The Kohonen network uses a different sort of competition, called "lateral inhibition" or "lateral competition." In this scheme, the neurodes in the competitive layer have many connections to each other, as well as the usual connections from the input layer and to the output layer. The strengths of these intralayer connections are fixed rather than modifiable, and are generally arranged so that a given neurode is linked to nearby neurodes by excitatory connections and to neurodes farther away by inhibitory connections. In other words, when any given neurode fires, the excitatory connections to its immediate neighbors tend to help them fire as well, and the inhibitory connections to neurodes farther away try to keep those neurodes from firing. All neurodes in the layer receive a complex mixture of excitatory and inhibitory signals from input-layer neurodes and from other competitive-layer neurodes. If properly designed, however, the layer's activity will quickly stabilize so that only a single neurode has a strong output; all others are suppressed. This kind of connection scheme is also sometimes called an on-center, off-surround architecture, a term used for biological structures that operate in the same way.

In lateral inhibition, an input is presented to all the neurodes in the competitive layer. Some of these are sufficiently excited that they try to generate output signals. These output signals are sent to the other neurodes in the layer through the intralayer connections, where they try to squash the receiver's output (an inhibitory connection) or try to assist it in firing (an excitatory connection). The result is that some of these receiving neurodes that were on the verge of firing have their activity suppressed. This strengthens the remaining neurode's outputs since the suppressed neurodes are no longer inhibiting their neighbors. Eventually one neurode's output will prove to be the strongest of all; that one neurode transmits a signal to the output layer for further processing. All other neurodes have their output suppressed in this winner-take-all scheme. A very real competition has occurred, with the strongest neurode winning the competition and thus winning the right to output to the next layer.

Several variations on this are possible. The number of neurodes that are excited and suppressed by the intralayer connections can vary, as can the values of the fixed excitatory and inhibitory weights. It is not necessary, for example, for all of these fixed weights to have the same value. Lateral inhibition has a number of subtleties of this sort that can make it reasonably complex to implement, but that are unimportant here. The point is that by using this scheme, we can enforce a system whereby the neurode with the strongest response to the input pattern is the single winner. Furthermore, we have a mechanism that makes this scheme work without having to call upon

The Capitalistic Neuron

At one time it was popular to consider this competitive view of learning as the individual neuron's attempts to maximize its own internal goals. The idea was that each neuron wants to fire as often and as strongly as possible. Thus, the neuron tries to do everything possible to maximize its likelihood of firing and to minimize the likelihood of other, competitive neurons' firing. This capitalistic view of the neuron's economy has caused some researchers to apply the mathematics of the marketplace to the analysis of neural networks. It has also generated the term *hedonistic neuron* to describe a neuron that consistently strives for its own reward.

some outside mediator to decide upon a winner arbitrarily. The need for the homunculus has disappeared.

The Network in Operation

The operation of a Kohonen network is relatively simple. A series of input patterns are presented to the network, and the neurodes are allowed to respond to each. After each presentation, the weights are adjusted using a learning rule. Then the next input pattern is presented, the weights are again adjusted, and so on. At no time is the network shown the correct output pattern. Its operation is such, in fact, that under ideal conditions, it can literally take continuous input, adjusting on the fly to the input data presented. This ability to accept continuous input data is essential if we want to model human learning in any nontrivial fashion. A Kohonen network thus has at least the primitive beginnings of real, biological learning models.

Let's explore the details of the learning law so that we can understand how it works. As we have seen, each neurode in the competitive layer receives the complete input pattern. Suppose we want to learn a series of multidimensional signals. These might be speech signals or some other complex input. To give a simple example, we might want the network to output a binary code that represents the words in a limited spoken vocabulary. In a competitive filter network, this is accomplished by having each neurode in the competitive layer associate itself with a particular set of similar input examples. Each example word in this collection of inputs has some resemblance to the others, and all can be characterized as being similar to some template pattern that represents an idealized pronunciation of the word. The template thus acts as a sort of ideal version of the corresponding word category.

Each neurode in the competitive layer receives the entire input vector. We compute the total input to each neurode in the usual manner—by taking the weighted sum of the input pattern using each neurode's individual set of weights on its input connections. Because each neurode has a unique set of input weights, this weighted sum generally will be different for each neurode. When all neurodes have computed their individual responses to the input pattern, we allow the neurodes to compete among themselves to decide which ones will learn. The competitive layer uses lateral inhibition to mediate this competition and decide which neurode has the strongest response to this input pattern. We designate this neurode the winning neurode. In this context, competition refers to the process of deciding which neurode(s) will have their weights adjusted and which one will output a signal.

Suppose competitive-layer neurode 3 has a larger net input than any other; it has successfully competed among its fellows, and it alone will be permitted to output a signal to the next layer. We say that this input pattern is classified as word 3, because it is neurode 3 that won the competition. This might correspond to the word tree in our oversimplified speech system. Now we have to adjust the weights of our network, and we see something we have not yet seen before: competitive learning.

A competitive filter network applies the idea of competitive learning literally. *Only the winning neurode and its neighbors are allowed to adjust their weights.* In other networks we have seen, all the neurodes adjusted their weights every time we presented an input pattern. But in a Kohonen network, only the winning neurode and its neighbors are allowed to learn.

This network is thus competitive in two senses: the neurodes are competing with each other for the right to learn and to generate an output to the next layer. We have not yet addressed the meaning of neighbor in this context, but we will in a moment.

How much do we adjust each weight? It is very simple: we subtract each of the neurode's weights from the input signal received

It's So Nice to Be Close

In the delta rule, we arrived at the new value of the weight vector by adding a delta vector to it term by term. This is by no means the only way we could have updated the weights, and in the competitive filter network, we find a slightly different rule in use. In this network, we define the "distance" between the new and the old weight vectors as their vector difference—the result of making a term-by-term algebraic subtraction between corresponding components of the new and old weight vectors. Here, the term *distance* refers to the geometrical distance between the tips of the previous and updated weight vectors.

The quantitative criterion for determining closeness differs in the two cases, and the networks each "guess" at unknown input patterns differently. When presented with an unfamiliar pattern, the adaline, or any other network usng the delta rule or any of its variations, chooses the stored pattern to present in a predictable way. In effect, it determines the term-by-term difference between the presented pattern and each stored pattern. It then adds these differences for each stored pattern and outputs that pattern having the smallest value of this sum of differences. When presented with an unfamiliar pattern, the Kohonen feature map, on the other hand, outputs the stored pattern having the largest geometric projection onto the presented pattern. Although these differences are subtle, they can result in considerably different guessing behavior, particularly on simple patterns.

along the interconnect associated with that weight and take some fraction of that difference as the change in the weight. The size of the fraction we take is the learning parameter (called the "gain" by Kohonen) and is usually about 20 percent or less. To complete this presentation of an input pattern, we compute and apply this weight change rule to every input weight attached to every neurode in the winning neighborhood. When we are done, we are ready to present the network with a new input pattern.

The Geometry of the Network

We have discussed the network from an operational perspective. Let's go through it again, this time looking at what is happening from a geometric perspective to try to understand better what transpires in the network. We want to pay close attention to two specific areas: the choice of the winning neurode and the adjustment of the weights of the winning neurode and its neighbors. In this discussion we will introduce some simple but important mathematical notions; readers preferring to avoid such mathematical detail may skip to the next section without loss of continuity.

First, consider what is happening when we choose the winning neurode. The computation of the weighted sum of the inputs has been seen before. We know from our earlier discussion that geometrically it is simply the dot product of the input vector and the weight vector.

The dot product is also equivalent to the lengths of the two vectors multiplied together and also multiplied by the cosine of the angle between the two vectors. We would like to correlate this dot product directly to that angle. But to do that, we have to take into account the lengths of the two vectors. For instance, if the length of one is much more than that of the other, the longer vector will dominate the value of the dot product. There is a way out of this, however. What if we normalize the two vectors first? For example, suppose we force the weight vector and the input vector each to have a length of 1 by performing some reasonable mathematical operation on them. One such operation is merely to divide each component of the vector by the total length of the vector; this guarantees that the total length of the resulting vector will exactly equal 1. If we do this on both the weight vector and the input vector, we end up with a nicely behaved pair of vectors, each of unit length.

Let's assume that both the input and the weight vectors have been normalized in this or some other fashion. This means that the

What's Dot?

The dot product of two vectors can be computed in several ways. For those who like matrix algebra, the dot product is just the sum of the products of the vector's corresponding elements. This is computed by multiplying the first elements of the two vectors together, adding the product of the second elements, and so on. This is the common form of the dot product for vectors expressed in our familiar Cartesian coordinate system of *x, y,* and *z.*

Geometrically the dot product is equivalent to taking the projection of the input vector onto the weight vector and multiplying by the length of the weight vector (or vice versa). We take a projection by dropping a line from the end of the input vector so that it intersects the weight vector at a right angle. The length of this projection times the length of the weight vector is the dot product. This is the usual form of the dot product in polar coordinates, where the position of a point is defined by its distance from the origin and by the angle between the vector from the origin to the point and some reference vector, which is often the *x* axis.

This latter formula for the dot product is also equivalent to the product of the lengths of the two vectors times the cosine of the angle between them. A few moments with a simple diagram and a bit of trigonometry should assure you that this is the case.

value of the dot product of the vectors becomes nothing more than the cosine of the angle between the weight vector and the input vector. Since the cosine of an angle gets larger as the angle gets smaller (for angles less than 90 degrees), the neurode with the weight vector making the smallest angle with the input vector has the largest dot product. Thus the closest weight vector—the one that points most nearly in the same direction as the input vector (and thus has the smallest angle between it and the input vector)—is the winner of the competition. This is important to understand. The network chooses the winning neurode on the basis of the dot product of the neurode's weight vector with the input vector. The winner is always that neurode with a weight vector pointing most nearly in the direction of the input vector. In order to make this work, remember that we had to normalize both the weight vectors and the input vector so that a meaningful dot product could be taken. Without normalization, the dot product does not necessarily measure the true closeness of each weight vector to the input vector.

What assurance do we have that weight vectors modified during training will remain normalized? Suppose for the moment that the input vectors (and therefore also the weight vectors) are limited to two dimensions. It turns out that as long as the weight changes in each learning cycle are kept small, they correspond to simple rota-

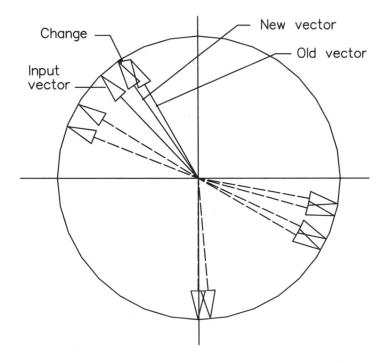

Figure 7.1 The weight change law rotates the weight vector nearer to the input vector.

tions of the weight vectors and not to magnitude changes. The net effect of the weight change rule is to push the weight vector closer to the input vector (which, because it is normalized, always lies on the surface of the unit circle, that is, a circle of radius 1). In other words, it serves primarily to rotate the weight vector along the surface of the unit circle so that it points more nearly in the direction of the input vector (figure 7.1).

Thus, if the weight vector initially pointed to the unit circle, it will still point to the unit circle (or nearly so) after it has been modified by training. Remember that this is true only as long as the size of the training step taken is reasonably small. In practice, the weight vectors do not always stay perfectly normalized during the course of training. They move along the chord that connects the weight vector's original position and the input vector, as opposed to moving along the perimeter of the unit circle; however, most do tend to stay more or less on or just under the surface of the unit circle, so that normalization is approximately maintained. Minor divergences from perfect normalization do not severely affect the network's performance, and, as training proceeds, the vectors eventually stabilize into near-normalized lengths.

The Crust Thickens...

Let's summarize what we have discovered. An input vector pointing in some direction on the unit circle is presented to the network. At the time of presentation, the weight vectors for the various neurodes point in a variety of directions around the circle. The weight vector pointing most nearly in the direction of the input vector determines the winning neurode. This neurode, along with each neurode in its immediate neighborhood, adjusts its weight vector by giving it a rotational nudge toward the input vector. We now apply another input vector and repeat the same process. We can imagine that after applying a large number of input pattern vectors representing some distributional pattern around the unit circle, the weight vectors have bumped, nudged, and jostled themselves to more or less the same distributional pattern around the circle.

This is shown in figure 7.2, where the thickness of the outer crust of the unit circle indicates the likelihood of an input vector's occurring from that direction. The crust thickness represents the probability distribution function of the training input patterns. Notice that the weight vectors after training are in fact distributed most thickly where the crust is thickest and more sparsely where the crust is thin.

We have made an important discovery: the network's weight vectors become a model for the distribution around the unit circle of the collection of input patterns presented to it. Effectively, they model the probability distribution function of the input patterns presented during training. This means that if 10 percent of the input pattern vectors point to a particular region of the unit circle, then after training, approximately 10 percent of the weight vectors will point to that same region of the unit circle. This will happen even though the network is not told what the distribution of the weight vectors should look like.

The network literally organizes itself based only on the input patterns presented to it, so that it models the distribution of input patterns. Furthermore, this distribution model appears even when we do not know an equation that describes the probability distribution pattern. The network merely extrapolates from the examples it sees to model the input distribution as best it can. Even when we cannot explicitly state the probability distribution in mathematical form, the network can model it.

In the discussion, we restricted ourselves to a case in which the input vectors and the weight vectors have only two elements. This allowed us to talk about a unit circle and to draw pictures of it easily. There is no reason, however, why we need to restrict the network in

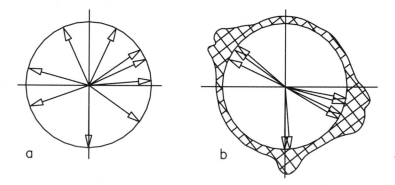

a   b

Figure 7.2 The weight vectors are clustered, with more pointing to those regions with a high probability of having an input vector (the thick portions of the circle's rim) and fewer pointing to those regions having a low probability of having an input vector.

this manner; the only change for such a larger-sized input is that the term *unit circle* is replaced by the equivalent term *unit hypersphere*, which covers a geometric form of any dimensionality. Of course, adding more dimensions also makes it difficult to impossible to draw on the printed page, which is why we limited the discussion above to two-dimensional circles.

Training Techniques

If we consider the way this network works, we can draw some conclusions about how it should be trained. For example, we know that the network models the statistical probability distribution of the input patterns; thus, we should present it with a large number of input patterns during training. If we use a training set that is too small, we will not get a valid model of the input distribution, just as too small a population sample will give invalid survey results. Similarly we also need to choose carefully the input patterns we use for training to ensure that they are representative of the actual input pattern distribution. Because of the need to use many input patterns and because we keep the nudges small so the weight vectors stay normalized, we can expect the training of this network to be fairly slow.

In fact, this network needs a great deal of careful thought when designing it for an application. We need to be concerned with exactly how to normalize the input and weight vectors. The simple normalization procedure discussed earlier may not be the most appropriate method for a given problem. We need also to consider how we should initialize the weight vectors before training. The simplest, and most obvious, solution is to place them randomly; however, this may not be the best solution. We have to assure ourselves, for example, that every neurode in the competitive layer is initialized so that it will have an opportunity to be the winner or at least to be the neighbor of a winner. Otherwise some of the neurodes may never participate in the training. These are called "dead vectors" when they occur, for obvious reasons.

Appropriate initialization procedures can be quite tricky to implement. Although the network designer does not need to have a detailed mathematical form for the distribution of input vectors, he or she must have an understanding of the characteristics of the input data. Only with such an understanding can proper normalization and weight randomization be defined. And of course the training set must be carefully selected so that it accurately portrays the statistical characteristics of the overall data set. This in itself is nontrivial in many cases.

There is still another important point about these networks: they are particularly useful in modeling the statistical characteristics of the input data, but the statistical models they create are only as accurate as the network size permits. A competitive layer of 100 neurodes produces a statistical model that is 10 times as detailed as one produced by a layer with only 10 neurodes but only a tenth as detailed as one from a layer with 1000 neurodes will be. The network will do its best to model the input data correctly, but the more neurodes it has available, the less area each weight vector must cover, and the more accurate the final trained network. For a perfect data set model, there would be one weight vector, or neurode, available for each possible input vector. A moment's thought reveals that this arrangement is not feasible. It is equivalent to saying that the ideal model of the input data set is the input data set itself. If we want a network capable of telling us something nontrivial about the data, we must use networks having fewer neurodes than the number of possible input vectors. For this reason, a Kohonen network will never be perfectly accurate.

On the other hand, there are some interesting possibilities for this kind of network. For example, suppose we train a network with a collection of input patterns and after training find that the weight vectors are clustered. We can then replace these clusters of weight vectors with single supervectors that serve to represent that cluster. As long as we keep the correct ratios of weight vectors in each cluster, we can use as few replacement supervectors as we like. For example, an initial set of weight vectors might have 100 vectors in one cluster and 200 in another. We can replace these with a single weight vector pointing to the average location of the first cluster and two vectors pointing to the average location of the second cluster. Since each weight vector corresponds to a single neurode in the competitive layer, this represents a dramatic reduction in the size of the network needed for this application.

When we have done this clustering replacement of the network, we have a smaller, more efficient network that effectively performs a data compression on the original patterns. Furthermore, we are guaranteed that this data compression scheme is statistically meaningful relative to the input data patterns. These clusters correspond to feature vectors of the input data set, and the scheme that produces them is sometimes called vector quantization.

As new input patterns are represented, we can relate the new inputs to the old by specifying how far away the new ones are from the nearest feature vector. If we have stored these original feature vectors somewhere, we can store the new inputs by simply saving the differences between the input and the stored feature vectors. This may not sound difficult, but for vectors with many elements, such as might be found in digital images, transmitting only the differences between the current image and some standard feature image can result in enormous efficiency improvements.

The Topology-Preserving Map

The one application of these networks that best illustrates their usefulness is the topology-preserving map, studied extensively by Teuvo Kohonen. The easiest way to understand what topology-preserving map means is to consider an example of how to create one. Imagine a sheet of paper and a robot arm, with a pencil in the robot's hand. Let's assume that we can move the hand to any location on the sheet of paper and have the robot make a dot. Suppose we connect sensors to the arm and hand that report back the position of the robot's arm as we make dots on the paper. When we are done making dots on the paper (and we must make many, many dots to make a valid statistical set), we have a pattern on the paper giving the distribution of locations where we placed the pencil point. Places that are very dark were visited many times and thus had a high probability of occurrence. Places that are still blank or contain few dots had a very low probability of being visited. The coordinates of each dot define the input vector for that dot. We use these vectors as input data to a Kohonen network. The competitive layer of the network is laid out as a two-dimensional grid, with connections between neighbors in rows and columns. Imagine a grid like that found on ordinary graph paper to understand the connections between the competitive layer neurodes.

Suppose we make 2000 dots on the surface of the paper, feeding each dot's coordinates into the Kohonen network as training data. Let's stop every 100 dots and make a note of the network's weight vectors, for a snapshot of the state of the network at these times. Now we take the snapshots and make a series of plots of the weight vectors in the network. As we plot the positions, we draw a line between the weight vectors of nearest-neighbor neurodes, defining neighbor as a neurode that is only one column or one row away in the layers grid. The plot we are making connects the weight vectors of neurodes that are physically positioned next to each other in the grid. It should be clear that there is no particular reason that neighboring neurodes in the grid should have weight vectors that point anywhere near each other. Remember that initialization of the network deliberately scrambled the weight vectors before we began, so we would expect the chart we make to be a jumbled tangle of connecting lines. Figure 7.3a shows that initially we have just such a tangled mess of lines. (In the figure, we initially forced all the weight vectors to be randomly located within the upper right quadrant.)

What will the snapshots of the network look like over time? The other sections of figure 7.3 show the weight vector chart after 100,

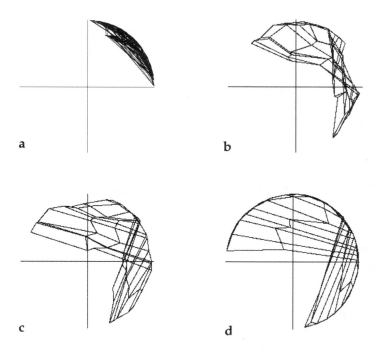

Figure 7.3. (a) The initial topology map. (b) The topology map after 100 input points. (c) The topology map after 200 input points. (d) The topology map after 2000 input points.

200, and 2000 data points have been passed through the network. In this case, about half of the input patterns came from points in the upper right quadrant of the circle, and the remaining input patterns were about evenly divided between the upper left and lower right quadrants. Notice that as the number of input patterns increases, there are fewer and fewer lines crossing the center of the circle and that the edges of the plot become closer and closer to an actual circle. This indicates that the physical ordering of the weight vectors over time becomes organized according to the characteristics of the input data. In other words, if a neurode's neighbor has a weight vector pointing in a particular direction, the neurode itself very likely has its weight vector point in a similar direction. The jumbled mass of lines is gone, replaced with an orderly mesh. It is as though the weight vectors form a stretchy fishnet that begins as a crumpled, tangled ball and tries to conform itself to the shape of the input pattern distribution, with more mesh intersections where input patterns are more likely and fewer mesh intersections where they are less likely.

It turns out that no matter what the input pattern distribution is, the network will organize itself so that the weight vector fishnet stretches and twists so that it makes a reasonably good mapping of the input pattern distribution. Furthermore, we can experiment and connect the neurodes in the competitive layer in a simple linear array instead of a grid, with each one connected only to the neurodes before and after it in the line. If we do this, the weight vectors behave as if they were a ball of twine, and their distribution after training becomes like a string twisting along the input vector pattern distribution.

These plots are topology-preserving maps because the topology, or shape, of the distribution of the input patterns in coordinate space is preserved in the physical organization of the weight vectors. Topology-preserving maps do not necessarily have to map physical locations. They can map frequencies, for example. A common name for a topology-preserving map when the input data corresponds to sound frequencies is a tonotopic map. In this case, the map represents an ascending or descending set of frequencies, and the neurodes are sensitive to a graduated scale of frequencies. In other words, the weight vectors of neighboring neurodes point to neighboring frequency inputs.

Because the robot arm example is truly a plot of spatial distributions, we call it a geotopic map. This may sound like a somewhat wild-eyed, and perhaps even useless, trait, but in fact topology-preserving maps exist in animals. It is known, for instance, that cer-

---

A Wrinkled Brow

We can reach a bit into the realm of speculation and note that when a network that is physically a two-dimensional grid is provided with three-dimensional input data, the resulting topology map strongly resembles a crumpled sheet of paper attempting to fill a thicker space. It bears a striking resemblance, in fact, to the furrows, wrinkles, and hollows of the cerebral cortex. If we also consider that physically the cerebral cortex is a thin, flat sheet, this becomes quite intriguing. While no one claims that the cerebral cortex is a giant topology-preserving map, the presence of small-scale topology maps in the brain, particularly in the sensory areas of sound, touch, and vision, provides fascinating possibilities for speculation.

---

tain structures in the brain that form part of the auditory system are physically organized by the acoustic pitch or frequencies they respond to. Quite literally, tonotopic maps exist in the brain for sound inputs. In addition, there appear to be other such abstract maps existing in the brain for such purposes as geographic-location mapping, such as retinotopic maps in vision and somatotopic maps in the sense of touch. For example, rats that have been trained in a maze have certain spatially ordered brain cells that fire when they are in a particular location in the maze. Such spatial ordering cannot possibly have existed in the animal before training unless we argue that it is that rat's destiny to learn that particular maze. Some mechanism must exist that allows the physical structure of the brain to modify during learning so that the neurons order themselves according to the layout of the maze. While competitive learning may not be exactly correct as a mechanism for this process, it certainly offers an elegant, simple model of how this might occur.

Why does the competitive filter network preserve input data topology? The fishnet analogy is quite apropos. As Kohonen has described, there are two forces working on the weight vectors. First, the vectors are trying to model the probability distribution function of the input data. Second, their interconnections are also trying to form into a continuous surface because of the synaptic links between each neurode and its neighbors. These different forces establish the model of the input data that we have seen. In other words, when each winning neurode adjusts its weight vector in the direction of an input vector, it pulls its neighbor's weight vectors along with it. Therefore, after training, the weight vectors have formed a more or less continuous surface. Finally, the continuity of the maps means that the trained network has the ability to generalize from its specific experiences to process novel data patterns.

Kohonen networks have several drawbacks, but their potential applications are many and intriguing. They are being used in research in speech- and image-processing applications and have potential for statistical or database applications as well. Moreover, as we will see when we look at the counterpropagation network in chapter 14, these networks can be used as building blocks in more complex hierarchical systems. Let's now examine more complex learning systems, ones that are even more directly modeled after biological systems. In the next part we explore some of these biologically based learning systems.

Application:
The Voice Typewriter

Teuvo Kohonen is a pioneer in the field of neural networks. Besides being the creator and unflagging proponent of one of the more useful network paradigms, he has contributed a number of practical devices using neural networks. One of the most recent is a phonetic typewriter.

Speech recognition is among the most difficult signal processing jobs that can be attacked. There are a few digital systems that can be successfully trained to recognize each word in the speech of a specific person who uses a limited vocabulary and pauses briefly between words; there are fewer that can be trained to recognize the separated-word, limited-vocabulary speech of a number of persons. There are none that can recognize natural speech of random speakers using an unlimited vocabulary.

But speech recognition is not just a matter of recognizing words. Researchers have long known that hearing someone is a psychological process. Humans do not understand speech by slavishly responding to one syllable at a time in serial order. Rather, we recognize only a fraction of the words spoken to us, and then use memories of previously understood speech fragments, context, guessed meanings, and other abstract information to piece together what is being said.

Even on the level of recognizing individual words, however, things are not really simple. The same words can be spoken rapidly or slowly and with differing emphases; they can be yelled or whispered; and they can be spoken in a noisy environment, even one including extraneous words from other nearby speakers. It's even worse. The basic speech sounds, called phonemes, are often run together by a speaker, and the same phoneme spoken by different speakers—even by a single speaker under different circumstances— can be pronounced differently.

Kohonen and his associates at Helsinki Technical University have stepped into this difficult arena with a phonetic typewriter based on the competitive filter network. Using the Japanese or Finnish language, this system achieves 92 to 97 percent accuracy with continuous speech from multiple speakers using an essentially unlimited vocabulary. The first 100 words of each new speaker are taken as training samples and usually show a lowered recognition rate. On isolated words taken from a 1000-word vocabulary, his machine achieves 96 to 98 percent accuracy. The phonetic typewriter illustrates well a characteristic that we believe should and will become common in neural network applications, a wedding of neural and standard digital techniques to utilize the best features of each technology.

When we speak, we cause small time-varying changes in the air pressure near us. The frequencies of the sounds contained in speech typically fall between 20 and 5000 Hz. (One hertz, abbreviated Hz, is 1 cycle per second.) These oscillatory pressure variations can be represented on a piece of paper by plotting the deviation from normal air pressure at some point for each instant of time. This kind of graph, in which the amplitude of some quantity is plotted against time, is called the time-domain representation of that quantity.

A fundamental theorem due to the French mathematician Jacques Fourier, however, tells us that any section of a time-dependent signal such as our sound wave can be represented as a sum of sines and cosines of a limited range of frequencies. A plot can be constructed of this; this plot is called the Fourier transform of the signal. The more rapidly something takes place in the time domain, the larger its contribution is at high frequencies in the frequency domain. For instance, the air is set in oscillatory motion quite rapidly by the high-frequencies in the *s* sound in *hiss* but much less rapidly by the lower-frequency *o* sound in *home*. Thus, the *s* sound requires much higher frequencies to represent it properly than does the *o* sound.

We used sound as an example, but any other time-varying signal can be transformed into a frequency-domain representation, and conversely the frequency-domain representation can be transformed to a time-domain version. This procedure is often called spectral analysis, spectral decomposition, time-series analysis, or Fourier analysis. It is important in all engineering and science disciplines, the social sciences, psychology, the medical disciplines, and even some humanities.

In the figure on the next page, the components of the voice typewriter's preprocessor are shown in block form. The signal from a noise-canceling microphone is first amplified and its spectrum limited to frequencies under about 5000 Hz. This is more than adequate to pass normal speech frequencies and, among other things, further limits the amount of noise introduced through the microphone. Kohonen uses a commercial microelectronic signal

processor chip to perform the remaining preprocessing operations. First, the analog signal is digitized to a 12-bit gray scale.

This means that the digitized and original analog signals are
the same to better than 1 part in 4000, or about 0.024 percent. The
chip then computes the fast Fourier transform of this signal every
10 milliseconds, calculates the frequency-smoothed logarithm of
this frequency-domain signal, and breaks it into 15 separate channels. Treating the 15 channels as a 15-component vector, the chip
then subtracts the average value from the signal and normalizes
the vector to unit length. You perhaps recognize many of these
steps as typical of those necessary to prepare a signal to be used
as input to a competitive filter network.

The preprocessed speech signal is now presented to such a
network, which can be viewed as a type of data compression
device. One of the data compression methods that the action of

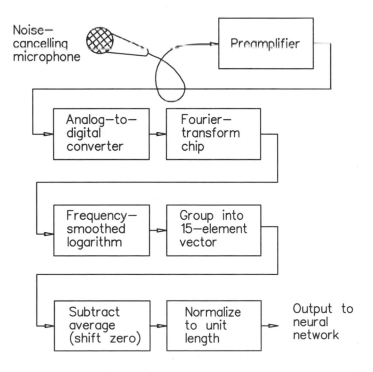

A block diagram of the Voice Typewriter.

the network parallels is called "vector quantization." In this method, the entire range of possible input vectors is divided into a set of contiguous areas, and one average output vector is chosen to represent each area. Any input vector that falls into that area is then replaced by the representative output vector. In other words, similar input vectors are lumped together in one category. This is exactly what is needed for a speaker-independent speech recognition system. It must classify a bewilderingly large number of sounds into a small set of basic, repeating sound patterns, which it can then reassociate to identify individual words.

During training, another of the properties of the feature map becomes apparent. As the network organizes the input vectors into groups, it places groups having similar characteristics physically next to each other in the network; it topologically orders them. As a result of the action of the network on the stream of 15-component speech vectors, the synaptic weights of the network come to represent a connected map of basic speech sounds. Without any attempt to make it do so, the system effectively invents phonemes and produces a phonotopic map in which related basic speech sounds are stored spatially near each other in the network. The reason that the network topologically orders related sounds is not mysterious and is discussed in chapter 7. Upon reflection, it is also not mysterious that the network reinvents phonemes. Phonemes are, after all, the result of intelligent humans having done exactly what the network did: analyzing words into their basic sounds. Beware, however, from drawing too close a parallel to human speech processing. There is no assurance in general that the internal representations of any artificial neural network will be meaningful or relevant to our intellectual analysis.

A single network cannot reliably discriminate among some types of speech sounds, such as the hard sounds *k, p,* and *t* when occurring at the beginning of a word. To increase the success of the system in these cases, separate smaller networks are trained expressly on each category of these sounds and accessed when needed.

Even with these procedures, coarticulation effects in natural speech prevent 100 percent success in identifying words. A coarticulation effect exists if the pronunciation of a phoneme is affected by the phoneme preceding or following it. Of course, the pronunciation of the preceding or following phoneme itself may have been affected by coarticulation effects, and so on. As a result, there are tens of thousands of rules in most languages governing pronunciation of specific phonemes under various circumstances. To correct for coarticulation effects, an efficient software database that contains many of these rules serves as a postprocessor. In principle, this database could be stored in an associative memory, but Kohonen, following good engineering practice, chose to use a known method that was already well developed and that was reliable and fast. The resulting system operates with only a small delay, though it runs on equipment that is only about a fifth the speed of currently available computers.

What are the problems of the system? The main one is the same as that experienced by all automatic dictation systems: accuracy is only marginally adequate when working in the large-vocabulary, speaker-independent mode. Secondarily, the one-quarter-second recognition delay caused by postprocessing is too long to qualify the system as a truly real-time device. This deficiency will undoubtedly be removed in later models, but addressing the first problem may prove more difficult. As Kohonen points out, the auditory system of humans seems to respond not only to the frequency spectrum of speech but also to timing and phase information contained in the sounds. A future typewriter system that adds temporal processing to the frequency-domain processing already employed may approach levels of performance that will make spoken data entry and phonetic typewriters commonplace.

Part III

A learned blockhead is a greater blockhead than an ignorant one.
—Benjamin Franklin

It is <u>not</u> a blob; it's my neurocomputer
in its learning mode!

Learning without thought is useless;
thought without learning is dangerous.
— Confucius

8   Learning

Neural networks are trained, not programmed; they learn. We have already seen two distinctly different types of learning in the adaline and the Kohonen feature map. The subject of learning and memory in artificial systems is so important, however, that we need to consider it in a more structured manner.

We will start this introduction to learning in artificial systems by looking at the ways animals and people learn and the kinds of memory that have been identified in humans by psychologists. We will then be in a position to relate these to the ways neural networks learn and remember. Finally, we will adopt a more operational view and discuss the major methods for training artificial systems.

Types of Learning

Learning has taken place—in an animal or in a neural network—when there is some lasting behavioral change or increase in knowledge resulting from an experience. For our purposes, we can break learning in animals and humans into three broad classes: instrumental conditioning, classical conditioning, and observational learning.

In instrumental conditioning, a subject is taught a certain behavior by being rewarded for that behavior or punished for the lack of it. Consider the famous pigeon experiments of B. F. Skinner. A pigeon

The Mind-Body Problem

The question of whether the mind and the brain are one and the same has been debated in Western culture since Plato's time and in Eastern culture perhaps even longer. The problem has profound humanistic and scientific ramifications. With some risk of oversimplification, we will phrase the mind-body problem as a question: "Can all mental states be accounted for by purely physical processes?" Despite debate over the centuries by some of the world's finest minds (or should we say brains?), no unassailable arguments exist on any of the several sides of this multifaceted problem. Reduced to what is, by comparison, the extremely simple arena of artificial systems, the mind-body problem gives rise to questions such as, "Can neural networks have emotions?" "Can neural networks be neurotic?" and "Can neural networks be sentient?" We leave our meager speculations on possible answers to these questions to the final chapter of the book. A thoughtful but predictably controversial treatment of the mind-body problem from the materialist standpoint can be found in Patricia Churchland's book, *Neurophilosophy,* (MIT Press, Cambridge, MA, 1986.) Treatments from a more metaphysical standpoint can be found listed in the extensive bibliography contained in that book.

is placed in a cage with a red disk mounted on one wall. At first the pigeon pecks only randomly around the cage. If it by chance pecks at the red disk, a door opens, and the pigeon receives a small amount of grain. If it pecks elsewhere, it receives no reward. Sooner or later the pigeon makes the connection between pecking at the red disk and receiving a reward. Once that connection is established, the pigeon pecks often at the red disk.

Obviously the pigeon learned something, as evidenced by the modification of its behavior. It discovered and remembered that pecking at the red disk was rewarded with food, while pecking elsewhere was not. This simple kind of learning is exhibited by most animals. Dogs learn to do tricks for a pat from their trainer; mice learn to run mazes for food; fish learn to swim to the top of an aquarium at feeding time; snails learn to avoid garlic-spiked tomatoes; even planaria, a kind of flatworm, learn to choose left or right in a T-maze.

The second type of learning in animals is classical conditioning, or Pavlovian conditioning. In the simplest classical conditioning experiment, two stimuli are presented to an animal at the same time. One is a neutral stimulus that by itself produces no response in the animal; the second always produces a response. The classic illustration of this kind of learning is Pavlov's experiments. The neutral stimulus in this case was the sound of a tone; the loaded stimulus was food, virtually guaranteed to produce a salivation response. Before training, presenting food alone to the dogs caused them to salivate and presenting the tone alone did not. Pavlov trained his dogs by repeatedly presenting food at the same time he sounded the tone. After a number of such presentations, the tone alone caused salivation. The dogs had learned to respond with salivation to a stimulus that would not normally have caused it. Perhaps you already see the similarity between classical conditioning and the training method used for the adaline.

Observational learning is a third way people and animals learn. In this kind of learning, an animal learns by watching or otherwise observing the activities or attitudes of others. A child who is scared to pet a large dog may learn by watching others that he can safely pet the animal. Conversely, a child who is totally unafraid to approach animals can learn appropriate caution by seeing the same dog snarl when another child approaches it while it is eating.

These are the major ways animals and people learn. There is one more topic we must take up in this introduction to learning before we proceed to learning in neural networks: memory.

Memory

Learning and memory are intimately entwined: there can be no learning if there is no memory. For this reason alone, it should not be surprising that the biochemical and structural bases of memory are among the most active areas in brain research. Although there is much that is yet to be learned, many of the general mechanisms of memory are known, and these are enough to give us the simple understanding we require for a discussion of memory in artificial systems. Before we discuss the biological aspects of memory, we will briefly look at it from a psychological standpoint.

The work of psychologists with amnesiacs and brain-damaged people has shown that there is no one thing called memory. The phenomenon we call memory is a collection of related and complex processes and abilities. For our purposes, though, we can functionally divide memory into three classes: sensory, short term, and long term. Sensory memory is the persistence time of sensory stimuli. Afterimages in the eye and the corresponding auditory afterimage—the length of time a sound remains available for processing—are examples of sensory memory. All are of short duration, a few seconds at most.

Short-term memory is the working memory of the brain; it is that part of permanent memory the mind is using at a given time. Only a few items—spoken or written words for instance—can be held in short-term memory at one time, and items in it tend to fade within a few seconds if not refreshed by concentration and rehearsal.

Long-term memory has been called the storehouse of the brain; information is stored in it more or less permanently. We can identify three kinds of long-term memory: linguistic, imaginal, and motor. Linguistic items are tagged. Concepts like chair, dog, and rain, and even more slippery concepts like love and cowardice are given concrete labels by the brain. When it becomes necessary to express such a concept, the tag can be communicated instead of the concept itself. Imaginal stores are not tagged; rather, the item itself is represented in the brain. When remembering the house you grew up in, you are more likely to recall actual images of its rooms, furnishings, and surroundings than you are to call up a set of tags that stand for these items and locations. Motor memories are ways of remembering motor skills. We are all aware that learning instructions for riding a bicycle does not help much in actually riding it. No matter how accurate our verbal understanding, it lies in our linguistic store of memories and does not allow us to mount a bicycle and ride away.

Learning and Memory in Neural Networks

There are parallels in artificial neural networks to nearly every kind of animal learning and memory. The one exception is instrumental conditioning. Artificial systems are probably not amenable to this form of learning. Animals will learn in order to improve their chances of obtaining a reward or to decrease their chances of receiving a punishment. We cannot attribute emotions and motives to present-day neural networks.

Artificial systems seem to offer many parallels to classical conditioning, on the other hand. Perhaps you have already seen the similarity between this type of learning and the training method used for the adaline or for crossbar heteroassociative memories.

Like classical conditioning, observational learning has analogies in the way we train neural networks. We will see such a learning technique used in two of the applications we present in chapter 18. In those applications, a network learns to perform a complex task by being allowed to "watch" an expert perform that task.

Each kind of memory outlined—sensory, short term, and long term—has rough correspondences in neural networks. Instrumental parameters like the persistence time of optical detectors are certainly equivalent to sensory memory. The spreading activation that occurs in a neural network as it comes to a consistent output state when presented with an input pattern, or the "top-down" priming signal we will see in adaptive resonance networks, perhaps offer analogies to short-term memory.

Finally, there are long-term memory functions in neural networks that are akin to all three types of human long-term memory. Heteroassociative storage of input signals and retrieval keys is reasonably analogous to linguistic memory. In this storage technique, an input pattern (concept) is replaced by a single output key (word) for recall. Just as in linguistic memory, both the concept and key are stored, and presentation of either one can recall the other.

Imaginal memory is similar to the way patterns are stored by two different kinds of associative memories. A simple autoassociative memory can be considered to approximate imaginal memory. The memory itself is stored; no key is associated with it. The Kohonen feature map also displays a function analogous to imaginal memory. In one version of the feature map, a somewhat idealized representation of each input pattern is constructed during training, with all similar patterns being replaced by one "iconic" pattern. When a pattern similar to an original input pattern is later presented, the network responds with the iconic pattern most closely matching it. This is reminiscent of the way the brain stores memories of events.

Networks intentionally built to imitate human motor memory are able to remember complex motor commands for robotic arms. In chapter 18, we will see that researchers have built robotic arms that actually utilize a not-too-simplified version of the feedback mechanisms used by the brain.

We have been comparing what might be called the psychological aspects of learning and memory in animals and artificial systems.

It's Not Nice to Imitate Mother Nature

The success of the delta rule is proof that it is not absolutely necessary to copy Mother Nature in designing learning laws for neural networks. The delta rule and the learning laws derived from it, however, are virtually the only ones in the neural network field that have little or no demonstrable biological foundation. In fact, one of the major arguments against using the delta rule and its variants is that they are not biologically plausible—that is, they are inconsistent with what we know about the way biological systems learn. We will deal with this argument more fully in chapter 13.

Unfortunately for those who make this argument, the delta rule has generated a variety of networks that are highly effective at solving real-world problems. Sometimes art does not have to imitate life to work well.

What about physiological similarities? There are many, of course, and we looked at most of them in earlier chapters when we outlined the basic structure and operation of neural networks. By this time, you know that those structural similarities are no accident. The main driving force of many neural network researchers has been a desire to copy the architecture of animal brains as closely as possible within the limitations of technology and neurophysiological knowledge. Because memory, learning, and processing are virtually inseparable from physical structure in neural architecture, a similarity of learning and memory in biological and artificial systems is inevitable.

That neural network researchers have begun to copy the architecture of the brain at both large-scale and cellular levels does not imply either that the biological mechanisms of learning and memory are understood in detail or that artificial systems necessarily resemble biological ones in more than a superficial way. For the purposes of devising learning laws for neural networks, however, the details of the biological mechanisms are largely unimportant; the general ideas provide researchers with enough information to create useful learning laws. As better understanding of biological systems develops, neural network researchers undoubtedly will devise yet more sophisticated and successful learning laws.

Do Neural Networks Learn Like People?

Learning is one of the fundamental characteristics of all but the simplest neural networks. But is learning in a neural network the same kind of process as learning in a biological system? Superficially networks use the same kind of process as animals do but they are not even remotely as complex as animals in their behaviors. Both the pigeon of our earlier example and an artificial neural network modify their behavior in response to an outside stimulus. But the central nervous system of a pigeon, or even a lowly leech, is exceedingly more complex than any existing artificial neural network. Humans and many other animals learn in a subtle and rich context of sensory inputs, emotions, and internal drives wholly beyond anything that can be ascribed to present-day artificial neural networks. It remains for a future generation to construct systems of large, interacting neural networks with organizations complex enough to rival the learning functions of the brains of the higher animals. In the meantime, we in the field of artificial neural systems should remember to be humble in the presence of a pigeon, a fly, or even a leech.

Learning models in neural networks are rules or procedures that tell a neurode how to modify its synaptic weights in response to stimuli. A neurode exists in a very limited environment. It knows nothing of the overall state of the network but receives inputs only from the neurodes to which it is directly connected. It uses these inputs to determine an internal level of activation and consequently outputs an appropriate response signal. Sometimes, depending on the kind of network it is in, it is provided with feedback to tell it how close it is to the correct response; in other kinds of networks, it receives no feedback at all. The neurode has no control over the input patterns presented to it; these are determined by some outside agent or condition. Nor can the neurodes in most network designs modify their activation functions or thresholds; for a given summed input, a neurode will always produce the same output signal. Thus, if a neurode is to modify its response to an input stimulus, its only means of doing so is to adjust its synaptic weights.

Training a Neural Network

We have been looking at learning and memory from a distinctly biological point of view. There is an operational perspective that is often more useful in everyday application of artificial systems; this perspective appears when we consider how to train neural networks to perform a task. We will now look at the matter of training methods. In the crossbar network, the adaline, and the Kohonen feature map, we have already seen examples of the three neural network training methods. Let's review each to point up their differences.

As it is generally practiced, the training method used with crossbar networks is more appropriately called "weight assignment." In most current crossbar simulations and implementations, interconnect weights are preassigned by a mathematical procedure and do not change during operation of the system. This is the equivalent to "hard wiring" the network; no iterative learning occurs.

The approach to training that we used with the adaline is called "supervised training." It is the equivalent of sending the network to school. In supervised training, we provide samples of the input patterns we expect our network to encounter during operation and also the output pattern we want it to produce when it encounters those patterns. We will see this kind of training again when we discuss the backpropagation network in chapter 13.

A variation of supervised training is called "graded training" or "graded learning." In it, we do not provide the network with the actual output pattern we want but only give it feedback on how well it is doing. This is equivalent to playing a children's guessing game with the network in which an object is hidden in a room, and the designated person has to find it, based on clues such as "You're getting warmer" and "You're getting colder." Because such training algorithms are highly experimental and often proprietary to the developer of the procedure, we will not discuss them further in this book.

The training approach we used with the Kohonen feature map is called "unsupervised training." With this method, we do not provide the responses the network is to give to the input patterns in the train-ing set. As we saw in chapter 7, systems trained in this way are use-ful for applications in which we do not know the "right" answers and in which the system itself must decide what features it will use to classify or partition the input data. As we also saw in the preced-ing chapter, this kind of training is frequently associated with net-works capable of self-organization. In our discussion of topology-preserving maps, we presented some of the many ways the brain uti-lizes this property to train itself, based solely on the input patterns it receives.

If you recall the subtleties involved in constructing a training set for a Kohonen feature map, you know that successfully employing unsupervised training with a neural network involves far more than presenting it with random information and waiting for it to learn. Yet a biological system is capable of learning many kinds of informa-tion without imposing any special requirements on the random flood of input data it receives. What we need is a form of self-organization that mimics this ability of biological systems to learn from random data—one that uses unsupervised training, is largely independent of the organization of the training set, can learn selectively, and does not require special constraints on the types of patterns presented. This special form of self-organization we call "autonomous learning."

The ability to glean useful information selectively from totally unconstrained data presented in random order and in the presence of confusing and irrelevant noise is so important that we discuss the subject separately in chapter 11. In chapter 16 we explore a network design, adaptive resonance, that displays many of the features of autonomous learning.

We refer to the supervised or unsupervised presentation of infor-mation to a network as training methods in order to distinguish them from the types of learning presented earlier in the chapter. In the neural network field, however, it is common to use the words *learning* and *training* interchangeably when referring to these approaches. In addition, supervised training is often referred to as constrained learning or tutored learning, and unsupervised training is often referred to as unconstrained learning or untutored learning.

We have discussed animal learning and memory and have related them to analogous processes in artificial systems. We have already encountered one biologically inspired learning paradigm in the discussion of the Kohonen network of chapter 7. In the next chapter, we introduce a second, hebbian learning.

Words are wind; learning is nothing but words;
ergo, learning is nothing but wind.
—Jonathan Swift

9 Hebbian Learning

Donald Hebb was not a neural network researcher in 1949 when he proposed his model for biological learning. He was a psychologist whose immediate goal was to understand how neurons in the brain change when learning occurs. His model was quickly picked up by neural network researchers, however.

Those seeking a new neural network design often adopt the ideas of biologists or psychologists. The reason, of course, is that it makes sense to copy a system already known to be successful—the brain. Of all the learning concepts appropriated from psychology by neural network researchers, hebbian learning is probably the best known and most used. The original statement of Hebb's law reads as follows: "When an axon of cell A is near enough to excite a cell B and repeatedly or persistently takes part in firing it, some growth process or metabolic change takes place in one or both cells such that A's efficiency, as one of the cells firing B, is increased." *

We will see that this deceptively simple statement is remarkable in its implications. It provides nearly all we need to know about learning to make useful neural networks. Hebb is saying that a neuron, A, that repeatedly happens to stimulate another neuron, B, at the times when B is firing, will have an increased effectiveness in

---

* D. O. Hebb, *The Organization of Behavior*, (New York: Wiley, 1949), p. 62.

stimulating B to fire in the future. If we translate this into "neurodes" and "weights," we can restate Hebb's law as follows: If neurode A repeatedly stimulates neurode B while B is generating an output signal, the weight of the synapse between A and B will increase in magnitude.

The net effect of this process is that the strength of the interconnect from A to B increases. This implies that neurode B will become more sensitive to neurode A's stimulus after appropriate training has occurred. During training, we sensitize the network's response to signals passing along certain pathways.

There are a number of details that are not addressed by this simple statement of Hebb's law, and it must usually be modified to be useful in actual neural network implementations. In the mid-1950s, when researchers began writing computer simulations of hebbian systems to determine their ability to learn, the inadequacy of the law for computational purposes quickly became apparent. For example, as the law is stated, the weights on the interconnects can rise without an upper bound; they can potentially rise to infinity. This kind of limitless growth, of course, is anathema to computer simulations. As a result, hebbian learning rules often have the additional constraint imposed on them that the weights of each neurode must be normalized; that is, the weight vector is constrained to have a fixed, constant length. This length is usually set to 1.0.

The impact of this constraint goes beyond the simple matter of confining the growth of the weights to manageable bounds. Assume that a particular neurode has several input interconnections and weights and that one of these weights is increased during training. If the neurode is to maintain a fixed-length weight vector while one of the weights increases, then one or more of the other weights must decrease. Because this decrease can come only from an interconnect that is not currently stimulating the neurode, the constraint effectively requires that a synapse that is consistently not stimulated when the neurode fires will gradually decrease in strength during training. Eventually this weight may even wither to a zero value. Here we have the neural network equivalent of "use it or lose it."

This is not the only modification of Hebb's law that is needed to use it as a neural network learning rule. We must provide for both positive and negative interconnect weights—excitatory and inhibitory synapses. With this feature, a positive stimulus from neurode A can have the effect of increasing or decreasing the tendency of neurode B to fire. Another way of saying this is that allowing negative interconnect weights permits inhibition as well as excitation of the stimulated neurode. Of course, this feature is also needed for it to be biologically accurate.

One way of accomplishing this is to alter our normalization procedure slightly. By picking the limits of the weights to be –1.0 and +1.0, and adding any one of several mathematical conditions that force the length of the weight vector to be equal to 1.0, we can provide for both inhibitory and excitatory synapses and for reduction as well as growth of weights during training.

Neohebbian Learning

One of the classical mathematical expressions of hebbian learning was produced by Stephen Grossberg in the mid-1960s. This version is sometimes called neohebbian learning because it expands the original statement of Hebb's law and provides an explicit mathematical model for Hebb's weight change rule.

The neohebbian model accounts for the fact that biological systems not only learn but also forget. This feature is essential if we want to explain the behavior of biological systems. At first glance, forgetting may not seem to be a useful feature in a learning model for artificial systems, but that is often not the case. It can be useful, for instance, to avoid overcrowding memory with seldom used detail or to correct mistakes in previously learned information.

To put it in its normal context, we'll state Grossberg's neohebbian weight change law as a computational rule. Before we actually state the rule, we need to talk a little about the stepwise manner in which such computations, or simulations, are made. Assume that we have presented an input pattern to the neural network and must now change the weights on each neurode so that it can begin learning the input pattern. In computations of this sort, we move the state of the network forward in small time increments; that is, we calculate the activity and value of the output for every neurode and update the weight of every synapse for one instant of time before moving on to the next instant. Because of this iterative procedure, we can state the law for only one neurode pair and apply it in turn to each synapse of each neurode. Let's assume that the synapse to be updated lies on neurode B, which receives output signals from neurode A. Since we are dealing with only one pair of neurodes, the output of neurode A in this case is unambiguously the input to neurode B, and we will use "output of neurode A" and "input to neurode B" synonymously in this discussion.

The content of this law can be summarized by writing it as a word equation. In this form, it is

    <new weight> =
        <old weight>
        $-F$ <amount forgotten between last and current cycle>
        $+L$ <new learning in this cycle>

Here, F and L are both constants that are in the range of 0 to 1.0. The constant F controls how quickly the network forgets, and L controls how quickly it learns.

Let's look at this rule for some special values of the forgetting and learning constants. First, if neither forgetting nor learning occurs (both F and L are zero in other words), the new weight value is the same as the old one; nothing is forgotten, and nothing is learned. If the forgetting constant, F, is very large, the hebbian term results in a new weight value, but the old weight is completely forgotten; nothing is retained from cycle to cycle. A very small value for F implies that little or no forgetting occurs. If the learning constant, L, is zero, the fraction of the old weight determined by the forgetting constant is retained, but no new changes are made. No learning takes place. Finally, the relative values of the forgetting and learning constants pick the relative importance of new and old knowledge.

The third term of this statement, the hebbian learning term, is just a computational statement of Hebb's law. It tells us that if both the incoming stimulus and the output of a neurode are large at the same time, the weight change of the affected synapse will be large and a lot of learning will occur. If, on the other hand, either the stimulus or the output is small or zero, little or no weight change will be made, and little or no learning will occur. Only when an input stimulus from neurode A coincides with an output from neurode B will learning occur.

Neohebbian learning does not resolve all the problems of hebbian learning; it merely provides a mathematical framework for the original concept and introduces the phenomenon of forgetting. It still has no way of dealing with inhibitory stimuli, so it does not model biological systems accurately. Neohebbian learning did, however, act as a precursor to Grossberg's later outstar learning paradigm.

Differential Hebbian Learning

In our discussion of simple hebbian learning, we had to introduce two features found in biological systems that are necessary for proper operation of a neural network: the possibility of both decreasing and increasing weights during learning and the presence of inhibitory as well as excitatory synapses. In differential hebbian learning, we finally have a learning system that provides both of these features in a natural way. In differential hebbian learning, the learning term of the weight change rule is not proportional to the product of the input and output signals of neurode B but instead is proportional to the product of the rates of change in those signals. In mathematical terms, the expression "rate of change" refers to the derivative of a neurode's output with respect to time.

Under this law, if the input signal from neurode A to neurode B increases in strength (a positive change) at the same time that the output signal of neurode B decreases in strength (a negative change), then their product is negative, and the weight itself becomes more negative. If the input signal decreases at the same time that the output signal increases, the product is similarly negative and the weight again becomes more negative. Only when both the input and the output signals increase or decrease at the same time is their product positive, and only under these circumstances will the weight increase and become more positive.

Differential hebbian learning at last provides us with a learning rule that can model a number of aspects of learning in biological systems with considerable accuracy. It is often the basis for neural network simulations today but rarely in this pure form. It has also inspired a variety of modifications to other network paradigms. For example, there is a version of backpropagation, called backpropagation with recirculation, that uses a differential hebbian learning approach.

Let's look at how classical conditioning is applied in artificial neural networks by discussing two network learning paradigms, the outstar and the drive reinforcement learning models. Both use a form of hebbian learning.

A retentive memory is a good thing,
but the ability to forget is the true token of greatness.
—Elbert Hubbard

10 Classical Conditioning

Many neural network learning laws are based on hebbian learning. We would like to see how hebbian learning can be used to construct a learning model that accurately portrays the classical conditioning described in chapter 8. In this chapter, therefore, we first investigate the outstar learning system, developed by Stephen Grossberg. It is an excellent example of how biological understanding can be used to inspire the development of neural network paradigms. We then look briefly at an even better model of classical conditioning based on differential hebbian learning, the drive-reinforcement theory of Harry Klopf. To do this, we first need to review classical or Pavlovian conditioning.

Classical or Pavlovian Conditioning

Pavlov's original experiments used dogs as subjects, but they have been repeated many times over the years with a wide assortment of subjects, including humans. The kernel of Pavlov's experiment is this: an untrained dog is tested for its response to both food and a ringing bell. The presence of food (naturally enough) causes the dog to begin to salivate even before the food is in reach. The bell ringing does not cause the dog to salivate, although it may bark, or startle, or have some other reaction. The food acts as an unconditioned stimulus because the dog does not have to be taught to salivate in response to it; the dog's salivation is the unconditioned response. We now begin to ring the bell and show the food at the same time. In each case the dog salivates. Eventually, after a number of such repetitions, we can ring the bell without showing the food, and the dog again salivates, though prior to training, the bell did not elicit a salivation response. The ringing bell is now called the conditioned stimulus, and the salivation that occurs as a response to the bell is called the conditioned response.

This simplified description of Pavlov's experiments is sufficient for us to begin to build a neural learning system to model it. Classical conditioning has been extensively studied, and there are many subtle effects to consider before claiming that it is accurately modeled by our learning system. For the moment, however, let's concentrate on these basic characteristics: we want a system that will learn to produce the desired response when stimulated simultaneously by the unconditioned stimulus (one that forces the desired output to occur) and the conditioned stimulus (one we hope will elicit the desired response after training). We can do this by building an outstar network.

The Instar and Outstar

Let's begin our discussion of the outstar by looking at the neurode from a new, geometric perspective. We describe here only those minimal characteristics needed to understand outstar learning. In Grossberg's work the concepts of instar and outstar imply much more than the simple physical structure we outline. We know that each neurode in a neural network receives input from hundreds or thousands of other neurodes. Thus, each neurode is at the focus of a vast array of other neurodes feeding signals to it. In three dimensions, this construct resembles a many-pointed star with all its radii directed inward. Stephen Grossberg terms this an "instar." From another, equally valid point of view, each neurode is a hub from which signals fan out to a vast array of other neurodes, since each neurode sends its output to hundreds or thousands of others. Grossberg, reasonably enough, calls this an "outstar."

Every neurode in any neural network is, at the same time, both the focus of an instar and the hub of an outstar. Thus, a neural network can be viewed as a highly complex, interwoven mesh of these structures, with the inwardly feeding inputs of each instar arising from the outwardly directed signals of other outstars. In a properly designed network, this complicated arrangement does not result in chaos. In fact, it is precisely this complex mesh in which the ever-changing activity takes place that generates the behavior characteristic of neural networks.

So far, we have not mentioned the synapses that we know lie at the end of every interconnect in both the instar and outstar. In an instar, the synapses form a tight cluster about the input end of the focus neurode. In an outstar, there is a synapse where each interconnect terminates at one of the outer, or "border," neurodes. If we could in some way make the weights on these synapses visible during learning, we would see a beehive of activity, with some weights tending upward, others tending downward, and yet others staying nearly constant.

We can use this instar-outstar concept to understand how a neural network can learn complex patterns. First let's consider how a network of instars and outstars might learn a static spatial pattern, one that does not change in time.

Outstar Learning

Let's build a small network that consists of a single neurode, acting as an outstar, connected to an array of neurodes that act as instars. For this network, we need to use only two inputs on each instar neurode: one from the outstar neurode that has an adjustable weight and a training input that has a fixed synapse weight of 1.0.

Imagine that we cluster the instar neurodes together into a two-dimensional grid, similar to the pixel grid that makes up the image on a computer monitor. (A pixel is the smallest element of light or dark a monitor can display.) So we can more easily visualize the operation of the outstar, we assume that we have arranged a way to make the output of each neurode visible. We see a tiny spot of light proportional to the output of each grid neurode. Thus whenever a grid neurode has an output near 1, we get a very bright spot on the grid at that neurode's position, and whenever a neurode has an output near zero, little light is emitted. In between these limits, the light output varies with the neurode's output. If we use enough neurodes in the instar grid, it will be able to produce an image much like that appearing on a computer screen. Finally, we will place a threshold on each of the incoming signals from the outstar neurode so that only stimuli that are at least as strong as the threshold value will be perceived by the grid neurodes; any smaller stimuli will be ignored. This threshold will suppress random noise firings in the network.

We would like to condition the grid to respond to a stimulus from the outstar neurode by reproducing some pattern, say, a picture of a rose. This picture will be the unconditioned response; it will also be the conditioned response after the network is trained. The input to each grid neurode is the conditioned stimulus. How shall we supply the unconditioned stimulus? That is, how shall we make the network produce the picture of the rose in the first place? That's where the training input on each grid neurode comes in: each time we stimulate the outstar neurode, we use the training inputs to stimulate the grid neurodes into reproducing the rose. A grid neurode corresponding to a very bright spot on the picture will receive a signal near 1 on its training input, while a grid neurode corresponding to a dark spot on the picture will receive a signal near 0.

Before we train the network, the grid's output makes a random pattern when we stimulate the outstar neurode. This is equivalent to Pavlov's ringing the bell for an untrained dog. While we may get some reaction, we certainly do not elicit the desired response because the weights between the outstar and the grid neurodes have random values. When the outstar neurode "fires," therefore, in the absence of a conditioned stimulus (the picture), we expect to see a pattern that looks much like the snow seen on a television set not tuned to a station.

Now we are ready to train the network to reproduce the rose when we stimulate the outstar neurode. To do this, we carry out the neural network equivalent of repeatedly ringing the bell while simultaneously showing the food. This means that we trigger the outstar neurode to send a stimulus signal to the grid at the same time that we use the training inputs to force the grid to reproduce the picture. As we do this, the network learns to respond with the picture even when the training inputs are not present. Let's consider how this happens.

Outstar learning is based on hebbian learning. According to this law, if a stimulus arrives at a synapse at a time when the receiving neurode is active, then the weight associated with that interconnect will increase. In outstar learning, the weight increase depends on the product of the input and output signals of the grid neurode. Thus, grid neurodes corresponding to bright spots in the picture will have large outputs at the time the outstar's stimulus arrives, and the corresponding weights will become somewhat stronger. The synapses of grid neurodes corresponding to intermediate brightnesses in the picture will have lower output and will be changed less. In either case, the next time the outstar neurode fires, the grid will be more likely to reproduce a bright spot in that position. After a number of repetitions and regardless of the initial values of the weights, the bright portions of the picture will be faithfully reproduced.

But what about those grid neurodes that correspond to dark spots in the image? Suppose that the initial, untrained weight between the outstar neurode and one particular such grid neurode is fairly strong. When the grid is stimulated, this neurode will generate a relatively bright spot in the image, though its corresponding image position is supposed to be dark. In contrast with the grid neurode at the bright image position, however, the weight will not increase (or at least not increase very much) because the output of the grid neurode at the time the outstar's stimulus arrived was very low. While the weight does not increase, however, there is no provision in the original hebbian learning model for it to decrease. Because we assumed that this particular weight was initially strong, its grid neurode produces a bright spot in the image instead of the dark spot needed.

Grossberg corrected this problem by using neohebbian learning. Recall that neohebbian learning adds forgetting to hebbian learning. The effect of this is to ensure that any weight not actively increasing in strength is slowly decreasing. As long as active, positive learning effects are being experienced, the forgetting effect is too small to matter, but if no learning is occurring (the weights are not actively increasing), the forgetting effect dominates, and the synaptic weight goes down.

This solves the problem with the grid neurodes that correspond to dark spots in the picture. We know that little or no learning will occur for these neurodes, and therefore when we add in the forgetting effect, the synaptic weights for these neurodes actually decrease slightly. Thus, even if these weights are very high when we begin training the network, after enough repetitions they decrease to a level that ensures that the dark picture elements remain dark.

We can now summarize how this little network learns to reproduce an image. During training, we artificially cause the grid neurodes to display the image we wish to condition the network to reproduce. As a result, grid neurodes corresponding to relatively bright portions of the image always have a correspondingly large output when the outstar's stimulus is received, and the synaptic weights leading from the outstar neurode to these neurodes are strengthened with each repetition. Eventually no matter what the ini-

How Soon We Forget

Before we go on, we ought to consider the two relative effects of the activity decay and forgetting terms to see their relationship. Activation decay governs the speed at which the activity of the neurode reduces to near-zero when inputs are removed. The forgetting term governs the speed at which the weights on the interconnects decay to near-zero when the interconnects are not exercised. Do these two different decays occur at the same speed? We certainly hope not! Let's spend a moment to see why.

The neurode's activity must decay very quickly as soon as the stimuli are removed so that the neurode can prepare to receive a new stimulus. If the activity decays too slowly, the neurode will not be able to respond to any new inputs for such a long time that the network's overall response time to changes in the environment will be unacceptably slow. Thus activation decay must occur quickly, and the activation decay parameter should reflect this. On the other hand, the pattern of weights and interconnects within the network literally is the network's working storehouse of memories. If that decays too rapidly, the network's working memory will literally be destroyed unless it is constantly refreshed. This means that the network would have to spend a lot of time doing such memory refresh operations, and it incidentally implies that there is some global authority—a homunculus, in other words—that can provide the appropriate direction to perform such a refresh. We can avoid both of these unacceptable conditions by permitting memories to decay but to do so only very slowly over many time periods.

tial value for the synaptic weights, the outstar's stimulus alone is sufficient to cause these neurodes to reproduce a bright spot.

Grid neurodes corresponding to dark portions of the image, in contrast, are never very active when the outstar's stimulus is received. As a result, these neurodes experience little or no hebbian learning, and the forgetting term dominates the weight change model. Each training repetition causes the synaptic weights for these neurodes to decrease slightly due to the forgetting term. Eventually the outstar's stimulus is never sufficient to cause these grid neurodes to become active, and the dark portions of the image are faithfully reproduced. This is true regardless of the strength of the stimulus and the initial value of the synapse's weight.

We can summarize the training process in Pavlovian terms. We present the network with the conditioned stimulus (the hub neurode's signal) at the same time that we present it with the unconditioned stimulus (the rose). This forces the network to produce the unconditioned response (reproduction of the image on the grid). If we do this often enough and frequently enough, sooner or later we get the conditioned response (the image) merely by presenting the conditioned stimulus.

Outstar Inconsistencies

The outstar seems to do a remarkable job of mimicking the behavior of classical conditioning. But there is a problem, and it hinges on the phrase "at the same time" in the previous paragraph. Animal experiments show that conditioning is more effective if the conditioned stimulus is presented before the unconditioned stimulus—if the bell rings before the dog sees the food, for instance. Providing both stimuli simultaneously turns out to be much less effective than placing them in a temporal (time) sequence. Despite the fact that the time for the outstar neurode's signal to reach the grid neurodes is carefully accounted for in the outstar learning model, learning takes place in the instar neurodes only if the stimuli reach them simultaneously. As a result, the model has no ability to mimic or account for the time-delay phenomenon.

If we consider conditioning as a survival tool to the animal, it is easy to see exactly why it works best when the bell rings before the food arrives. From the dog's perspective, learning to recognize that the food (or, perhaps, some dangerous predator) is about to appear gives it time to react to that event so that it can effectively prepare to

The Virtue of Forgetting

Why would we want to introduce forgetting deliberately into a neural network? Don't we have enough problems getting these things to work correctly without letting them forget whatever we have managed to train them to do? There are actually a couple of reasons why forgetting can be a virtue as well as a problem when designing a neural network. First, if we want systems to truly model biological systems, we have to model all aspects of biological behaviors, not just the best ones. In particular, this means enabling the model to forget as well as learn. More important, however, we also want the system to respond to an environment that changes over time. If the environment can change, the responses appropriate to a particular stimulus can also change. If we do not permit the system ever to forget, it will be difficult to retrain it to a new, more appropriate behavior when circumstances change.

An example might occur when training a robot to deal with weather. We might first introduce the idea that when it rains, the robot is supposed to get under whatever cover is available. The result of such training might be for the robot to seek a tree as shelter, which would be fine as long as there was no lightning. We would then have to retrain the robot to stay away from trees when the rain is accompanied by lightning (assuming we don't want fricasseed robot after the storm). If the robot cannot forget the earlier training in favor of the new response, we would likely be faced with a completely neurotic robot that dashed back and forth from the tree to the open field in the rain.

eat—or avoid being eaten. Associating a simultaneous stimulus with the appearance of the food or predator has little point because by then the dog can directly sense that it has arrived and can immediately begin to eat, or flee, or fight. Learning such a simultaneous association has provided the animal with no improved ability to survive. On the other hand, if through experience one animal learns an association with a particular stimulus that occurs before the food or danger arrives, it has an opportunity to prepare to react. Thus, that animal may be a bit faster than its fellows to seize a juicy morsel or a bit more likely to avoid a predator. The overall survival benefits of learning such temporally related associations are clear.

This inability to mimic the dependence on time delay has a more subtle meaning for the outstar as a model of learning. As constituted, it cannot learn sequences of patterns and cannot perceive causal relationships. As a result, the neurodes of an outstar network are forever trapped in a single, continuously changing moment of time.

There are a number of other problems with the outstar as a model of conditioning, most having to do with secondary or subtle details of the process. For example, the grid neurodes learn in a more or less linear fashion, with the weights increasing in a straight line. In actual animal experiments, however, learning curves are S-shaped, with a slow beginning, a sharp increase in weights in the middle trials, and slow learning at the end of the training. There are a number of other discrepancies between actual animal experimental results and the outstar model's predictions. Nearly all of these problems are corrected by Harry Klopf's drive-reinforcement theory.

Drive-Reinforcement Theory

Drive-reinforcement is a learning system developed by Harry Klopf of the Air Force Wright Aeronautical Laboratories. It is a modification of differential hebbian learning. Recall that in differential hebbian learning, weight changes result from changes in the stimulus and response signals rather than from the stimulus and response signals themselves. In drive-reinforcement learning, the weight increase depends on the product of the change in the output signal of the receiving neurode and the weighted sum of the changes of the inputs to that neurode over some time period. Thus, it is not only the current change in the input stimulus that determines learning but also the accumulation of such changes over some significant time period, with each such change being weighted by the synaptic strengths in effect at the time that change occurred. This mechanism permits a network using drive-reinforcement training to perceive causal relationships between stimuli separated in time. To use our Pavlovian example, it allows the network to relate a ringing bell to later presentation of food. Let's see how such a system changes the weights during training.

Consider the case in which the incoming stimulus is increasing in strength. If the output of the receiving neurode is also increasing, the changes in both input and output are positive, and the weight associated with that neurode increases in value. It can become more positive if it is greater than zero or less negative if it is less than zero. The stimulating neurode will thus find it easier to excite the receiving neurode in the future. But what if the receiving neurode's output is decreasing as the incoming stimulus is increasing? Then the output change is negative rather than positive, and the weight associated with that neurode decreases in value. In the future, the stimulating neurode will find it harder to excite the receiving neurode, but easier to inhibit it from firing.

We can similarly analyze the remaining cases in which the stimulating signal is decreasing at the same time the output of the receiving neurode is either increasing or decreasing. The result of our analysis is this: if the stimulus and the output of the receiving neurode simultaneously change in the same direction, the weight of the synapse becomes more positive and the input signal has an excitatory effect. If, on the other hand, the stimulus and the output of the receiving neurode simultaneously change in the opposite direction, the weight of the synapse becomes more negative and the input signal has an inhibitory effect.

In drive-reinforcement training, only those incoming signal changes that are positive (that is, in which the input is increasing in strength) are normally acted on; other changes are ignored. Furthermore, the system places a minimum magnitude on each weight. This means that weights are never permitted to go completely to zero. There are two reasons for this latter restriction. The first is pragmatic: because of the form of the equations governing the weight change, if any weight ever does exactly equal zero, it can never change again; a weight that goes to zero is permanently stuck there. This would remove it from any future usefulness to the network. The second reason for not permitting zero values is for biological consistency. Permitting zero weight values would allow a synapse to begin as a positive (excitatory) one and then pass through the zero point to become a negative (inhibitory) synapse, and vice

And the Beat Goes On...

In our brief digression into neurobiology in chapter 2, we noted that biological neurons are actually pulse devices that determine the incoming signal strength not by the volume of the signal (which is more or less constant) but rather by the relative number of signal pulses received over a given period of time. It turns out that this pulsed-frequency encoding is quite robust with regard to noise. Determining the correct exact strength of a noisy analog signal can be quite difficult, but even a fairly low-resolution receptor can easily determine that a signal pulse has arrived, just as a digital computer can much more easily distinguish the 0 and 1 of a binary pulse as opposed to distinguishing between two nearly equal analog values. A pulsed frequency encoding that simply counts the number of such signal pulses in some standard time interval is thus robust, simple and efficient.

versa. As far as we know now, there are no synapses in the brain that are sometimes excitatory and sometimes inhibitory. By prohibiting such a change of functionality, we force the network's synapses to be more consistent with their biological counterparts.

Drive-reinforcement network responses have been compared to the results of classical conditioning experiments carried out on animals in order to determine the network's consistency with biological behaviors. For example, a simulation of drive-reinforcement training using pulse-frequency signal encoding (rather than the easier signal-strength encoding usually used for artificial systems) has been done by researchers Mark Gluck, David Parker, and Eric Reifsnider of Stanford University. Carefully following Klopf's guidelines, these researchers found that all of the behaviors claimed for drive-reinforcement networks were exhibited by their system and that agreement with classical conditioning experiments was remarkably good.

There are two key reasons we should care about a system that correctly models classical conditioning. The first is that the success of a network paradigm in modeling known biological learning models provides a good measure of its potential to solve real-world problems. Thus, drive-reinforcement networks are more likely to be able to solve real-world problems than the relatively less sophisticated outstar networks. The second reason is that drive-reinforcement training offers a means by which we can have a network learn the concept of causality. With this model, a network exists that can correlate the past to the present; no other existing network model has this capability. This seems to us to be a great step forward in the quest to create naturally intelligent systems.

Even the drive-reinforcement network, however, still looks at the world only one step at a time. If we truly want naturally intelligent systems, we must do more than process a series of single moments; we must deal with continuity of actions and events. We must be able to handle patterns that change in time rather than just patterns that are static; in the next chapter we look at some ways neural networks can handle such sequences of patterns.

There is nothing permanent except change.
—Heraclitus

11 Learning Sequences of Patterns

For us to survive, it is not sufficient merely to be able to respond to individual, distinct patterns. Life does not present us with a series of unrelated still frames. Rather, we are constantly bombarded with continuously changing but related cues and stimuli. Researchers trying to model biological behavior must take this into account and must generate artificial neural systems that have some ability to process and recognize sequences of related patterns. In this chapter we will look at a few of the ways neural networks can be built to learn such sequences, often called "spatiotemporal patterns."

The Music Box Associative Memory

One of the simplest ways to build a network that learns sequences of patterns is to modify slightly a heteroassociative memory. Suppose we want the network to learn to recite the alphabet in order. What do we have to do to make the network generate the output sequence "A-B-C-D" when given an appropriate cue? It turns out to be almost a trivial task.

Recall that a heteroassociative memory is one that associates two different patterns together. Let's set up the system so that we associate some arbitrary trigger starting signal with the pattern for A and then train the network to associate each succeeding letter of the alphabet with the letter following it: A with B, B with C, and so on. In principle, although not necessarily in practice, it is a simple matter to connect the output of the network to the input so that as each letter is output, it becomes the input that calls up the next letter of the alphabet. Upon supplying the trigger cue, the output of the network quickly reproduces the alphabet in a fixed, rote sequence.

This network does not truly learn a sequence of patterns. In order for the sequence to appear, we must explicitly take the output of one step and use it as an input stimulus to get the next pattern. It is a crude way, however, to learn and recall a sequence of patterns. The "music box" name for this technique derives from its similarity to the frozen sequence of notes that a music box plays. The sequence can be repeated indefinitely, and there is no variation or alteration; each replay is exactly the same as the one before. This style of associative memory operation is also called the "tape recorder" mode, for obvious reasons.

Single-Neurode Systems

We can make a system that recalls sequences of patterns with a much simpler layout, however. In fact, Stephen Grossberg has shown that a single outstar neurode can initiate and sustain a lengthy spatiotemporal sequence. An example system is shown in figure 11.1a.

Think of what this means. A single initiating pulse to a single neurode could result in the generation of a complex series of spatiotemporal patterns. Let's assume that we want to cause a robot arm to draw a picture. To do this, the output resulting from the initial stimulus would be fanned out among a large number of interconnects of differing lengths. At the end of each interconnect would be an actuator that caused a specific movement of the arm. Because the output would travel along the interconnects with a fixed velocity, the time of arrival of the output at the various actuators could be chosen in such a way that the arm would draw the picture we wanted.

As Grossberg points out, there is a hitch. Once started, there would be no way to stop the picture from being drawn to completion, and there would be nothing to permit variations of the illustration on successive repetitions. The action of the neurode would be as automatic as an eyeblink and the outcome as predictable as a tape recording because every detail of the procedure would be dictated by the order in which the neurode's output signal arrived at the various actuators.

We clearly need more than this simple arrangement if we are to be able to interrupt or vary an activity. A more elaborate structure that permits some flexibility is shown in figure 11.1b. It uses a single outstar with a single set of receiving instar neurodes. The outstar is connected to each of its border neurodes many times by means of a scheme similar to that used in the single-neurode approach. Once again, different delays of the single output signal are accomplished by sending it over paths of varying length. Here, however, each set of delayed signals arrives at a different set of synapses on the border neurodes, creating the same effect as if the hub cell sequentially activated a series of separate outstars. By combining the arrival times of signals at the border neurodes with the particular action each neurode controls, some degree of versatility and control can be obtained.

A third structure, one that actually uses the series of outstars suggested, is shown in figure 11.1c. The signal from the original hub neurode is sequentially intercepted by a series of appropriately spaced secondary hub neurodes. (We can call these "interneurodes" because of their functional similarity to the interneurons of biology.) Because the border neurodes in the principal and secondary outstars can communicate with other similar networks or with networks of other types, this structure offers a means of creating a rich set of spatiotemporal patterns and controlling them in subtle ways. It allows each pattern in the sequence to be a completely different kind of response, for example, so that the sequence might include a motor control pattern for a robot arm, a speech pattern for a voice synthesizer, and an image pattern for a visual system.

All of these approaches possess the capability to produce complex spatiotemporal patterns, but probably none is easily usable for practical applications. For one thing, such networks would be time-consuming and difficult to construct. The spacing of interneurodes (or the axon collaterals) along the axon is crucial but would have to be redetermined each time the designer wanted to vary the process the network controlled. Another way of saying this is that the schemes depend more heavily on finding the correct interconnect lengths and wiring schemes than on training the synapse weights. While we could possibly let the networks effectively wire themselves by clever training techniques, the scheme to do this successfully is not at all obvious.

Is there no practical way to build spatiotemporal capabilities into a network that uses the outstar learning model? The answer is, yes, there is; and one way to do it is with Grossberg's avalanche network.

143

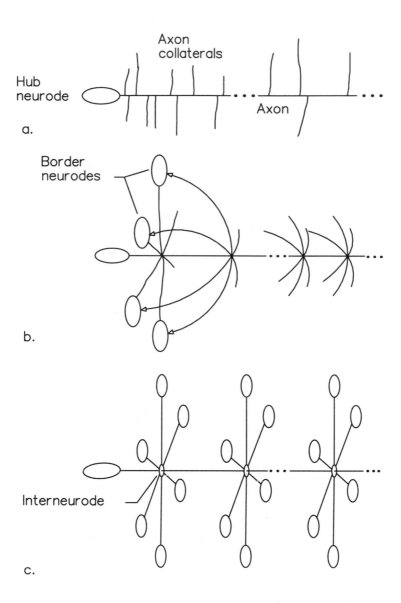

Figure 11.1 (a) The simplest outstar capable of learning sequences. (b) The outstar connected to different synapses of the same grid neurodes is a more versatile system. (c) A single outstar connected to a series of grids via a set of "interneurons" that pass the signal through. This is more versatile yet.

144

The Outstar Avalanche

We can use the outstar learning model to build a network that can learn pattern sequences by making one basic change to the model: we must use neurodes that are slow to lose their activity once they become activated.

Until now, we have ignored the reaction time of the neurodes in our networks. We have implicitly assumed an instantaneous model of activation. When an incoming signal was presented, we assumed the neurode reacted instantly; if the incoming signal was removed, we assumed the neurode's activity disappeared instantly. Biological neurons do not act in this way. It takes a finite amount of time for a neuron's activity to build to its maximum value when it is stimulated, and it takes a finite amount of time for it to return to its quiescent state when the stimulation is removed. We will have to go at least part of the way toward this biological model of activation to make the spatiotemporal network function properly.

In the outstar network of chapter 10 that learned static patterns, we implicitly assumed an instantaneous model of activation. As a first-order approximation, it is not bad. For patterns that change in time, however, we need to modify this model and assume at least that the activity of a neurode does not decay instantly when excitation stops. Grossberg uses a simple exponential to describe this decay. This allows the activation falloff to be controlled by a single constant, called the activation decay constant. When this constant is large, the neurode's activity rapidly drops to zero; when it is small, the neurode's activity decays much more slowly. The neurodes of the static outstar network effectively had a very large activation decay constant, so that activity died off quickly when stimulation was removed. We will see below why this must be changed to build an avalanche network.

As a simple application for our network, we will look at a problem we have used before: given the correct input cue, we want the network to learn to display the alphabet in the correct sequence. We also want the network to be more flexible than the simple systems discussed; we want it to be able to stop its display at any time if so prompted and to be able to start from some letter other than "A" if we signal it to do so.

For the network, we use an input, middle, and output layer. The input layer provides fan-out. It transmits every element of the initiating or "trigger" pattern to every middle-layer neurode and starts the replay of the sequence of letters. Thus, each input neurode is the hub of an outstar.

The output layer comprises the grid that displays the appropriate letters. Its purpose is thus the same as the corresponding layer of the static outstar network. Its structure is also the same: each grid neurode is the focus of an instar beginning on neurodes in the previous layer. In the static network, there was only a single neurode in the previous layer; in this case, however, there are many. Also as in the previous network, these output neurodes each have an additional external input used during training to impress the pattern for each letter on the output grid.

The middle layer is the most complex. These neurodes receive inputs from the input layer and from some number of other neurodes within the middle layer itself. We will be a bit vague about how many other neurodes each middle layer unit connects to, but it should be some small number, say between 1 and 10. These intra-layer connections are essential for the correct operation of the network.

Now we need only two more things before describing the way a trained system works. First, although the operation of the avalanche network is continuous, it will be helpful in our description if we break time into short intervals as with the crossbar network. Second, we need to indicate the size of the activation decay constant of the input- and middle-layer neurodes. For this qualitative description, let's assume that the activity of a neurode will decay in a matter of seconds or tenths of seconds—several time periods. Thus, once a middle- or input-layer neurode becomes active, it will stay active for several time periods, even though the stimulus that initially excited it has been removed. Without this feature, the avalanche network will not operate correctly.

Operation of the trained avalanche is exquisitely simple in concept. The neurodes in the middle, avalanche layer are trained to fire only if they receive a stimulus from the currently active neurode and if the previously firing neurodes in the sequence are still at least partially active. Each succeeding neurode can thus be triggered only if the correct combination of stimuli is received at the correct time. For example, if the correct sequence of neurode firings in the middle layer is 1, then 5, then 3, then 6, the network is set so that neurode 3 will not fire unless it sees stimulating activity from neurode 5 and at least partial activity from neurode 1. Neurode 6 will not fire unless it sees stimulating activity from neurode 3 and partial activity from neurode 5, and so on. The intralayer connections enforce the temporal relationships between the avalanche layer neurodes.

There are a number of points to note about the operation of this network. For instance, if the middle-layer neurodes are excited in the wrong order or accidentally stimulated with noise, any resulting spurious activity in the layer soon dies out, and the process continues as if nothing happened. Also, for complex patterns, we can require more than one neurode to be active for the pattern to continue. We can also arrange for operator interaction. At any point in the process, for instance, we can require a reinforcing command from the input layer in order for the recollection to continue; thus, for instance, a single input prod will not necessarily cause the network to run through the entire alphabet. Finally, we can store many sequences with a relatively small number of neurodes since it is their temporal relationship during stimulation that determines whether or not they activate.

How do we train the network? It may seem that designing the interconnection pattern of the middle layer would be tedious and that training the network would be difficult, if not impossible. For simple spatiotemporal patterns like the alphabet example, only single-neurode middle layer sequences need to be considered, and network design is easy. More complex patterns take more thought and effort. Training is not especially difficult in either case. We first initiate the middle layer's activity sequence by presenting the desired input cue to the network. As this sequence progresses, we successively impress each item in the spatiotemporal pattern to be memorized on the network. This we do by means of the training inputs of the final layer neurodes. Of course, we must choose the interval between succeeding presentations to be commensurate with the chosen activation decay constant of the network's neurodes. With repeated presentations of this training routine, the outstar learning law built into the adaptive synapses of the middle and output layers causes the network to learn to reproduce the desired sequence.

The avalanche network gives one possible mechanism to save and recall complex temporal patterns and interactions. The architecture of the network and the conditions under which it can react and learn can be varied so that they are appropriate to the specific needs of our application. We can permit the network to start the recall at any point in the sequence by making appropriate middle-layer neurodes that have strong sensitivities to special input signals, sensitivities strong enough to overcome the fact that the previous patterns have not been output. We can stop the sequence at any time by making the middle-layer neurodes have appropriate inhibitory sensitivities to other special input layer signals. Thus, we not only can have "start" inputs, but also "stop" inputs and "start-from-here" inputs.

These are fundamental properties of voluntary behavior; we can stop and start such behaviors at will. Simpler networks than the avalanche can learn spatiotemporal sequences like the alphabet but these designs actually only provide involuntary temporal learning; once started, they cannot easily be altered or stopped. Other, more complex designs exist that can successfully learn and recall sequences and that can be interrupted or started from an arbitrary point in a sequence. The avalanche is the simplest approach that shows real power in learning spatiotemporal sequences of patterns.

Recognizing Sequences of Patterns

You may have noticed that the primary capability of the avalanche is in learning to reproduce temporally related pattern sequences. What if we want the network to be able to recognize such sequences as well?

Robert Hecht-Nielsen of HNC has shown that the avalanche can be modified for this purpose. He suggests that Kohonen learning be used in the avalanche layer to allow it to model the probability distribution function of some standard sequence of known patterns. This training sequence is sampled at regular time intervals, and these samples used as input to the network, maintaining the temporal order and separation of the samples. We can think of this training sequence as some action that is being filmed, and each sample as an individual frame in the movie. To compare an unknown sequence to the learned one, we present it to the network inputs as we did the standard patterns and allow the neurodes in the avalanche layer to compete. Only the neurode combinations that encode sequences similar to the unknown one will fire; the others will lose the competition and remain off.

The essential strategy is to overlay a Kohonen learning scheme (or any similar learning scheme) on the avalanche architecture. Permitting the avalanche layer competition to include the total input—the unknown input pattern as well as signals from the other neurodes in the layer—generates a system that correctly classifies spatiotemporal patterns.

We have nearly concluded our discussion of learning, but before we go on to other issues we should step back to assess how well current learning systems perform. In the next chapter, we consider just what the requirements really are for naturally intelligent learning, and how well we are doing relative to those requirements.

Who learns by Finding Out has sevenfold
The Skill of him who learns by Being Told.
—Guiterman

12 Autonomous Learning

We have discussed several important learning models in this part. Let's now step back and take one last, broader look at autonomous learning systems. We will distinguish autonomous learning from the more general unsupervised learning of, say, the competitive filter associative memory by the following characteristic: an ordinary unsupervised learning system learns every input pattern, whether or not it is important; the only way to prevent an input pattern from being learned is temporarily to disable—turn off—learning. An autonomous system, on the other hand, can learn selectively; it learns only "important" input patterns. As a result, learning can be enabled—left on—at all times.

Neural networks capable of autonomous learning provide the foundation for some exciting applications, including the possibility of genuinely independent machines, true robots. We will need autonomous learning for many subsystems in such a robot: vision, speech, language processing, motor control, context understanding, and perhaps even mass storage. Let's explore some of the characteristics an ideal autonomous learning model must have and assess how well we are doing relative to that ideal.

Chapter 12

Characteristics of Autonomous Learning Systems

The competitive filter associative memory is capable of ordinary unsupervised learning; for example, it can learn the statistical properties of its input data set without a tutor. But we must provide the network with a carefully controlled schooling experience for it to learn correctly. For instance, we must arrange for the learning data set to be a balanced and rich representation of the real-world data we expect the network to experience in operation.

What are the characteristics we would like to build into a system capable of truly autonomous learning? We suggest the following, based on a list originally set forth by Gail Carpenter and Stephen Grossberg.

1. The system functions as an autonomous associative memory; it organizes its knowledge into associated categories with no help from us and reliably retrieves related information from partial or even garbled input cues.

2. It responds rapidly when asked to recall information or to recognize some input pattern it has already learned. This means that the system utilizes parallel architecture and parallel search techniques.

3. Since it must function in the real world, the system learns and recalls arbitrarily complex input patterns. Further, it places no mathematical restrictions on the form of those patterns. A mathematician would say that the input does not need to be orthogonal or linearly separable, for instance.

4. The system learns constantly but learns only significant information, and it does not have to be told what information is significant.

5. New knowledge does not cover or destroy information that the system has already learned.

6. It automatically learns more detail in a particular associative category if feedback information indicates that this is necessary.

The autonomous system may suddenly begin treating as significant some input that it had previously been ignoring, or vice versa.

7. It reorganizes its associative categories if new knowledge indicates that its present ones are inefficient or inadequate.

8. It can generalize from specific examples to general categories.

9. Its storage capacity is essentially unlimited.

These are ambitious requirements, but some of the neural network designs we will describe display almost all of them. Let's explore each requirement in more detail to see what it might mean in the operation of an autonomous system.

Recall by Association

In chapter 4 we looked in detail at the capabilities of associative memory systems and illustrated through Sue and George's conversation about Joe Flamespitter that our own memories operate in this way. It is difficult, if not impossible, to visualize how any autonomous system could learn and function without these capabilities.

Seek and Ye Shall Find

An autonomous system must have rapid recall of data. Associative memories store patterns by correlating or associating them with other patterns that are in some way similar. Think of oranges, for instance. We can find oranges in our heads in the category "fruit," "round things," "orange-colored things," or in any other of a number of other categories as the need arises—literally without thinking about it. Also, we don't think of elephants first when we want to decide what fruit to eat, and we don't think of oranges first when asked to name a large land mammal. In placing "orange" in the appropriate categories, in deciding what fruit to eat, and in searching for the name of an animal that has been described, we naturally adopt the optimal search strategy. A good autonomous learning system must do the same.

Nobody's Perfect

It is not difficult to illustrate that the "search strategy" of an associative memory has faults. We have all experienced the phenomenon of meeting someone unexpectedly, in an unusual place or circumstance, and having difficulty recalling the person's name. Possibly we don't recognize him at all. This happens because we don't associate that person with that particular location or circumstance; he is not stored in the right place. Yet, although the search strategy of an associative memory is not foolproof, it is far better for an autonomous entity—animate or inanimate—than strategies currently used by serial computers.

Rapid recall implies that both the architecture and search strategy of the associative memory of an autonomous system must be parallel. In our brain and in a neural network system, all possible paths must be searched at the same time. Serial strategies simply will not do for real-time searches of the very large knowledge bases needed for getting along on our own in the real world.

A serial search strategy that works well on a standard computer for a database containing only a few items may fail miserably if the database is enlarged. Moreover, a serial search strategy that works well for items organized in one way will often become inefficient if the same items are organized differently.

A key feature of human recognition and one we would want for any autonomous system is direct access to learned patterns. We do not have to search through our memories when we see the face of a person we know well. The identity of the person and a great deal of other information is immediately available to us. This attribute is virtually impossible to obtain with serial or fixed-strategy ·search algorithms.

Dealing with Reality

Our world is complex and difficult. A rich cacophony of sounds, scents, sights, and other sensations bombards us constantly. This sensory stimulation continues night and day, every day, for our entire lives. As human beings, we have gotten so used to processing the cacophony that we suffer considerable discomfort if we are denied sensory input. Psychologists experimenting with volunteers in sensory deprivation environments have found that a complete lack of sensory input soon causes even the most stable human to hallucinate and sometimes to become nearly psychotic. Our brains have the ability, even the need, to process input data; deprived of it, we lose our bearing and rapidly develop psychological difficulties.

The input we receive in no way consists of simple binary data patterns. Instead we are constantly bombarded with electromagnetic radiation we interpret as heat and light, pressure waves we interpret as sound, mechanical stimuli we interpret as touch, and traces of chemicals we interpret as smell and taste. This information is not cleaned up or preprocessed for us; we have to do that ourselves with our sensory and cognitive systems. It does not consist of convenient, dissimilar patterns or of handy, precategorized data sets. Yet somehow we manage to make sense of it all and generate a coherent view of the world. Any autonomous system that leaves the laboratory needs similar capabilities and must be able to process such a plethora of inputs, or at least to filter out the meaningless data and process the rest.

The Importance of Being Significant

The ideal self-organizing network should be able to use context and historical experience to decide what it will learn and ignore. In other words, it should be able to determine for itself what inputs are significant and what are not. In our everyday experience, whether we label a particular piece of sensory information as meaningful or irrelevant often depends on the context we experience it in and our past experiences. The sound of a chain rattling causes no particular curiosity if we are in a machine shop. The same sound probably generates a great deal of curiosity, and even alarm, if we are alone at night in an abandoned house. Similarly, a short mark over a vowel is easily dismissed as a misprint or a flaw in the paper when reading English but must be carefully taken into account when reading French or Spanish because its presence can change the entire meaning of the sentence.

To illustrate that what is judged an obviously important feature of one pattern may be ignored as irrelevant in another, look at the two parts of figure 12.1. We will almost certainly separate the two patterns of figure 12.1a into distinct categories. When they are incorporated in a more complex pattern such as that in figure 12.1b, however, we will probably decide that both of these two patterns correspond to an "E." That is, we will judge them as variants of a more general, single pattern type and will consider the extra portions of the patterns as "noise." An ideal neural network should do the same.

On with the New, On with the Old

Human beings have a great capacity to learn. Moreover, we can learn things that are new to us without forgetting or erasing what we have already learned. We may learn to drive a car and later learn to ride a motorcycle. These skills are different but have many similarities; they are nonorthogonal. Yet we do not forget the first skill when we add the second.

In our discussion of associative memories in part II, particularly the adaline and the crossbar, we found that training the network on a new pattern often has the unfortunate effect of causing it to "forget" an old pattern. Clearly this kind of behavior is not acceptable in an autonomous system. Autonomy requires the system to be able to learn and adapt based on its experience with the world around it; no system can function if it can recall only its most recent experiences.

a.   b.

Figure 12.1 Two pattern sets with common features. Patterns (a) would likely be judged different while patterns (b) would very likely be judged as slightly different examples of the same pattern.

An autonomous system must thus be able to expand its learning, adding new patterns that do not destroy the old ones, so that its knowledge and aptitude increase over time. This is especially difficult in the light of the complex and unstructured nature of the data patterns presented to it.

Categorically Speaking

If we are told or find from experience that the two patterns in figure 12.1b are individually significant, we would like to be able to split up our earlier single cognitive category and remember that the two kinds of "E" had separate meanings. An everyday example of this occurs when we train in a new job. For instance, nearly everyone has an idea of what a computer is. However, a trainee in computers must learn to distinguish microprocessors, minicomputers, superminicomputers, and mainframe computers, as well as a host of other specialty categories.

A similar thing occurs in every field of endeavor. When we see a pretty flower in a store, we don't necessarily know or care what specific name it has. If all we want to do is to add an attractive color accent to a room or table, the variety of flower used doesn't matter at all. We go to the nursery or florist and choose an orchid solely on its superficial appearance and its appropriateness for the decorating scheme we have in mind. However, if we become a professional orchid grower, we now care very much whether we have an epiphytic or a terrestrial orchid or whether it is a cymbidium, dendrobium, or cattleya. When we learn such distinctions we have split our original "orchid"/"not orchid" categorization into much finer categories. Differences among orchids that were previously perceived as insignificant are now meaningful and important.

This process can go the other way: fine details can be discarded and categories merged as the need for subtle distinctions is removed. A child might pick over a bowl of M&M candies and select only the red ones because "they taste better." As an adult, that person might well perceive all colors as tasting equally delicious and place all M&M candies in the same category. (Of course, some of us still pick out the red ones.)

One key way we have of knowing that some particular feature of a pattern is unimportant is if it is not stable while we are viewing the pattern or if it is not repeated in every appearance of that pattern. We usually identify such unrepeated or randomly occurring features as meaningless noise. We would like an autonomous system to do the same.

There are networks that can keep from learning or responding to either unstable or unrepeated features of patterns. These networks do not learn unstable noise in a pattern because it does not persist long enough to cause significant, correlated changes in any synaptic weights. These networks do not learn unrepeated noise because any modification it may cause in the synaptic weights associated with that pattern is "averaged out" during other presentations of the pattern.

The Memory Shell Game

Wholesale reorganization of our knowledge is not common in every-day living, but small changes in the way we associate the things we learn and know occur constantly. We can reorganize the categories in which we store information in several ways. First, we can broaden a category to include new classes of objects and concepts. When Europeans introduced the horse to North America, one of the Native Americans' first words for it meant "big dog." The Indians' first reaction was to broaden an existing category to accommodate the new animal. Only as the horse gained in importance to the Indians did it merit a cognitive category of its own. Similarly, when moving from one part of the country to another, we often are introduced to new decorative shrubs or new foods. It is usually not necessary to invent a new cognitive category for these; rather, we enlarge existing ones to include the new items.

A second way we can change the way we store information is to partition an existing category into finer divisions. Some Eskimos, for instance, have a very large number of words for "snow" and "sky." Their experience has taught them that the particular type of snow falling or the exact condition of the sky can be crucial to their survival. In the temperate zones, however, people need and use a much more limited vocabulary to describe the condition of the sky or the type of snow falling. Yet a person moving from the southwestern United States to northwestern Canada quickly learns the additional words and concepts required. Other examples of this type of category partitioning abound. Farmers in one area of Africa have over 200 nouns that stand for "cow." They presumably need them. An American farmer has nowhere near that number, and a native of Manhattan might have only one—or fewer. Either the farmer or the city slicker, however, could partition the "cow" category into finer divisions if it became necessary.

We perform a similar kind of partitioning on a dynamic basis every day when we apply coarse or fine discrimination among the same set of objects in different environments. In fact, our categorization of objects is quite slippery. Compared to an artificial sweetener, a sugar cube can change from being considered essentially the same (both are sweet) to complete opposites (one has calories, one does not), depending on whether the observer is on a diet. Similarly we perform dizzying scale changes in the blink of an eye. Depending on context, a group of three people can be a congenial discussion group, a tiny audience in a huge auditorium—or a crowd.

A third way of changing how we store information is to rearrange completely existing categories to accommodate new information. Some of the best examples of such restructuring are found in the history of science and philosophy. In the 1600s Newton revolutionized scientific understanding by presenting his laws of motion and of gravity. Among them, these laws govern the motion of objects ranging from hockey pucks to interplanetary rockets to galaxies. Philosophers presented with this revolutionary new information probably had to do a lot of rearranging of their cognitive categories. In the early 1900s Einstein's theory of relativity produced a similar revolution in thought for the motion of objects that move near the speed of light. The concept that the speed of light measured by any observer is the same did not fit into the cognitive systems of most scientists of the day.

The discovery that every object is a collection of a vast number of atoms produced not only a revolution in scientific thought but also filtered into the world of art, being partially responsible for the beautiful paintings of the impressionists. This change in our perspective of solid objects altered our art, our philosophy, and our view of the world around us.

For an autonomous learning system to have the ability to absorb such enormous changes requires an extreme flexibility in the way categories are created and destroyed, as well as a willingness to embrace new categorizations.

Elementary, My Dear Watson

When we cope with the world around us, we rarely have the luxury of having someone tell us how the things we perceive relate to each

The Grand Canyon Effect

Lest we become so enamored with totally unsupervised learning that we lose contact with reality, let's remember that we do send children to school for supervised learning and that we train new employees to perform difficult tasks instead of just throwing them into the job. Thus, we do not entirely rely on experience as a teacher, even in autonomous humans. Similarly, it will probably be wise to pretrain autonomous machines to some minimum level of competence. We might, for instance, want to teach an autonomous pattern classifier the basic types of patterns we expect it to encounter. We would even want to provide a totally autonomous robot with a set of prelearned "truths." Perhaps, for example, we should teach our autonomous machine the simple rule, "Don't step off highledges," so that it need not learn this, for instance, by walking over the edge of the Grand Canyon—once.

other. We must sort the objects and sensations we encounter into meaningful categories. Even more than this, we need to be able to predict what characteristics new items might have based on our experience with similar objects. We need the ability to generalize from specific instances to general categories. This is similar to saying we need to be able to induce the characteristics of new objects based on those of objects we already know about. We tend to generalize from specific experiences and assume, for instance, that new objects have the characteristics of similar known objects until shown otherwise. While people may carry this to extremes at times ("Japanese cars are always more reliable than American ones because my Toyota lasted longer than my Ford"), such shorthand reasoning frees us from having to do extensive—and possibly dangerous—testing of every newly perceived object. It should be evident that this is a primary survival mechanism. Any autonomous robot will have to make similar inductions and generalizations, as a survival technique and to keep from immediately saturating its ability to process the amount of sensory input it receives.

An Ocean of Experience

The world around us does not stop just because we are tired. Our sensory input is continuous, which means that our learning experience continues every day we live. Do our brains ever fill up? Is there a limit to how much we can learn? If so, what is that limit? So far, we know of no limit to the human brain's capacity that can be reached in the human life span. For all intents and purposes, our brains have an unlimited capacity to store data.

An autonomous learning system must have a similarly unlimited capacity for data, where "unlimited" is defined as significantly greater than the number of patterns required to be stored during the working lifetime of the system. This may sound like an excessive or extreme storage capacity requirement. Not so! In principle, a system composed of even a thousand neurodes, each of which can support ten distinct activity levels, can store a number of patterns equal to 10 followed by 1000 zeros—many, many times the number of atoms in the universe. Thus, the need to have an unlimited capacity for an autonomous system is possibly the simplest of all to meet.

Autonomous Learning Redux

We do not have neural networks today that display all of the characteristics needed to build a system capable of truly autonomous learning. Some designs, however, possess a number of these qualities, and a few possess nearly all of them in some degree. We'll discuss these designs later in this book. Producing an autonomous learning system with all of the above qualities will be challenging, but it must be done if we are ever to build a real R2-D2 or C3-P0. The difficulties in accomplishing such a goal are obvious, but getting there is half the fun.

The simple systems we have seen thus far lack the power and flexibility required for completely autonomous learning. We need networks that are much more complex in order to approach this level of performance; in fact, we need networks that are hierarchical. In the next chapter, we will discover why this is so.

A Classic System:
The Perceptron

The perceptron was the first neural learning model. The historical importance of this model to the field is so great that it merits a special discussion here.

Early in the 1940s, Warren McCulloch and Walter Pitts published a paper called "A Logical Calculus of the Ideas Immanent in Nervous Activity." In this landmark paper, they described a simplified model of biological neurons governed by five principles: (1) the activity of the neuron is an all-or-none process (i.e., the neuron is binary); (2) the neuron has a fixed activation function so that any given input pattern always generates the same resulting output; (3) the neuron has no transmission delays except for those that are a result of the synaptic junction itself; (4) any inhibitory input to the neuron is sufficient to prevent it from turning on; and (5) the connections among neurons do not change in time. These assumptions comprise a highly simplified model of biological neurons. They are quite inconsistent with the way we now know neurons behave; however, in the 1940s they were not unreasonable given the available knowledge about the nervous system.

The way this neuron model works is quite simple. If the neurode's summed input is greater than some threshold value and if there is no inhibitory input to the neurode, the neurode outputs a +1. If the summed input is less than the threshold or if there is any inhibitory input to the neurode, the output is a 1. This neurode is the McCulloch-Pitts neurode and is still referenced as such in the literature.

McCulloch and Pitts demonstrated that a collection of these neurodes could be used to compute logical operators, such as OR (a OR b returns a 1 if either a or b or both are 1). By combining them together into networks, highly complex logical propositions could be computed. At the time scientists thought that this must be the way we reason, so it seemed that McCulloch and Pitts had devised a model for the way human brains work.

There was a fundamental problem with the McCulloch and Pitts neurode: no one knew how to connect the neurodes to make them solve arbitrary problems. Certainly it seemed that if this was a model of the brain, there had to be some kind of autonomous means for the network to figure out how to wire itself up. In essence, the McCulloch-Pitts neurode has no learning law.

The learning law is precisely what Frank Rosenblatt added to the McCulloch-Pitts neurode to make it into a perceptron. In 1958 he published the first of a series of papers describing and later proving that his training scheme, called the perceptron training algorithm, would work. Let's explore this learning law.

Suppose we want to use the perceptron to sort data points into two categories, X and O. If we plot the data points in space, we know that as long as we can draw a straight line between the X points and the O points, the perceptron can separate them properly. We say such data points are linearly separable. What is the likelihood that the data points are linearly separable? You might think this would be impossible to predict, and it is for specific cases, but while we cannot say much about any individual example without analyzing it, we can talk about the probability that the data points are linearly separable.

It is possible to demonstrate that if the number of data points in our collection is less than about twice the dimensionality of the weight vector, then we have a fifty-fifty chance of having linearly separable data. In other words, if we have an input pattern and weight vector with ten components (10-dimensional space), we should be able to separate collections of up to about 20 data points about half the time on average.

If the data points are linearly separable, there is an infinite number of possible lines that separate the two categories. Let's choose one arbitrary line. We draw any one such separating line between the data points and through the origin of our axes. Now let's draw a weight vector that has its tail at the origin and is perpendicular to the line, such that its arrow points toward the data points that are to produce a +1 output. This vector is the weight vector we are looking for in the trained perceptron. We still face a problem, however: how do we get the perceptron to modify its weights so that it can generate that weight vector? Rosenblatt provided such a training method.

Rosenblatt's perceptron training algorithm is a marvel of simplicity. We begin with a McCulloch-Pitts neurode with a weight vector that has its tail at the origin and that points in any arbitrary direction. For each data point in the training set, we input the data point to the neurode and allow it to respond with either a +1 or –1 output. After each input pattern, we adjust the weight vector by adding to it the input vector multiplied by the correct category, +1 or −1. We do this until all the data points are presented and the neurode recognizes them all correctly.

Let's explore this training scheme geometrically to get a better understanding of how it works. To keep things simple, we use a two-dimensional example, but remember that the scheme holds for any size of input pattern. We start with the data points shown in the figure below, and with an arbitrary weight vector. We want the O points to generate a +1 output and the X points to generate a −1 output. Clearly this data set is linearly separable, so there should be no difficulty in solving this problem. Finally, we use a threshold of zero for the perceptron; any net input greater than zero generates a +1, and any net input less than or equal to zero generates a −1.

Let's begin training by presenting the neurode with the pattern O_1. We have been speaking of these patterns as data points, but they really are vectors that point from the origin to the point referred to. When we present pattern O_1 to the neurode, the net input will be positive because the angle between the neurode's weight vector and the vector corresponding to O_1 is less than 90. Remember that the summed, weighted input is the dot product of the input vector and the weight vector and that this is also equal to the product of the two vectors' lengths, both of which are always positive, times the cosine of the angle between the vectors. The cosine function is always positive for angles less than 90 and is always negative for angles between 90 and 180. We know

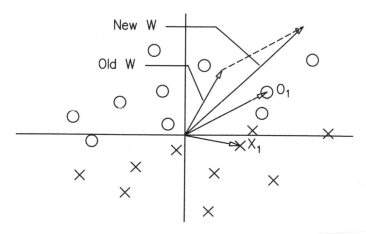

The perceptron training algorithm.

therefore that if the weight vector is less than 90 from the input pattern vector, then the neurode will output a +1, and if it is more than 90 from the input pattern vector, the neurode will output a −1.

We present pattern O_1 to the neurode and get a +1 response. We then modify the weight vector by adding to it the input vector multiplied by the correct response, +1. The addition of two vectors is simple to do graphically; we draw a vector that has its tail at the arrow of the weight vector and has length and direction the same as the input vector. The sum of the two vectors is a vector drawn from the tail of the weight vector to the arrow of the input vector copy. This is the new weight vector for the neurode.

We now present pattern X_1 to the neurode. We can see from the drawing that we will get a +1 response because the angle between X_1 and the new weight vector is less than 90 degrees. We modify the weight vector by again adding the input pattern vector multiplied by the desired response, −1. Multiplying any vector by −1 does nothing except reverse the direction of the arrow: if it pointed left, it will now point right; if it pointed up, it will now point down. We add this reversed vector to the weight vector just as before and continue.

No matter what the original weight vector is, this training algorithm finds a weight vector that separates the X and O patterns successfully.

Over the course of half a dozen years, Frank Rosenblatt and other researchers were able to demonstrate mathematically that the perceptron training algorithm can always solve any linearly separable problem in a finite number of steps. This training algorithm, simple as it is, was the first to be written explicitly as a series of algorithmic steps, making it immediately suitable for computer simulation. Rosenblatt's enthusiasm drew many other researchers into the field, resulting in significant progress in the span of a few years. Modifications to this training algorithm abounded, such as modifying the weights only when the answer was wrong. Actual models of the perceptron were built in hardware and demonstrated to fascinated audiences. Things seemed rosy indeed.

This blissful state did not last forever. By the mid-1960s there was a falloff of interest in perceptron systems, due partly to a growing realization that the class of problems they can solve is quite limited and partly to a lack of tools (hardware and software) with which to continue research. Some researchers tended to describe their systems with extensive hyperbole, which alienated more prudent scientists. Finally, Minsky and Papert's brilliant analysis of the perceptron published in 1969 delivered the killing blow, as we will see in the next chapter.

The perceptron never became a viable application system. In spite of this, Its position as a historical landmark in the field makes it important to understand. As a practical system, it was a failure. As a guiding light that has influenced researchers for three decades as much by its failures as by its successes, it has served nobly and well.

Part IV

*If the human brain were so simple
that we could understand it,
we would be so simple that we couldn't.*
— Emerson Pugh

Normally, Wentworth, we feel that intelligent systems are an extension and supplement to our human intellectual capacities. Now what we're looking for in you is a place to extend from!

If you think to build a tower, first reckon up the cost.
— St. Jerome

13   Hierarchical Systems

So far the networks we have looked at have consisted of only one or two layers of neurodes: an input layer and possibly an output layer. Because they have so few layers, they are only able to take advantage of any natural coding of information that already exists in their input. These networks do not have the ability to interpret their input data or to organize them into any kind of internal worldview.

About twenty years ago, Marvin Minsky and Seymour Papert of MIT wrote a book, *Perceptrons*, which proved that 1- or 2-layered perceptron networks were inadequate for many real-world problems. Their book, combined with other contributing factors of the time, was so influential that neural network research and development was brought to a near-standstill for almost two decades. Only a few die-hard researchers continued to work in the field, and they had a great deal of difficulty in obtaining funding, tenure, and promotions. We need to look at Minsky and Papert's arguments to understand why they wrote what they did and why it had such a tremendous impact on the field.

The discussion in *Perceptrons* was a thorough piece of reasoning. Minsky and Papert performed a careful analysis of the problem of mapping one pattern to another. In this context, mapping simply means association. That is, when we map A to 1, B to 2, and so on, we are correlating the letters with numbers. In this view, a mathematical function is a mapping of the function's value to each value of the variable(s). In many cases, all we want a neural network to do is to provide such a mapping. For example, we might map a visual image of our friend to his name or a particular sonic pattern to the word *hello*.

In many mappings, we find that similar input patterns generate similar output patterns. For example, if we are doing speech understanding, the input pattern we want to map to the word *show* is similar to the input pattern we want to map to the word *shown*. (Of course, in English especially, similarly spelled words are not always pronounced similarly.) If we are doing a mathematical function, say, $f(x) = x/2$, then nearby x input values of 2 and 2.4 will give output mappings of 1 and 1.2, which are also close to each other. For this kind of mapping, the closer the two input values are to each other, the closer the resulting mapped values are to each other.

But there are mappings where similar input values do not map to similar output values. There are two classic examples of this: the exclusive OR function, and the parity problem. Let's look at each of these. The exclusive OR (XOR) function is a logical function that accepts two binary inputs and generates a single binary output. The output will be 1 if either of the two inputs, but not both inputs, is 1. The output will be 0 if both inputs are 0, or if both are 1. The problem with this function is that the two input patterns that are the most dissimilar, 0-0 and 1-1, have to map to the same output of 0. In addition, the input patterns of 0-1 and 1-0, which are exact opposites of each other as inputs, also have to map to the same output of 1.

In the parity problem, we find the same difficulty. Parity checking is a method of confirming that a binary pattern has not been altered from its original pattern. It is often used in data communications and by computer memories to confirm that the data value stored is valid. Parity is quite easy to compute. One scheme works like this (there are several variations on this idea). If we have a 16-bit binary value, we first attach a special parity bit to that word to make it 17 bits long. We then count the number of bits in the original 16 that have the value 1 (as opposed to 0). If this count is even, we set the parity bit to 1. If the count of 1-bits is odd, we set the parity bit to 0. Now we can transmit this 17-bit word to another computer. When the second system receives it, it counts the number of 1-bits and compares its result to the parity bit value. If a single bit was accidentally changed (from 0 to 1 or from 1 to 0) during the transmission process, this simple scheme will detect the fact that the error occurred. (Of course, changes in two different bits may not be detectable in this scheme, but this is usually much less likely and we won't worry about that here.) If an error is detected by an incorrect parity bit, the second computer can ask that the word be retransmitted.

The parity problem from the neural network perspective is difficult. Let's look at two 16-bit patterns:

0000 1000 0000 0000
17th parity bit = 0 (one 1-bit set)

and

0000 1100 0000 0000
17th parity bit = 1 (two 1-bits set)

These two patterns differ in only one bit position; they are as similar as possible without being identical. But their parity bit values are as different as it is possible for them to be.

Linear Separability

We can classify both the exclusive OR problem and the parity problem as instances of mappings that are not linearly separable. This mathematical term can be easily understood by plotting the values of the exclusive OR function on a graph (figure 13.1). There is no way to draw a single straight line through the plot so that all the Xs are on one side of the line and all the Os are on the other side. The Xs and Os cannot be separated by a straight line, so the exclusive OR function is nonlinearly separable.

Minsky and Papert concluded that it would be impossible for simple perceptron networks ever to solve problems with this charac-

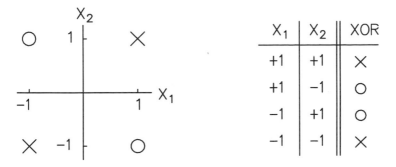

Figure 13.1 There is no way to draw a single line separating all the 'X' values from all the 'O' values.

teristic. In other words, it appeared at the time that neural networks could solve only problems where similar input patterns mapped to similar output patterns. Unfortunately, many real-world problems, such as the parity problem and the exclusive OR problem, do not have this characteristic. The outlook appeared gloomy for neural networks researchers.

Minsky and Papert were correct in their analysis of perceptron neural networks. It eventually became clear, however, that what was needed to correct the problem was to make the networks slightly more complex. In other words, although a two-layer network cannot solve such problems, a three-layer network can. While Minsky and Papert recognized that this was possible, they felt it unlikely that a training method could be developed to find a multilayered network that could solve these problems.

As it turns out, there is strong evidence that multilayered networks intrinsically have significantly greater capabilities than one- or two-layered networks. A mathematical theorem exists that proves that a three-layer network can perform all real mappings; it is called Kolmogorov's theorem.

Kolmogorov's Theorem

In the mid-1950s Soviet mathematician A. N. Kolmogorov published the proof of a mathematical theorem that provides a sound basis for mapping networks. Although the problem originally addressed by this theorem had nothing to do with neural networks, Robert Hecht-Nielsen has shown its application to neural network theory. (In explaining this theorem, we will consider only the world of numbers, but bear in mind that we can always represent nonnumerical data similarly.)

Suppose we want to perform any mapping at all. We allow the input pattern to be a pattern of numbers, say m total numbers, where each number is between 0 and 1 and m can be any size at all. We can always scale our input to make this true.

We will allow the resulting output pattern to be any size number pattern, say n total numbers, where each number is real, that is, not complex. Specifically there are no constraints on the relative sizes of the input patterns and the output patterns; they can be the same size ($m=n$), or either m or n can be larger than the other by any amount. The mapping is thus totally arbitrary between any two sets of number pattern pairs.

Kolmogorov's theorem says that this completely arbitrary mapping can be exactly implemented by a 3-layer neural network. The implementation will not be an approximation of the mapping but will precisely map each input pattern to the exact output pattern specified. This represents a major advance in neural network theory. What we are talking about goes beyond simple analytic expressions of mappings (those mappings that can be expressed by an equation). In fact, it does not matter whether we can write down an analytic expression (an equation) for the mapping. It does not even matter whether we know a sequence of mathematical steps to perform the mapping. We can implement the exact mapping by simply building the appropriate neural network.

As astounding as this seems, Kolmogorov's theorem goes even further and tells us something about how to construct the neural network to implement this mapping. The network consists of three layers. The first layer, or input layer, contains one neurode for each number in the input pattern—that is, m total neurodes. The middle layer has $(2m + 1)$ total neurodes. The third layer contains one neurode for each number in the output pattern, or n total neurodes. We also know a bit about the architecture of the network as well. The first layer is a fan-out layer: each input number in the input pattern goes to one neurode in the first layer. This first layer does nothing more than distribute the input values to every neurode in the second layer. The second layer has a fairly complex transfer function that implements the sum of a set of functions, g, each of which is continuous, real, and monotonically increasing. (This is a category that includes the sigmoid functions, for example.) The third layer's transfer function is the sum of a set of functions of the output signals of the second layer.

Clearly this is not enough information to build the appropriate neural network with all weights preset, but Kolmogorov's theorem has told us that it is possible to solve any mapping problem exactly by using a three-layer neural network of limited size.

Let's step back from this theoretical discussion and try to describe Kolmogorov's result more concretely. When we build a neural network of three layers, we are generating a system that performs the desired mapping in a two-step process. First, in moving from layer 1 to layer 2, the input pattern is translated into an internal representation that is specific and private to this network (thus the frequently used term *hidden* for the middle layer of a multilayer network). Second, when the activity of the network moves from layer 2 to layer 3, this internal representation of the pattern is translated into the desired output pattern. The middle layer of the network somehow implements an internal code that the network uses to store the correct mapping instructions. This is important to understand because it is one of the chief reasons that a hierarchical, multilayer neural network is so much more powerful than a simple neural network. Adding a hierarchy of layers to the system allows for complex internal representations of the input patterns that are not possible with simpler systems.

The internal representation generated by the hierarchical network may or may not be one that is meaningful to us as humans. Researchers have spent a great deal of time reverse engineering trained, multilayer networks to try to decipher the codes they use. A couple of important points emerge from such studies. First, the representation that the network develops is not cast in concrete. If the network is reinitialized (the weights are randomly set to new initial values) and the network retrained on the same training data in the same training regimen, the internal represention developed the second time will generally be similar to but not identical with the first representation. Furthermore, there is no way to predict which neurode will encode any specific portion of the representation. The second important point is that the encoding used by the network may or may not have a bearing on any encoding scheme animals use in their brains, nor need it make any particular sense to us. While reverse engineering a trained neural network can provide clues to the operation of biological networks, it is dangerous to take such clues too seriously and assume that biological networks have to work the same way.

What Kolmogorov Didn't Say

There are some questions that Kolmogorov's theorem does not answer. For example, it does not tell us that the network described is the most efficient implementation of a network for this mapping. Nor does it tell us whether there is a network with fewer neurodes that can also do this mapping. And, of course, the functions used in the Kolmogorov network are not specifically defined by the theorem.

Kolmogorov's theorem assures us that we need not go to hundreds or thousands of layers to make a good mapping; there is no need for neural network skyscrapers. Instead the theorem demonstrates that there is in fact a way to do any mapping we choose in as few as three layers. This agrees with our knowledge about biological systems. Our brains are incredibly complex, but the number of processing layers for any particular subsystem is remarkably small for the power of its operation.

You may notice something else about the Kolmogorov multilayer network. It appears that within each layer of the network, there is little interaction among neurodes. Instead neurodes take inputs from the previous layer and fan their output to the next layer, but they do not receive inputs or generate outputs to other neurodes on the same layer. This is quite typical of many neural network architectures.

Such a hierarchical structure is similar to the organization of biological systems. In fact, it now appears that much of the brain is organized as functional modules arranged in a parallel set of increasing hierarchies. At many vertical levels within a given subsystem of the brain, additional interaction occurs from other hierarchical subsystems, allowing, for example, the visual system to interact with the motor system.

In the next chapters, we take a close look at some hierarchical neural network architectures. Even the brief taste that Kolmogorov's theorem has given us makes clear that such systems have enormous potential for real world applications. Let's begin our study of hierarchical systems by looking at the most successful network developed to date: the backpropagation network.

Application:
The Neocognitron

Hierarchical networks offer some advantages over nonhierarchical systems. But just how complex a hierarchical network can we build? In 1975 Kunihiko Fukushima of the NHK Laboratories in Japan introduced a hierarchical neural network he called the Cognitron. In 1980 he announced an advanced design, the neocognitron, which he has continued to modify and improve.

Fukushima's aim was to construct a biologically plausible adaptive neural network for pattern recognition. He wanted the network to recognize learned patterns if they were slightly distorted, regardless of their relative size and whether they were centered on the neocognitron's input grid. These are often referred to as distortion, size, and position invariance, respectively. These three attributes make his system valuable for handwritten character recognition, and we will analyze the operation of the neocognitron with this application in mind.

The original design uses a purely feed-forward architecture in which succeeding layers detect increasingly higher-level features of the presented character. This design is shown schematically in the figure on the next page.

Let's first review the neocognitron's general operation. The analog pattern to be recognized—one of a set of memorized symbols, for instance—is presented to the input stage. The second stage recognizes the constituent small features, or geometric primitives, of the symbol, and each succeeding stage responds to larger and larger groupings of these small features. Finally, one neurode in the output stage recognizes the complete symbol. There must be as many neurodes in the output stage as there are symbols in the set to be recognized.

To accomplish the task of broadening the focus of each successive stage on larger and larger features of the input pattern, Fukushima was forced to give the neocognitron an exceptionally complex structure. We will not give a complete description here but will sketch the organization of the system in enough detail to make its operation plausible.

The first stage of neurodes accepts the analog image to be recognized from a sensor array such as a solid-state video camera or a digitizing tablet. Succeeding stages have a two-layer structure, with each layer being composed, in turn, of a number of square arrays of neurodes that Fukushima calls planes. Thus, there

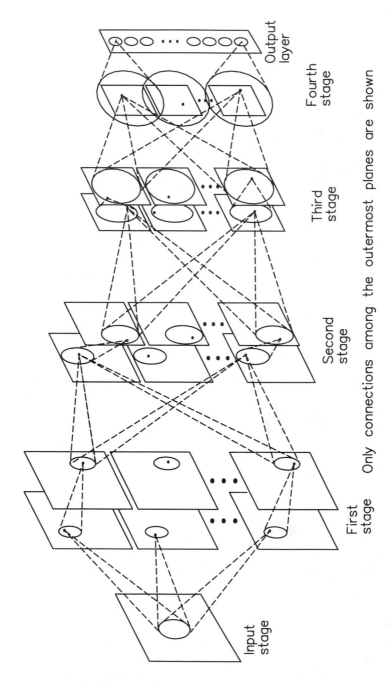

The design of the Neocognitron

Input stage · First stage · Second stage · Third stage · Fourth stage · Output layer

Only connections among the outermost planes are shown

is an input stage and several succeeding compound stages. Each compound stage is divided into two layers, each consisting of a number of planes of neurodes.

The first layer of each stage contains a set of feature-detecting neurodes fed by a large number of modifiable excitatory synapses and an equal number of control neurodes with a large number of fixed excitatory input synapses. The control neurodes are also connected by a modifiable inhibitory synapse to the corresponding feature neurode. During training, the excitatory feature neurodes learn to recognize specific characteristics of the input images, while the inhibitory control neurodes keep their feature neurodes from responding to more than one pattern feature. The second layer of each stage contains neurodes with nonmodifiable excitatory synapses. These neurodes are connected to the next stage in such a way that the image detection is insensitive to small distortions and positional errors of the input image.

Fukushima introduces a gradual broadening of the size of feature attended to by each succeeding stage. He does this by the way he connects groups of neurodes in the second layer of a stage to the first layer of the next stage. Each neurode in each plane of the first layer of a stage accepts input only from a small neighborhood on each plane of the preceding stage. Because the neighborhoods overlap, every neurode in a first layer receives input from several adjacent neighborhoods on each plane of the previous layer. The result of this elaborate interconnection scheme is that information from small areas of the first stage becomes spread over increasingly large areas of succeeding stages. Eventually every neurode on the input stage is represented in the signal arriving at the grandmother nodes of the output layer of the final stage.

For many applications, an operator can teach the neocognitron a set of patterns using unsupervised training techniques. In this mode, the patterns are presented to the input one at a time. It is not necessary to tell the system which pattern to associate with each node in the output stage. Of course, it is also not possible to select the output neurode that corresponds to any particular input pattern. The system automatically picks features into which it decomposes each input pattern. If it has been properly designed and if the input patterns are sufficiently dissimilar, it will learn to recognize a complete set of patterns with only one presentation of the input set.

Fukushima uses two learning laws to train his system. To decide the amount to change a synapse weight, he uses a hebbian law.

By means of the control neurodes, he introduces lateral competition among the feature neurodes at corresponding places on the various planes of a layer in order to decide which one of those neurodes will be updated. He designates this as the seed neurode. All neurodes in the immediate vicinity of the seed neurode are updated by the same amount as the seed using a variant of Hebb's law. These learning procedures are reminiscent of those used in the competitive filter feature-mapping network, although Kohonen and Fukushima apparently arrived at their laws independently.

If there are a number of distinct patterns that have very similar characteristics, an operator can use supervised learning to prepare the neocognitron. The procedure for this teaching mode, however, is complicated and somewhat ad hoc, and we will not consider it here.

How well does the neocognitron perform? It is difficult to obtain quantitative performance measures using handwritten symbols since there is almost an infinite number of ways to write even a small set of characters such as the 10 Arabic numerals. In demonstrations, though, the neocognitron has shown a good ability to recognize individual members of small sets of symbols even when they were badly distorted and without regard to their relative size or position.

Despite this demonstrated recognition ability, the neocognitron so far has not been implemented in hardware. This may be partly due to some serious drawbacks of the design. First, it possesses an exceedingly complex interconnect structure. Second, it uses neurodes in an apparently inefficient manner. Most of the system's modifiable neurodes recognize only a single feature or group of features. This inescapably gives rise to a third undesirable feature: the neocognitron requires many, many neurodes to accomplish its recognition tasks. The system developed by Fukushima to recognize handwritten versions of the 10 Arabic numerals, for instance, contains nearly 63,000 neurodes—over 27,000 each of feature and control neurodes and nearly 8000 neurodes dedicated to obtaining the distortion, size, and position invariance that the system displays. Finally, although it can hardly be faulted for not having every possible invariance, the neocognitron offers little rotation invariance; that is, the system may not recognize a learned symbol presented to it rotated by a significant angle.

Even with its drawbacks, however, the neocognitron remains a landmark in the history of neural network development and a monument to the creativity of its inventor.

Like the pace of a crab, backward.
—Robert Greene

14 Backpropagation Networks

Arguably the most successful and certainly one of the most studied learning systems in the neural network arena is backward error propagation learning or, more commonly, backpropagation. Backpropagation has perhaps more near-term application potential than any other learning system in use today. Researchers have used this method to teach neural networks to speak, play games such as backgammon, and distinguish between sonar echoes from rocks and mines. In these and other applications, backpropagation has demonstrated impressive performance, often comparable only to the far more complex adaptive resonance systems discussed in chapter 16.

Features of Backpropagation Systems

Each training pattern presented to a backpropagation network is processed in two stages. In the first stage, the input pattern presented to the network generates a forward flow of activation from the input to the output layer. In the second stage, errors in the network's output generate a flow of information from the output layer backward to the input layer. It is this feature that gives the network its name. This backward propagation of errors is used to modify the weights on the interconnects of the network, allowing the network to learn.

Backpropagation is actually a learning algorithm rather than a network design. It can be used with a variety of architectures. The architectures themselves are less important than their common features: all are hierarchical, all use a high degree of interconnection between layers, and all have nonlinear transfer functions. Before we think through construction of a backpropagation network, let's look at the need for the first two of these features; the need for a nonlinear transfer function will become clear later.

A hierarchical network structure is essential. At a minimum, the network must have three layers: an input layer to accept patterns from the outside world, an output layer to present the network's response back to the outside world, and at least one middle layer. During training, the middle layer or layers build an internal model of the way the input patterns are related to the desired outputs. These middle layers are often called hidden layers in research literature.

Another way to think of the action of the middle layer is that it creates a map relating each input pattern to a unique output response. We have already seen one such mapping network, the Kohonen feature map. Because the backward transmission of errors allows backpropagation networks to generate a sophisticated and accurate internal representation of the input data, they are often more versatile than these other mapping networks. For example, counterpropagation networks, discussed in chapter 15, can have difficulty with discontinuous mappings or with mappings in which small changes in the input do not correspond to small changes in the output. Backpropagation networks can generally learn these mappings, often with great reliability.

The middle layer, and thus the hierarchical structure of the system, is the source of the improved internal representation of backpropagation networks. Physically this representation exists within the synapses of the interconnects of the middle layers of the network; the higher the interlayer connectivity is, the better is the ability of the network to build a representation or model of the input data.

Building a Backpropagation System

Let's construct a typical backpropagation system in our minds and see the way in which it works. First we need to select an appropriate architecture. For our purposes, three feed-forward hierarchical layers are sufficient, with each layer fully connected to the following layer.

(As with earlier networks, if you are not interested at this moment in how backpropagation works, you can skip this and the next section with no loss of continuity.)

The input, activation, and output functions of a neurode can usually be combined into one function, the neurode transfer function. To see how backpropagation works, we will need to consider these functions separately.

We can assume the additive input function discussed in chapter 2. Recall this means that we obtain the summed input for each neurode by the following recipe: multiplying the output of every neurode connected to the neurode by the synaptic weight associated with that connection and summing the results. This summed input is then used as the input to the activation function.

For the backpropagation network, we must choose a sigmoid activation function. The characteristics of this S-shaped curve that are important to the operation of a backpropagation network are that it levels off at some lower and upper value of summed input and that it always increases between these limits. We place no constraints on the details of the function such as its slope, threshold value, or the upper and lower limiting values. For instance, we can choose lower and upper limits of 0 and +1, –1 and +1, –0.5 and +0.5, or some other convenient set of values.

The third component of the neurode transfer function is the output function. We can use a very simple function here: the output of the neurode will be the same as the activation. The overall neurode transfer function, then, is just a sigmoid, with the vertical axis representing the neurode's output and the horizontal axis representing the summed input.

We will use the input layer of the network as a fan-out layer whose only duty is to supply a complete copy of the input pattern to every neurode in the middle layer. As a result, the synapse weights between the input pattern and the neurodes of the input layer will be fixed at 1.0; they will not be modified during the learning process. The synapses between the input and middle layer and those between the middle and output layer will be plastic, or modifiable. Our architecture is now complete.

The arrangement described is typical of networks used to perform research in backpropagation. Remember, though, that backpropagation can be applied to many architectures. For example, it is not necessary to use only one middle layer, to fix the weights on the input layer, or to use the input layer strictly to provide a fan-out function. In general, however, it is best to use the simplest architecture that accomplishes the desired aim, and it often makes sense to start with the simple architecture we have adopted.

The Backpropagation Process

To teach our imaginary network something using backpropagation, we must start by setting all the adaptive weights on all the neurodes in it to random values. It won't matter what those values are, as long as they are not all the same and not equal to 1. To train the network, we need a training set of input patterns along with a corresponding set of desired output patterns.

The first step is to apply the first pattern from the training set and observe the resulting output pattern. Since we know what result we are supposed to get, we can easily compute an error for the network's output; it is the difference between the actual and the desired outputs.

This should sound familiar. We encountered the same rationale when we talked about the adaline in chapter 6. In that chapter, we used the delta rule which computed the distance of the current weight vector from some ideal value and then adjusted the weights according to that computed distance. The learning rule that backpropagation uses is quite similar. It is a variation of the original delta rule called the "generalized delta rule."

The original delta rule allowed us to adjust the weights using the following formula: multiply the error on each neurode's output by the size of that output and by a learning constant to determine the amount to change each neurode's weights. By this formula, the change in the weight vector is proportional to the error and parallel to the input vector. This rule is easy to apply to the output layer of our network since we know both the desired and actual outputs. But what about the middle layer? How do we compute the difference between the actual and desired output for a neurode in the middle layer without knowing what the middle layer's output is supposed to be?

We begin to solve this problem by listing the possible sources of the error in the output layer. A neurode in the output layer may generate the wrong output value for one of several reasons: the output layer's neurode might have incorrect weights on its interconnects, the inputs from the middle layer to the output layer might be incorrect, or both the output layer's weights and the inputs from the middle layer might be incorrect. For any one of these error sources, we

The Derivative As a Slope

The derivative of a function can be thought of as the slope of the function at each point along its curve. Just as with a hill, the slope of a function can be positive, negative, or zero. A positive slope means that the function increases as the value of its variable increases, so that the curve rises when we move our eyes along it from left to right near the point in question. A negative slope means that the function decreases in value as the value of its variable increases, and the curve descends as we move our eyes from left to right. A zero slope indicates that the value of the function does not change for small changes in the value of the variable. The slope of a straight line is constant and is equal to the vertical change over any section of the line divided by the horizontal change over that same section.

need a procedure to calculate how much an error in the output of a middle-layer neurode contributes to the error of an output-layer neurode. We can then use this effective error procedure to compute how to modify the weights in the middle layer.

Backpropagation computes this error in the following manner. First, we pass, or propagate, the weighted output error from each neurode in the output layer back to the neurodes of the middle layer. The weights used to compute these errors are those on the interconnects between the various neurodes. Thus, each middle-layer neurode can calculate exactly how big a contribution it made to the error of each neurode in the output layer. This means that an output neurode with a large weight from a particular neurode in the middle layer can probably "blame" much of its output error on input signals from that particular middle-layer neurode. Thus a large weight and a large error in the output layer will generate a large contribution to that middle-layer neurode's own error.

So far so good. But suppose a middle-layer neurode has a large weight on the interconnect between it and an output-layer neurode that produced a large output error. As things stand now, the error computation would tell us to generate a large weight change for that middle-layer neurode even if the middle-layer neurode had generated a very small or even zero output. With a small or zero output, it could not have contributed much to the output layer's error, and it would not be correct to penalize it when it could not have caused that error. The generalized delta rule addresses this problem in a clever way; it factors in the derivative of the neurode activation function.

Recall that we chose a sigmoid for this activation function. The derivative, or slope, of a sigmoid curve is shaped like a bell, with the largest values in the mid-range of summed inputs and very small values at both extremes. Even if the sigmoid itself permits negative values, as between −1.0 and +1.0, for example, its derivative will always be positive. Multiplying the error correction term by this bell-shaped derivative function ensures us that the weights on the neurode we are considering will change only slightly as the summed input approaches either very low or very high values. Previously, we said that we would make the need for a nonlinear neurode transfer function clear later in the chapter. This is it; we could not limit the weight change for low activation values by taking the derivative of a linear transfer function, since its slope would be constant and have the same value for all values of the summed input.

Applying the derivative to the error-propagation flow serves two purposes. As we just pointed out, it ensures that middle-layer neurodes are not unfairly blamed for errors in the output layer. More important, it helps ensure the stability of the network as a whole. By this we mean that it helps to prevent the weights from cyclically see-sawing through a range of values and thus assists in settling the weights to a set of stable values.

We are now ready to compute the error on a particular middle-layer neurode. To do this, first add up the contributions to that error from each output neurode. To obtain the contribution from each output neurode, we multiply the measured error for that neurode by the weight of the synapse between it and the middle-layer neurode. We then add the contributions from each output neurode together and multiply the result by the derivative of the activation function. This derivative is taken at the point on the activation function corresponding to the actual value of activation of the middle-layer neurode.

All that effort computed only the error on one of the middle-layer neurodes. We still must compute the corresponding weight changes for that neurode, which we do with the same delta rule used for the adaline, except that the error we use is the value just computed, rather than the simple distance used in the earlier case.

Are we done yet? No. We have only modified the weights on a single middle-layer neurode. We have to repeat this process for each middle-layer neurodes. For each middle-layer neurode, we must propagate the error from the output layer back to it, compute the sum of the weighted errors, multiply it by the derivative of the sigmoid function, and then use this computed error value in the delta rule to modify the weights. When these computations have been made for all of the middle-layer neurodes, this particular iteration of the network is complete.

Let's review the entire backpropagation process. First we present an input pattern at the input layer of the network, and this generates activity in the input-layer neurodes. We allow this activity to propagate forward through each of the layers of the network until the output layer generates an output pattern. Remember that we initially set the weights on all modifiable interconnects randomly, so we are almost guaranteed that the first pass through the network will generate the wrong output. We compare this output pattern to the desired output pattern in order to evaluate errors that are propagated backward through the layers of the network, changing the weights of each layer as it passes.

This complete round of forward activation propagation and backward error propagation constitutes one iteration of the network. From here, we can present the same input pattern to the network again, or we can modify it and present a different input pattern, depending on what we are trying to accomplish. In any event, we do complete iterations of the network every time we present an input pattern for as long as we are training the network.

Limitations of Backpropagation Networks

Backpropagation is computationally quite complex. Many iterations, often hundreds or even thousands, are usually required for the network to learn a set of input patterns. This causes a backpropagation network to be a risky choice for applications that require learning to occur in real time, that is, on the fly. Of course, many applications do not require that learning occur in real time, only that the network be able to respond to input patterns as they are presented after it has been trained.

There is still more bad news about backpropagation systems, however. Backpropagation, unlike the counterpropagation system we will look at in chapter 15, is not guaranteed to arrive at a correct solution. It is a gradient descent system, just as the adaline was. For this reason it is bound by the problems of a class of systems called hill-climbing algorithms—or rather hill descent in this case. Readers familiar with AI jargon will have heard this term before. The hill-descent problem asks, "How do you find the bottom of a hill?"

One commonsense solution is simply to always walk downhill, which is exactly what gradient-descent algorithms do. If you have ever tried this on a real hill, however, you know that there is a hitch: you sometimes find yourself in the bottom of a dip halfway down the hill and are forced to climb out of the dip in order to continue downhill. If the dip has steep sides, this commonsense approach to getting down the hill may not actually get you there at all but may strand you in a dip partway down. The feature corresponding to a dip in the gradient descent method is called a local minimum.

Gradient-descent algorithms are always subject to this problem. There is no guarantee that they will lead the network to the bottom of the hill; they can be sidetracked by local minima and end up stranded with no further means of arriving at the bottom of the hill. In particular, although the adaline had a smooth parabolic bowl for its error function, the complex architecture of the backpropagation network has an equally complex error function with the potential of having many local hills and dips between the network's starting error and the desired minimum error position. In practice, backprop-agation systems have been found to be remarkably good at finding the bottom of the hill. Even so, nearly every researcher has found that some trials do not work, and their backpropagation system fails to find the correct answer. A great deal of research is being con-ducted to determine how to identify such cases in advance or other-wise escape from local minima.

One method modifies the delta rule still more than the general-ized delta rule does by adding a feature called the "momentum term." Consider how this might work. A sled moving down a snow-covered hill is a perfect example of a gradient-descent system. It has no internal power to move itself uphill unless the rider gets off and pulls it. However, a sled can overcome small bumps or even short rises in its path if it has generated enough physical momentum to carry it over such perturbations and to allow it to continue in its orig-inal direction, downhill. The momentum term in the modified delta rule works in the same fashion.

Adding momentum to the weight change law is easy. We just add a term to the existing formula that depends on the size and direction of the weight change in the previous iteration of the network. To use our sled analogy, each new iteration "remembers" the direction and speed it had in the last iteration. If the algorithm finds itself in a local minimum, this momentum term may make enough contribution to the formula to carry the system out the other side so it can continue on its way "downhill."

This momentum term adds to the complexity of an already tedious calculation. Do we really need it? The answer is that we do not need it, but we may want it. Research suggests that we can accomplish nearly the same result by making the weight change for each learning step very small. Of course, this action causes the network to require many more iterations to learn a pattern, and including the momentum term is usually the more desirable solution of the two.

The generalized delta rule is the most common implementation of backpropagation; however, there are variations on this scheme.

Variations of the Generalized Delta Rule

Many researchers have offered variations on the generalized delta rule theme. In general, these attempt to decrease the number of iterations required for the network to learn, to reduce the computational complexity of the network, or to improve the local computability of the network.

A number of researchers have suggested ways of reducing the computational burden of backpropagation. One of the more popular schemes is to estimate some of the quantities in the error computation. There are two primary candidates for estimation. The first of these is the derivative of the signal function.

Derivatives are difficult and slow for digital computers to compute and are notoriously susceptible to small numerical errors (noise) in the function being differentiated. Some schemes attempt to avoid these problems by performing only an estimate of the slope of the transfer function rather than computing it exactly. Others attempt to improve the update speed by choosing an activation function whose derivative is especially easy to compute. For example, the derivative of one popular sigmoid function happens to be equal to the function itself minus the square of the function. An exact derivative of this function can be speedily calculated without the computer's having to perform a differentiation operation at all.

The second primary candidate for estimation is the error value being backpropagated. One popular estimation method adds an extra, global input to every neurode in, say, the middle layer. Once the forward pass is complete, a single, aggregate error in the output pattern is computed and broadcast to all middle-layer neurodes over the extra global interconnects. In this scheme, all middle-layer neurodes receive the same error input, but this aggregate error is easy and rapid to calculate, and even such a global error signal provides guidance in correcting middle-layer weights.

Researchers using both of these methods have reported good results, and somewhat shortened iteration times.

Scaling Problems

There is one more serious drawback to backpropagation networks: they do not scale up very well from small research systems to the larger ones required for real-world uses. For example, a network with 50 middle-layer units might learn a particular problem in about 200 iterations. The same network with 100 hidden units might take 2000 iterations to learn the same problem. And if we had 100 units, split between two or three middle layers, it might require well over a million iterations to learn. While too few neurodes in the middle layer can cause the network to learn slowly, too many neurodes in the middle layer can have the same result. (There is nothing precise about the numbers suggested in this example; they are simply illustrative.) Worse, every middle-layer neurode we add increases the computational complexity of each iteration so that each iteration takes proportionately more time.

This scaling problem restricts the applicability of backpropagation to problems that can be solved with relatively small networks. There are many such problems, however, and sometimes a collection of small backpropagation networks can be used to solve large problems. Also even small backpropagation networks can master surprisingly difficult tasks. Finally, there is some hope that a further modification to the generalized delta rule may be able to overcome this problem. One of many such possibilities has been reported by Tariq Samad of Honeywell. His variation is to modify the weight change computation by anticipating the error in each neurode's output and to modify the weights on neurodes both ahead of and behind the neurode in question. Thus the error adjustment for a middle-layer neurode changes not only the input weights for that neurode but also the weights on its own output signal, that is, the weights between it and the output-layer neurodes.

There is obviously a computational penalty in using this approach; each middle layer's error must be computed twice instead of once. However, Samad's experimental results, while preliminary, indicate orders of magnitude better performance in terms of the number of iterations required to learn. In fact, the relative performance advantage actually seems to get larger for bigger or more complex networks. A network that is small and simple learns only marginally faster using his idea than does a standard backpropagation network. One that is simply bigger—has more middle-layer units—learns about twice as fast as a standard network. But one that is larger and has several middle layers may learn several orders of magnitude faster. This modification and others being suggested show promise for increasing the utility of the backpropagation scheme approach for applications requiring large networks.

Biological Arguments against Backpropagation

In addition to these pragmatic difficulties, backpropagation also faces other objections. One argument is that this learning system is not biologically plausible. These critics deem it unlikely that animal brains use backpropagation for learning. One reason they believe this is that while our brains do have reverse neural pathways—for instance, from the brain back to the eye—these are not the same interconnects and synapses that provide the "forward" activity. Recall that a backpropagation system traditionally uses the same interconnects for both the forward and backward passes through the network.

A second and more serious reason that some critics believe backpropagation is not biologically plausible is that it requires each neurode in the network to compute its output and weight changes based on conditions that are not local to that neurode. Specifically the neurode relies on knowledge of the errors in the next higher layer of the network to compute changes in its own weights. Most current research seems to support the idea that real synapses change their weights in response only to locally available information rather than relying on information about the activity of neurons farther up the computational chain. This lack of reliance on locally available information is thought by many to disqualify backpropagation systems as serious biological models.

Recently researchers investigating this issue have suggested that there is a backpropagation formulation consistent with biological systems and that requires only locally available information at each neurode to adjust synapse weights. If this proves to be the case, some critics of backpropagation will be silenced. To many supporters of the method, however, nothing will be changed because they were never concerned that it did not possess biological plausibility. We suggest that biological plausibility need not be weighted too heavily in the development of neural network paradigms. It is true that biological systems are good models for network architectures; they furnish architectures we know will work. Except for researchers who are actually trying to model the brain, however, there seems little reason to reject an effective system just because it is unlikely to be an accurate model of biological systems.

Applications of Backpropagation Systems

Backpropagation has been applied to an enormous number of applications, and the number grows almost daily. Most of these applications have been only at the level of research systems, but the potential for useful real-world problem solving is tremendous. Let's take a quick look at some actual problems that have been successfully attacked using backpropagation.

Medical instrumentation. Backpropagation has been used to teach a neural network to remove the noise from medical instrument readouts. In a demonstration system, a network was provided with the input from an electrocardiograph. After training, the backpropagation network was able to clean up the input so that the output could be more easily interpreted. In a fully implemented system, the network would remove the noise in the electrocardiograph, allowing the physician to see easily whether a particular signal variation was significant.

Sonar signal processing. Backpropagation was used to teach a neural network to distinguish between the sonar echoes of an undersea rock and those of a mine. The network equaled or exceeded the performance of human operators, and it took only a few weeks to build. A traditional digital signal processing system took months to build and was less successful. This backpropagation system is described in more detail in chapter 18.

Speech. A network was taught to mimic human speech by repetitively trying to match its output to preprocessed input from a tape recording, by using standard voice synthesizers for its speech generation. Its output changed over the course of only a few hours from unintelligible gibberish to clear, precise pronunciation.

Games. A backpropagation system has been taught to play backgammon. It reached an intermediate to advanced skill level and was able to demonstrate that it could generalize from its experience. Other backpropagation networks have learned chess, checkers, and other games.

These examples are only a sampling of the kinds of applications that have been approached with backpropagation systems. Not all attempts have been successful, but many different kinds of problems have been successfully solved.

Application:
NETtalk

In 1986 Terrence Sejnowski and Charles Rosenberg described a simple backpropagation network simulation that reads and properly pronounces unrestricted English text with good accuracy. They named their system NETtalk. Large computer programs exist that accomplish the same task, but these programs, which take many hundreds of hours to write, painstakingly encode each English pronunciation rule and provide lookup tables to cover the many exceptions in the language. The NETtalk simulation program took only a short time to write and contains no explicit pronunciation rules or lookup tables.

Sejnowski and Rosenberg trained their net to produce the speech sounds corresponding to a printed text that stepped past its simulated input sensors one letter at a time. The speech sound produced at any instant corresponded to the letter being presented to the center of its field of view. That field of view consisted of the central letter plus a few letters on either side. These extra letters provided the network with contextual information so it could choose the best pronunciation in ambiguous cases. Early versions of the network used a 5-letter field of view, but the researchers eventually increased this number to seven.

NETtalk is a hierarchical backpropagation system with three layers. The input layer, actually was a superlayer composed of one parallel network for each position in the field of view. Each of these input networks contained 29 neurodes: 26 to recognize the letters of the alphabet and one each for the comma, period, and space. Sejnowski and Rosenberg used 21 output neurodes to represent the symbols for the standard English speech sounds (phonemes) and 5 more to allow the system to produce stresses and syllable boundaries. The final system had 120 neurodes in the middle layer, but they studied the effects of using 0 and 60 neurodes in this layer as well. The smaller networks they studied had about 230 neurodes and 10,000 synapses; the final, larger one has 349 neurodes and over 27,000 synapses.

Sejnowski and Rosenberg's aim was to find out if a relatively simple neural network could learn to pronounce standard English. To do this, they only needed to teach NETtalk to produce the cor-

rect symbols for the standard English pronunciations corresponding to the input text. The training system they used was backpropagation learning. As the text was stepped past the sensors, the
symbol for the correct pronunciation of the central letter was
impressed on the proper output neurode. Unvoiced or silent letters
were given a special symbol. Once the network was trained, they
used a sophisticated commercial program to produce actual
sounds from NETtalks output.

In one experiment, the researchers trained NETtalk using a
1000 word section of text transcribed from a recording of a 6 year
old who was talking about visits to his grandmother's house. At the
start of training, NETtalk quickly learned to recognize the difference between vowels and consonants. It picked out only one
vowel and one consonant sound, however, and used these for all
vowels and all consonants. The result was much like the babbling
sound made by infants. As its training progressed, NETtalk learned
to recognize word boundaries, and its output began to resemble
the earnest but totally unintelligible pseudo-talk familiar to parents
of slightly older infants. After only 10 passes through the 1000-word
sample input, the text was intelligible.

After about 50 passes, the network was able to come very
close to a perfect pronunciation over 95 percent of the time. The
fully trained net seldom made large errors; its mistakes mainly consisted of confusing sounds that are nearly identical, such as the difference between "th" in *these* and *throw*. When they had the
network read an unfamiliar section of the same transcription that it
had been trained on, one with a number of words it had not
experienced, it still was able to come close to the correct pronunciation for over three-quarters of the words it encountered.

NETtalk also exhibits failsoftness or graceful degradation.
Sejnowski and Rosenberg trained a network and then altered the
weights of every synapse upward or downward by a random
amount D where D was different for each neurode, but equally
likely to fall somewhere within a range which was varied as the
experiment proceeded. For instance, in a trial for which $D = 0.2$,
the change in the weight of a particular neurode could have fal-
len anywhere in the range from -0.2 to $+0.2$ weight units with
equal likelihood. For our purposes, these weight units can be considered arbitrary. When fully trained, this network design had an
average synaptic weight of 0.77 unit and could come very close
to a correct pronunciation about 92 percent of the time. They
then increased D in steps, testing the performance of the network

after each step. The network continued to perform as if nothing had happened until *D* reached 0.3 or 0.4, roughly half the original average weight. At this point, the weights of each neurode had been damaged by random values of up to 50 percent of the trained network's average weights. Moreover, the pronunciation success rate of the network decreased smoothly as they increased *D* to higher and higher values and was still 80 percent when the weights had been damaged by random values up to approximately the average synaptic weight of 0.77.

NETtalk is not a practical system that can easily be used in commercial applications. In a way, Sejnowski and Rosenberg cheated when compared to the operation of biological speech systems. They reduced the text to the symbols for its component sounds by hand and then told NETtalk exactly what symbol to use for each letter in the words it read. (Recall that backpropagation demands such supervised learning.) Ideally we would like the network to create its own internal symbology for sounds. We might want to train it, for instance, using spoken and printed training input combined in some clever way. Similarly we might want it to obtain contextual information from a much wider portion of the text so it could speak with natural rhythm and inflection instead of the flat, monotonal speech we have come to associate with talking computers. Research proceeds in small steps, however, and NETtalk represents a good first step on the long road to systems that can read out loud.

Striving to better, oft we mar what's well.
— Shakespeare

15 Hybrid Networks

We have considered several networks that have a uniform architecture throughout and have looked at various styles of nets and several distinct learning rules. Each of these learning systems has
advantages and disadvantages, strengths and weaknesses. It would
be useful if we could make a network that combined the strengths of
several networks into a new, more powerful architecture. We would
like to make an alloy or hybrid network: a combination of neural network building blocks that is stronger than any of the individual
components.

This is a concept we have not seen before. In creating such systems, we treat the networks seen until now as the building blocks for
more complex networks that ideally will have properties better
suited to our application needs than those simpler structures. In this
chapter we will concentrate on a simple hybrid network that combines the competitive filter network with the outstar. While the discussion here will be specific to this network, called a
"counterpropagation network," you should consider it as only one
possible way to combine the simple building block networks
together to create new systems.

The counterpropagation network was developed in 1986 by
Robert Hecht-Nielsen, and it combines the data modeling power of
competitive filter associative memories with the pattern reproduc-

tion capability of outstars. Unlike the backpropagation network, a counterpropagation network cannot be fooled into finding a local minimum solution. This means that the network is guaranteed to find the correct response (or the nearest stored response) to an input, no matter what.

The Counterpropagation Network

The name *counterpropagation* derives from the initial presentation of this network as a five-layered network with data flowing inward from both sides, through the middle layer and out the opposite sides. There is literally a counterflow of data through the network. Although this is an accurate picture of the network, it is unnecessarily complex; we can simplify it considerably with no loss of accuracy.

In the simpler view of the counterpropagation network, it is a three-layered network. The input layer is a simple fan-out layer presenting the input pattern to every neurode in the middle layer. The middle layer is a straightforward Kohonen layer, using the competitive filter learning scheme discussed in chapter 7. Such a scheme ensures that the middle layer will categorize the input patterns presented to it and will model the statistical distribution of the input pattern vectors. The third, or output layer of the counterpropagation network is a simple outstar array. The outstar, you may recall, can be used to associate a stimulus from a single neurode with an output pattern of arbitrary complexity.

In operation, an input pattern is presented to the counterpropagation network and distributed by the input layer to the middle, Kohonen layer. Here the neurodes compete to determine that neurode with the strongest response (the closest weight vector) to the input pattern vector. That winning neurode generates a strong output signal (usually a +1) to the next layer; all other neurodes transmit nothing. At the output layer we have a collection of outstar grid neurodes. These are neurodes that have been trained by classical (Pavlovian) conditioning to generate specific output patterns in response to specific stimuli from the middle layer. The neurode from the middle layer that has fired is the hub neurode of the outstar, and it corresponds to some pattern of outputs. Because the outstar-layer neurodes have been trained to do so, they obediently reproduce the appropriate pattern at the output layer of the network.

In essence then, the counterpropagation network is exquisitely simple: the Kohonen layer categorizes each input pattern, and the outstar layer reproduces whatever output pattern is appropriate to that category.

What do we really have here? The counterpropagation network boils down to a simple lookup table. An input pattern is presented to the net, which causes one particular winning neurode in the middle layer to fire. The output layer has learned to reproduce some specific output pattern when it is stimulated by a signal from this winner. Presenting the input stimulus merely causes the network to determine that this stimulus is closest to stored pattern 17, for example, and the output layer obediently reproduces pattern 17. The counterpropagation network thus performs a direct mapping of the input to the output.

Training Techniques and Problems

The counterpropagation network presents us with the difficulty of trying to train two different layers, the middle layer and the output layer, that use very different learning laws. To accomplish this feat, normally we train a counterpropagation network in two stages. The first order of business is to convince the middle layer to categorize the input data patterns properly. Thus we set the constants in the middle-layer learning system to allow it to learn in some reasonably optimal fashion. While it is adjusting its weight vectors, we fix the output-layer learning constants at some small (near-zero) value. In this learning phase, we are not concerned whether the network produces the correct output.

Once the middle-layer weight vectors are appropriately distributed, we concentrate on training the output outstars. Depending on how much they have managed to learn in the first phase of training, we can either increase the size of their learning constants to make the outstars learn faster or decrease their learning constants to make them learn more slowly. As their output patterns approach the desired answers, we slowly decrease their learning constants until learning is complete.

One problem is often encountered with the counterpropagation network during training. For this network to work correctly, we need to be sure that each distinct input pattern (or category of patterns) has a unique winning neurode in the middle layer so that the outstar layer can know what output pattern to reproduce. In practice this is often not a trivial task.

In order to ensure unique middle-layer winners, we need to initialize the weight vectors in the middle layer so that each neurode in it has a chance of winning. Alternatively it is sometimes helpful to use middle layers that are much larger than the total number of distinct input categories; we might want to use a middle layer two to ten times larger than we normally need. While this adds to the physical complexity of the network, it also provides more middle-layer weight vectors and decreases the likelihood of any single weight vector's being the winner all the time. Duane DeSieno of Logical Designs (San Diego) has proposed adding a conscience to the middle-layer neurodes to monitor the number of times each neurode wins and prohibit the neurode from further firings for some period of time after a specified number of wins is reached.

The Size of the Middle Layer

Now let's consider the size of the middle layer not in the context of training issues but in terms of the accuracy of the networks response. If we are trying to model a mapping with 100 possible patterns, and we set up a counterpropagation network with 10 middle-layer neurodes, then we can expect some inaccuracies in the network's answer. It is not, by the way, so straightforward as saying we will get 10 percent accuracy; we might find a much higher degree of accuracy depending on how densely packed the probability density distribution of the input pattern data is.

In the simplest case, the input patterns form a uniform probability density function. If the data patterns are evenly distributed throughout the unit circle, we expect that the weight vectors will also be equally distributed after training. In the two-dimensional case, each weight vector will have to cover about 36 degrees (360 degrees divided by 10 vectors) of the unit circle. In other words, any input vector within this 36 degree arc of the circle will generate precisely the same output. If we use 100 weight vectors to cover this 360 degree span, we would expect that each weight vector will correspond to about 3.6 degrees of arc, so any input vector within 3.6 degrees of a weight vector will count as a hit.

The situation becomes more complex if the input patterns are not evenly distributed about the unit circle. In this case the weight vectors are clustered during training about the areas of the unit circle most likely to contain input vectors. Regions outside the most common input areas may end up with very few weight vectors in their region. Thus the occasional input vector that occurs in one of these sparsely populated regions may end up being approximated by a weight vector that is only a gross estimate of the actual input vector. On the other hand, input vectors that do occur in the area densely clustered with weight vectors will be quite closely approximated.

In reality, a nonuniform distribution of input patterns is much more likely in a real application than a uniform one. This means that the accuracy of the network's mapping is better in those parts of the unit circle that are more likely to contain input vectors. Rather than having a uniform accuracy, counterpropagation networks have higher accuracy in the more commonly used areas of the unit circle and lower accuracy in the areas less likely to receive input vectors. For many applications, this is quite acceptable and possibly preferable.

We still have not answered the question of how many neurodes we need to have in the middle layer. We have only indicated that the answer depends on how accurate the network's output needs to be. The more neurodes we have, the more accurate our mapping can be. This is one of the key drawbacks to the counterpropagation network (and the Kohonen network as well), in fact, because real problems may well demand middle-layer sizes too large to build today. If we can afford to have only a limited number of neurodes, the mapping will still work, of course, but it may be less precise than we need. There is no hard and fast rule to apply to this question. As in many other situations with neural networks, the answer is: It depends.

There is a way to improve the counterpropagation networks accuracy without requiring an unacceptably large middle layer: we can allow the network to interpolate its output. In other words, if we have trained the network to respond with a 1.0 to a blue input and a 2.0 to a red input, we train the network to output, say, a 1.5 to a magenta input. It is quite simple to implement this kind of interpolation in the counterpropagation network. All we have to do is to change the middle layer to allow more than one winner. For example, we might allow the middle layer to have two winners: the two neurodes with weight vectors closest to the input vector. In this case, the network's output will be a melding of the outputs from the neurode categories in the middle layer. If we want to broaden its response, we might allow three winners. We must be careful not to allow too many winners, or the output pattern will be too ambiguous to be useful. However, permitting multiple winners in the middle layer does give the network the ability to interpolate between known patterns.

Chapter 15

Using the Counterpropagation Network

Papers describing the counterpropagation network became generally available only in late 1987 and 1988, so there are few applications to date using this architecture. Certainly, though, this network holds promise for use in some unique applications. We can foresee two areas in which counterpropagation may be extremely useful. The first is signal processing. There are many signal processing applications, including speech, radar, sonar, and noise filtering, that can be greatly affected by a system with the pattern distribution modeling ability of the counterpropagation network. In many cases there are no analytic expressions that accurately express the input distributions, so a system that can learn and model an arbitrary input can be quite useful.

A second area in which these networks may be useful is statistical applications, including statistical databases. Robert Hecht-Nielsen has outlined one possible way of using a counterpropagation network to generate inferences from statistical databases without waiting for an operator to make an appropriate query. For example, the U.S. Census information may show that people who live in blue houses come down with fewer colds than people who live in brown houses. Such information, if true, might well provide a clue on how to cure the common cold. But because no one has ever asked the question, we have never had that information available to us. It is not that the information is not in the database; the problem is that we literally do not know what questions to ask to get the answers needed. Hecht-Nielsen's highly speculative proposal would perceive that such a relationship exists and tell the operator to ask the appropriate question. Researchers could then apply standard statistical techniques to the query results to see if they were meaningful. We do not know whether his idea will work because no one has yet tried to build it. But this kind of statistical inferencing system, if demonstrated to be feasible, may well prove to be one of the most broadly useful neural network applications of all.

The counterpropagation network makes a good initial foray into the world of hybrid networks. It is simple and easy to understand. In the next chapter, however, we will review what is probably the most complex network to date, the adaptive resonance network.

The true art of memory is the art of attention.
— Samuel Johnson

16 Adaptive Resonance Networks

In this chapter we will look closely at one of the most complex network designs available today. Like the counterpropagation network, this is a hybrid network, containing various types of neurodes arranged in several network subsystems. One of the key values of adaptive resonance networks is that they provide a glimpse of what will be required to make truly autonomous systems. These networks are based on a theory developed by Stephen Grossberg and Gail Carpenter called adaptive resonance theory (ART).

Grossberg shaped ART during the same period of time in which he developed outstar learning. In 1986 Grossberg, working with Gail Carpenter, introduced ART 1, a neural network based on adaptive resonance theory. This network can process only binary input data. In 1987 they followed their original design with the more complex ART 2, which can process gray-scale input data. In this chapter, we present the principles of adaptive resonance theory and describe the operation of ART 1 networks. We will also briefly touch on the kinds of changes that must be made in the ART 1 network so that it can handle gray-scale data.

The ideas of adaptive resonance theory can be confusing initially, but the effort expended in understanding them is well spent. ART supplies a foundation upon which we may eventually be able to build genuinely autonomous machines. These networks are as close as anyone has yet come to achieving the goals for the autonomous systems listed in chapter 12.

Chapter 16

The Principle of Adaptive Resonance

We can best present the basic idea of adaptive resonance with the two-layer network shown in figure 16.1. The broad arrows in the figure are a shorthand way of indicating that the network layers are fully interconnected with modifiable synaptic weights. Although it will not be important to our immediate discussion, let's assume our net uses the outstar learning model.

Each pattern presented to the network initially stimulates a pattern of activity in the input layer. We call this the "bottom-up" pattern; it is also called the "trial" pattern. Because of the outstar structure, this bottom-up pattern is presented to every neurode of the upper, storage layer. This pattern is modified (in the normal weighted-sum fashion) during its transmission through the synapses to the upper layer and stimulates a response pattern in the storage layer. We call this new activity the "top-down" pattern of activity; it may also be called the "expectation" pattern. It generally is quite different from the bottom-up pattern. Since the two layers are fully interconnected, this top-down pattern is in turn presented (by the synapses on the top-down interconnects) back to the input layer.

We can think of the operation of these two layers in another way. The basic mode of operation is one of hypothesis testing. The input pattern is passed to the upper layer, which attempts to recognize it. The upper layer makes a guess about the category this bottom-up pattern belongs in and sends it, in the guise of the top-down pattern, to the lower layer. The result is then compared to the original pattern; if the guess is correct (or, rather, is close enough as determined by a network parameter), the bottom-up trial pattern and the top-down guess mutually reinforce each other and all is well. If the guess is incorrect (too far away from the correct category), the upper layer will make another guess. Eventually either the pattern will be placed in an existing category or learned as the first example of a new category. Thus, the upper layer forms a "hypothesis" of the correct category for each input pattern; this hypothesis is then tested by sending it back down to the lower layer to see if a correct match has been made. A good match results in a validated hypothesis; a poor match results in a new hypothesis.

If the pattern of activity excited in the input-layer neurodes by the top-down input is a close match to the pattern excited in the input layer by the external input—if the guess is correct, in other words—then the system is said to be in adaptive resonance. The ART systems that we will describe are built on this principle. We will see, however, that we must introduce several complexities into this basic scheme in order to make a working neural network design.

If the top-down pattern does not match the bottom-up pattern sufficiently well, the ART network automatically searches its stored patterns for a better match. This search process continues until either an adequate match is found or the input pattern is learned as a new data item. Note that such a search occurs only if the first guess is incorrect. When the first guess matches the input pattern, the network immediately recognizes the input without having to search through all stored patterns, a characteristic important for practical autonomous systems.

Before we go on, we need to make a note of the internal architecture of these two layers. Recall that the lower layer is devoted to processing the input pattern and achieving adaptive resonance and that the top layer is devoted to pattern storage. In our discussion of the adaptive resonance principle, we concentrated on the interconnec-

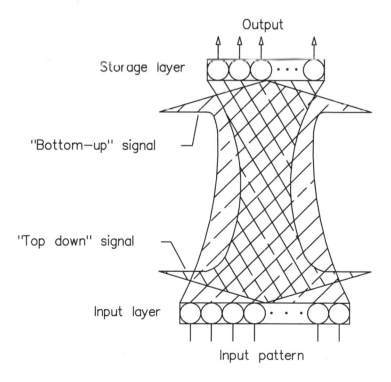

Figure 16.1 Adaptive resonance in a two-layered network.

tions between the input and storage layers. We now need to concentrate on the interconnections within layers, the intralayer connections, of the input and storage layers.

For the minimal ART 1 structure we will consider here, the nodes of the input layer are individual neurodes connected into a competitive internal architecture of the type presented in chapter 7. To simplify the discussion, only one winner will be allowed. In general, multiple winners can be permitted, but nearly all ART systems actually built force a single winner. The rivalry for activity inherent in the competitive structure is essential to the adaptive resonance process. (While this single-winner strategy is not inherent in the design of the network, it is much easier to implement and operate than a multiwinner strategy. Significant architectural changes would have to be made to the network to permit multiple winning neurodes in the storage layer. See the discussion of grandmother nodes at the end of this chapter for the ramifications of this design decision.)

The nodes of the storage layer are more complex than the simple neurodes used in previous networks. The individual neurodes of this layer are arranged in groupings Grossberg calls "dipoles." These dipoles act as simple on-off toggles and are interconnected as units into a competitive architecture, just as the Kohonen network had a competitive architecture. We will talk more about toggles; for now, just be aware that each "node" in the storage layer is actually a group of neurodes connected together in a specific structure.

Operation of the ART 1 Network

Let's move on to the nitty-gritty of the network and see how an ART 1 network operates in detail. Such an exploration will tell us much about the delicate balances necessary to build a good hybrid network.

An external pattern presented to the input layer causes some of the nodes in that layer to become active. Because ART 1 allows only binary inputs and the neurodes have binary output functions, this pattern will be identical to the external input pattern. Nevertheless, for consistency of discussion we call the pattern that becomes active in the input layer the "trial pattern."

Each of the neurodes in the input layer is connected to each of the neurodes in the upper, storage layer. By this means, the pattern of activity in the input layer is transmitted to the storage layer. In the

---

Nodes and Neurodes

In complex artificial neural systems such as the ART family of networks, the fundamental unit in a particular layer may not be the single neurode. We have already seen one example of this in the lateral inhibition or competitive groupings described in chapter 7. For cases like this, we use the term *node*. Recall that we used the word in an analogous way in chapter 3. There it referred to a functional grouping of computing elements in a parallel computer. In the present context, a node is a functional grouping of neurodes that acts as a single unit within a particular layer of a neural network.

---

process of moving across the synaptic junctions between the two layers, the pattern is modified so that the activity generated in the storage layer differs from the trial pattern.

The pattern arriving at the storage layer signals the beginning of a competition among the nodes in this layer. The winner of this competition generates an output signal and all others are suppressed. The resulting output-layer activity pattern is called the "expectation" pattern. For the moment we will assume that this pattern consists of exactly one active node because we have designed it so that only one node can win the competition. This expectation pattern is, of course, transmitted (via the top-down synaptic junctions) back to the input layer.

Everything we have said about the interconnection of the input layer to the storage layer is true of the return path from the storage layer to the input layer. Because the expectation pattern must pass through the synaptic junctions, it will be modified en route; thus, the pattern of activity generated in the input layer will be quite different from the expectation pattern itself. The pattern generated by the expectation pattern in general will involve a number of nodes in the input layer.

The input layer now has two inputs presented to it: the external input, which originally excited the trial pattern, and the top-down expectation pattern. These merge and generate a new pattern of activity, which replaces the old trial pattern. If this new and the original trial pattern are very similar, the network is in adaptive resonance, and the output of the storage layer becomes stable. The corresponding expectation (top-down) pattern is the stored symbol, or icon, for the external input pattern presented.

We have not yet considered all possibilities, however. What if the expectation pattern excites a pattern in the input layer entirely different from the original trial pattern? This will happen, for example, when the ART network is presented with a pattern very different from any it has yet seen. Such an input does not match any of the network's "known" patterns and results in a mismatch between the trial and expectation patterns. The ART network must be able to cope with the novelty arising from unusual patterns. We have already seen that its method of coping is hypothesis testing. In order to understand how it actually implements this strategy, we need to add a subsystem to the basic two-layer system of figure 16.1.

The Reset Subsystem

Figure 16.2 is nearly identical to figure 16.1, with the exception of a subsystem we call the "reset unit." The reset unit has two sets of inputs: the external input pattern and the pattern from the input layer. The structure of the reset unit depends on the details of the ART 1 system being considered. For our network, we can assume that it is a single neurode with a fixed-weight, inhibitory input from every node in the input layer and a fixed-weight, excitatory input from each external input line.

The reset unit's output is simple; it is linked by a fixed-weight connection to every node in the storage layer. By now, you know another way of saying this: the reset unit is the hub of an outstar whose border is all the nodes of the storage layer. There are no reverse connections from the storage layer to the reset unit.

Before we go on, we must fully understand the structure of the nodes in this storage layer. We have briefly mentioned that these nodes are little groupings of neurodes called dipoles or toggles. Let's explore what that implies.

These toggles have several useful properties. First, they act just like an individual neurode most of the time. Second, and the one of interest to us here, is the property called "reset." Reset is the process of persistently shutting off all currently active nodes in a layer without interfering with the ability of inactive nodes in that layer to become active. The reset action of a toggle can be summarized in two statements: (1) If the toggle is active and it receives a special signal, called a "global reset," then it will become inactive, and it will be inhibited from reactivating for some period of time. (2) If the toggle is not active when it receives a global reset, then it is not inhibited from becoming active in the immediate future. With these two characteristics, it should be evident that sending a global reset signal to every toggle in the storage layer will shut off only the currently active toggles and furthermore will prevent only those toggles from becoming active in the immediate future.

In general, we can think of the storage layer as simply being made of special nodes that have this reset characteristic. It is not especially important here whether we call them toggles, dipoles, or nodes. It is important to realize, however, that no matter what we

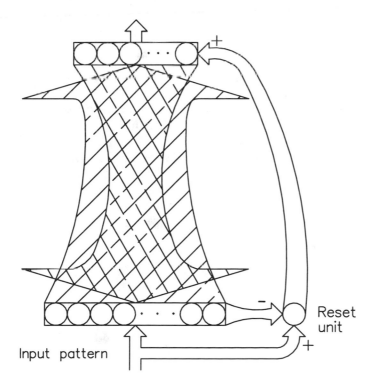

Figure 16.2 The reset system added to the network.

call them, they act as outstars and instars, just as an individual neu-rode does in any network.

Now we are ready to see what happens if the network does not reach adaptive resonance—that is, if the original bottom-up and the newly generated bottom-up patterns do not match. If they do match, the two inputs to the reset unit (one from the external pattern and one from the input layer) balance, and it produces no output. If the original and the new trial patterns do not match, the activity of the input layer temporarily decreases as its nodes try to reconcile these two patterns. In fact, for reasons we will see, we can be absolutely guaranteed that if the bottom-up and top-down patterns do not match, the net activity (that is, the total number of active nodes) in the input layer will always decrease. As a result, the inhibitory input to the reset unit no longer exactly balances the excitatory input from the external pattern, and thus the reset unit becomes active.

The active reset unit now sends its global reset signal to the nodes of the storage layer. Because these nodes are toggles, this reset signal causes any active nodes to turn off and stay off for some period of time. This destroys the pattern then active in that layer and suppresses its immediate reemergence. With the old pattern destroyed, a new pattern of nodes is now free to attempt to reach res-onance with the input layer's pattern.

In effect, when the old and new trial patterns do not match, the reset subsystem signals the storage layer that that particular guess was wrong. That guess is "turned off," allowing another one to take its place. The cycle repeats as many times as necessary. When reso-nance is reached and the guess is deemed acceptable, the search automatically terminates.

This is not the only way a search may terminate: the system can end its search by learning the unfamiliar pattern being presented. As each trial of the parallel search is carried out, small weight changes occur in the synapses of both the bottom-up and the top-down path-ways. These weight changes mean that the next time the trial pattern is passed up to the storage layer, a slightly different activity pattern will be received providing a mechanism for the storage layer to change its guess. If a match is quickly found, the amount of modifi-cation of these synapses is insignificant. If the system cannot find a match, however, and if the input pattern persists long enough, the synapse weights eventually will modify enough that an uncommit-ted node in the storage layer learns to respond to the new pattern.

This also explains why the storage layer's second or third guess may prove to be a better choice than the original one. The small weight changes ensure that the activity generated by the bottom-up pattern in the second pass is somewhat different from the activity generated in the first pass. Thus a node that was second-best the first time, may well prove to be the best guess the second time. If the input is a slightly noisy version of a stored pattern, it may require a few synaptic weight changes before the truly best guess can be matched.

We can also supply ART 1 with the property of vigilance. This means that the accuracy with which the network guesses the correct match can be varied. By setting a new value for the reset threshold, we can control whether the network fusses with trifling details or concerns itself only with global features. Because of the way vigilance is defined, a low reset threshold implies high vigilance and thus close attention to detail, while a high threshold implies low vigilance and a more global view of the pattern. By controlling the threshold of the reset unit, we thus govern what the system calls "insignificant noise" and what it identifies as a "significant new pattern."

We can interpret vigilance in another way. In effect, by setting the threshold of the reset unit, we choose the coarseness of the categories into which the system sorts patterns. A low threshold (high vigilance) forces the system to separate patterns into a large number of fine categories, and a high threshold (low vigilance) causes the same set of patterns to be lumped into a small number of coarse categories.

The Gain Control Subsystem and the 2/3 Rule

We still do not have an operational ART 1 system. We must provide a way for the input layer to tell genuine input signals from spurious top-down signals that might be present even when no real-world input is being presented. Such a situation would exist, for instance, if some random system noise or other extraneous inputs activated the storage layer even when no external input was present. We must also make sure that a genuine external input always creates a pattern in the input layer in order to start the adaptive resonance process. Furthermore, we have not yet justified the assurance we made that the input layer's total activity is guaranteed to decrease in the event of a mismatch. The gain control added to the system in figure 16.3 ensures these actions. With it, our minimal ART 1 system is complete.

What is the structure of the input gain control? As you can see in the figure, it has two inputs: the excitatory external input signal and an inhibitory signal from the storage layer. Just as for the reset unit, the exact structure of the input gain control depends on the complexity of the particular ART 1 net it controls. For our purposes, we can assume that it is a single neurode. The inhibitory effect from the storage layer is sufficient to overcome any excitatory effect from the external input pattern. If both signals are present or if only the inhibitory signal from the storage layer is present, the gain control produces no output. If the external input is present alone, however, the gain control is not inhibited; it is forced above threshold and produces an output. That output is sent to every node of the input layer.

ART 1 uses a scheme called the 2/3 rule to decide whether the nodes of the input layer should be allowed to become active. There are three input sources to that layer: the top-down pattern, the exter-

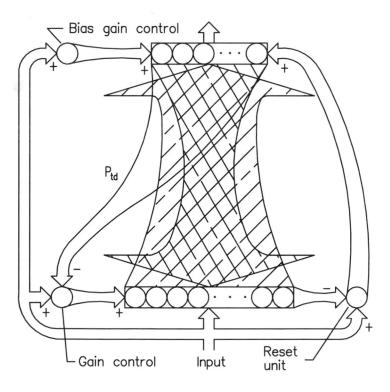

Figure 16.3 The gain control system added to the network. The ART 1 network is now complete.

nal pattern signals, and the signal from the input gain control. Any two of these three inputs allow the nodes of the input layer to become active.

Ideally the external input pattern is presented to the input layer, the gain control system, and the reset system more or less simultaneously. The gain control system turns on, providing the second necessary source of stimulus to the input layer and in turn allowing that layer to become active and generate the original trial pattern. In the meantime, the external input has also turned on the reset system, which shuts off any active pattern in the storage layer. The input layer's activity is translated into a bottom-up pattern and sent to the storage layer. In addition, it goes to the reset system where it matches the external input and shuts off the global reset. This combination of actions allows the storage layer to respond to the bottom-up pattern.

The storage layer now generates a top-down expectation pattern, which it sends to the input layer. This same expectation pattern also is sent as an inhibitory signal to the gain control; as a result the gain control system turns off. This removes one of the input layer's two sources of stimulation, but because the input layer now sees the top-down pattern (the new trial pattern) as well as the external pattern, it has sufficient stimulation to stay active.

The 2/3 rule explains why the total activity of the input layer is guaranteed to drop in the event of a mismatch. Any node active in both the input pattern and the top-down pattern can stay active; any node active in only one of these must shut off because of the 2/3 rule. The top-down pattern by itself is not sufficient to turn on a node not already turned on by the input pattern, nor can the input pattern by itself maintain the activity of any node not matched by the top-down pattern. Thus the total number of active nodes can decrease only if the two patterns do not match exactly.

The 2/3 rule also keeps noise damped in the network. Any activity in the storage layer keeps the input gain control from exciting the input layer. If the storage layer is firing, the only other available stimulus for the input layer is the external pattern; if this is present, the input layer's neurodes can activate. If the storage layer fires spontaneously, without an appropriate external pattern being present, the 2/3 rule will not be met and the input layer will not be stimulated into action. Noise from the storage layer thus immediately damps out.

The input layer can also be the source of noise and spontaneous firings. If this happens when there is no external pattern to support it, the noise pattern gets transmitted to the storage layer. But the top-down pattern will shut off the gain control (assuming it was on), so that the input layer will be left with only one source of input (the top-down pattern response) and the noise will be once more damped out. This keeps the storage layer from being bombarded with meaningless bottom-up signals that do not correspond to real inputs. If this were not done, the storage layer would constantly be learning nonsense, and its stored patterns would not be stable.

We have so far not addressed the bias gain control shown in figure 16.3. Its function is to allow the presence of an external input to predispose the nodes of the storage layer toward activity even before receiving a trial pattern from the input layer. It does this by applying a small excitatory signal to the nodes of the storage layer when an external input signal is applied to the network. In this way, the activity of the system is correlated with, or paced by, the rate of presentation of external inputs. In some implementations it also helps mediate the competition of the nodes in the storage layer, enhancing the activity of any node that gets an edge on its competitors and suppressing other nodes.

Troubles with ART 1

ART 1, even the simple version described, is a pretty good system. It possesses several of the characteristics listed in chapter 11 for a system or machine capable of truly autonomous learning. It learns constantly but learns only significant information and does not have to be told what information is significant; new knowledge does not destroy already learned information; it rapidly recalls an input pattern it has already learned; it functions as an autonomous associative memory; it can (by changing the vigilance parameter) learn more detail if that becomes necessary; and it reorganizes its associative categories as needed. Theoretically it can even be made to have an unrestricted storage capacity by moving away from single-node patterns in the storage layer.

This leaves, however, at least one major unsatisfied criterion: a truly autonomous machine must place no restriction on the form of its input signal. Unfortunately, an ART 1 network can handle only binary patterns. This limitation is built into the way the network subsystems interact, implying that it is fundamental to this architecture. This has two ramifications. First, it limits the total number of distinct input patterns that an n–node input layer can allow to 2^n. This is an important limitation only for small networks. Ten input nodes, for instance, can handle only 1023 distinct patterns. One hundred nodes, however, allow input of over 10^{30} separate patterns. The second ramification of binary input nodes is that they place requirements on the type of preprocessing we must give real-world input signals. Under some circumstances, this can be costly in hardware complexity, hardware price, processing time, and total system power. For an application in which the ART 1 system is used with equipment already operating in a digital mode, however, this need not be a serious restriction.

ART 2

ART 2 removes the binary input limitation of ART 1; it can process gray-scale input signals. The cost of this fix, however, is a considerable increase in complexity. ART 2 systems proposed so far have as many as five input sublayers, each with its own gain control subsystem. Further, each sublayer typically contains two networks.

There are two major reasons for ART 2's added complexity. The first concerns noise immunity. The noise problem of a network such as ART 1 designed to recognize binary patterns is relatively minor. Individual pattern elements have a sharp "yes–or–no" nature. Thus, to change one element of a binary pattern, a noise signal must be of virtually the same magnitude as the pattern element. The noise problem of a network designed to recognize gray-scale patterns is much more severe, however. Individual elements of such patterns do not have the sharp yes–or–no nature binary patterns possess; instead they can take on a range of values. Two patterns that differ by only one gray-scale value in one element are treated as quantitatively different. As a result, noise that changes only a single pattern element by one gray-scale value may make the input pattern unrecognizable.

The second reason for ART 2's added complexity is that alikeness becomes a much fuzzier concept with analog signals, even with no noise present, because each input element can take on as many values as are in the gray scale being used. *Identical, similar, different,* and *very different* are ambiguous terms that must be quantified by the network in some way.

Several ART 2 architectures have been designed by Carpenter and Grossberg and by others. All of these systems accept gray-scale inputs, and they differ mainly in the number and function of the sublayers in the input superlayer.

Gray Scales

Binary signals can take on only one of two values. These might be −1 and +1, or 0 and 1, for instance. In visual terms, we can think of binary signals as all or nothing, black or white. Gray-scale signals, on the other hand, can assume a number of specific values between their lower and upper limits. The range between −1 and +1 might be broken, for instance, into 20 subranges or steps, each 0.1 units in width. In visual terms, these correspond to values between black and white, or grays. Accordingly, the scale of discrete values that a signal may take on is called a gray scale. A gray-scale measurement is not at all the same as an analog measurement. An analog measurement in the range of −1 to +1 can have an infinite number of possible values, since any real number in that range is acceptable; on the other hand a gray-scale measurement must have one of a specific, finite number of values. The number of gray-scale values determines how much two adjacent portions of a pattern must differ for us to recognize them as unequal. Generally speaking, the smaller the step size between gray-scale values, that is, the more steps there are in the measurement range, the more complex the system must be to deal properly with the measurements. This is true for neural networks as well as any other system.

An excellent example of such a gray scale is a color monitor. Such monitors often have various modes from monochrome (1 bit per picture element), which simply determines black or white (or amber or green!) values, to full color, which can range as high as 32 bits per picture element; this latter setting allows more than 4.2 billion color values in each picture element, ranging between black (no color) and white (all colors).

Grandmother Nodes and ART

As they are usually presented, both ART 1 and ART 2 use "grand-mother" nodes in their storage layer. A grandmother node is one that alone represents a particular input pattern. This winner-take-all feature does not appear to be essential to the operation of either type of ART system. We have seen that more than one winner may be allowed in a competitive architecture. However, nearly all actual implementations of ART networks (both ART 1 and ART 2) use this scheme. If the output of a system must operate a relay or be viewed by a human, having a single output node correspond to a particular class of input patterns may make sense. If the output of the system is to be interfaced to other neural networks or to a digital system, however, using grandmother nodes may make no sense at all. Let's see why.

First, using grandmother nodes limits the storage capacity of an ART system to the number of nodes in its storage layer. The severity of this limitation becomes clear when we realize that even with binary storage-layer nodes, the memory capacity we could obtain if each combination of n nodes could be used to store a separate binary pattern would be 2^n. This leads to the same numbers we gave for the input capacity of the binary input layer: 100 nodes could potentially store over 10^{30} pattern classes instead of only 100.

Even allowing storage-layer activity patterns to contain a limited number of nodes can gain a great deal. Two-, three-, and four-node storage patterns in a 100-node storage layer can represent approximately 5000, 300,000, and 23,000,000 input-pattern classes, respectively. There are many applications in which such capacities are not needed or even desirable. But there are others, such as large data or knowledge bases and sequence storage, for which these or even larger capacities are essential.

A second way in which grandmother nodes may be a problem is that they reduce the reliability of a system. Failure of a single component in one node can cause the pattern coded into that node to be lost. Although there are ways to compensate for this danger, it is one we would rather not have in machines that we expect to use in applications requiring high fault tolerance.

Third, restricting the storage layer to patterns containing only one node limits the ability of the network to represent a hierarchy of concepts or objects. To understand this, we must look at the effect of pattern complexity not on how many input patterns we can store but on the way those stored patterns can be associated.

Grandmother Nodes

A single binary output-layer node that by itself represents a particular input pattern is often called a "grandmother node." The term alludes to an indirect proof of
the existence of distributed memory in humans. An old
theory held that there is a single brain cell dedicated to
each memory. The refutation observes that many brain
cells die each day and suggests that we could reasonably expect to wake up some morning and not be
able to recognize, for instance, our grandmother's
face. Since this does not happen, it must be true that
more than one brain cell holds each separate piece of
information.

It may not be intuitively obvious, but it takes fewer storage
nodes to encode an input pattern representing a high-level general
concept or complex object than it does to encode an input pattern
representing a single specific concept or object. The broad concept
"tree" needs fewer nodes to encode it than the concept "cherry tree."
Treeness must be part of the pattern for cherry tree, as must fruit-
treeness, hardwoodness, deciduousness, and a host of other concepts
needed to distinguish cherry trees from other kinds and classes of
trees. "The cherry tree in my front yard," a specific object, requires
still more nodes to encode because its coding pattern must carry the
extra information required to identify it as a particular tree yet still
contain the subpatterns representing "cherry tree" and "tree." Thus,
a layer designed to allow storage of hierarchical information must
have the ability to form patterns consisting of different numbers of
nodes. A storage layer that consists only of grandmother nodes
simply will not do.

Are there cases in which we would want to use the same complexity in both the input and storage layers of an ART network?
Perhaps, but not normally. We usually want to reduce the complexity, or the dimensionality, of the input signal before we store in the
storage layer in order to let only the essential features of the input
pattern be preserved. That is one reason that we use a competitive
structure in the storage layer; allowing competition in that layer
guarantees just this outcome.

The Limitations of ART Networks in General

ART systems have a number of advantages for applications requiring continuous autonomous learning. What are the limitations of ART systems? We have already listed two problems which ART 1 possesses: the need for binary input patterns and a reliance on grandmother nodes in its storage layer. ART 2 obviates one of these; the other can be overcome if the designer is willing to pay a considerable penalty in complexity.

There are yet two other drawbacks to present-day ART systems. One is the inability of present designs to function well if the input signals are even moderately noisy. Current ART network designs do not appear to have a particularly good track record when there is noise in the input pattern. A second potential limitation of ART systems is their relative complexity. These systems also tend to be quite tricky to implement and tune for a given problem.

Because of their complexity, ART 2 networks have not met with immediate successes in applications. While the research group that originally specified these networks have claimed some extremely good results using ART 2 architectures, few, if any, outside researchers have been able to duplicate these findings to date. Part of the reason for this lack of substantiation is that published information on ART 2 is insufficient to build a working application network. Another part of the problem is that even commercial simulations of ART 2 appear to be highly sensitive to precise values of the many network parameters. Changing certain parameter values as little as 5 percent can have disastrous consequences for the network's operation. Such fine-tuning requirements make clear that ART 2 has serious problems as a model of our fuzzy, imprecise biological brains.

In fact, both ART 1 and ART 2 have one more serious drawback as a biological model: the requirement that the input and storage layers, as well as the reset and gain subsystems, must be fully interconnected with each other. The connectivity requirements implied by this, and comparisons to the structure of the brain, make it unlikely that the brain widely uses an ART-like architecture. When added to the grandmother node architecture, ART 1 and ART 2 have some serious drawbacks as models of the biological brain.

In parts II, III, and IV of this book, we have described the major neural network architectures. In part V, we will look first at some of the ways in which neural networks can be implemented and then at a number of applications to illustrate some of the ways they can be applied.

Part V

What is not today will be tomorrow.
—Petronius

Practice is better than theory.
— Latin proverb

17 Neural Network Implementations

We have come a long way from chapter 1, and it is time to ask the dollar-and-cents question: what can neural networks do in real-world applications? The truth is that no one yet fully knows. At least, nobody knows the limits of their abilities. The reason is simple. Ideas of how to accomplish complex, meaningful tasks using neural networks have been around for a long time, but the means of implementing large networks capable of performing these tasks have not. Such means are relatively recent developments. As a result, it will be several years before we begin to understand thoroughly the limits of the present generation of practical neural network implementations in real-world applications. We have seen a few of these ideas as we explored some actual network applications throughout the previous part of the book. Now it is time to talk in detail about how we actually build network implementations and application solutions.

There are three ways to make practical implementations of neural networks: (1) write a software simulation program that directs a general-purpose digital computer to perform the actions characteristic of a true neural network; (2) build special-purpose digital network emulators that connect to a general-purpose host system; or (3) construct true electronic or optical neural networks. The first two implementation methods involve emulating the network using a mathematical model of its behavior; the last involves a direct implementation of the network's physical elements in hardware.

Netware

In the realm of neural networks, the word *netware* is used in two ways: it is applied to the private and commercial software programs used to simulate neural networks on standard serial computers, and it is used to refer to the programs supplied with neurocomputers to realize specific neural network designs. A third use of the word, unrelated to neural networks, is also popular; the software that runs local area networks (LANs) is often referred to as netware.

Generally the cheapest and fastest implementation method to create is that of a software simulator; a competent programmer can produce a skeleton simulator for a single network design in a few hours. The next easiest implementation to produce is the hardware emulator; these take a few months or years to design and build and are substantially more expensive than the software-only implementation. Hardest of all is the direct physical implementation of the network. After many years of effort, we are still struggling to produce the first commercial hardware implementations. The three methods are also ordered in terms of increasing effectiveness and power, with software simulations being the least effective and direct hardware implementations being the most effective.

Software Simulations

Many software simulations of neural network designs exist. These simulations work because all neural networks can, in principle, be modeled or described by equations, and equations can be solved numerically on a serial computer. That's one of the things digital computers do well.

So a simulation is just a computer program that replicates the temporal behavior of a complex neural network system over time. A simulation program numerically solves the system's equations for successive instants of time, using as the starting point for each iteration the values of the system parameters obtained from the previous solution. The behavior of the system then unfolds as the simulation generates successive solutions. To the extent that the programmer crafted model equations well, the simulation approximates the behavior of the real system being modeled.

This sounds like a good way to go, but a few evenings at the computer writing and using simulations teaches us two sobering lessons. The first is that writing usable simulations is time-consuming. This is not an insurmountable obstacle, and a little later we will describe one way of partially overcoming it. We learn our second sobering lesson as we encounter a much larger obstacle: simulations are inherently slow and very demanding on computer resources such as memory, disk storage, and processor time. They are slow even on large computers if we try to use more than a few hundred neurodes in the net. This makes simulations virtually useless for any application in which a network of substantial size must learn and respond in real time.

In addition to these problems, neural simulations are subject to the pitfalls that await any other modeling activity. One is that models based on observed behavior—so-called phenomenological models—are notoriously brittle; they cannot be pushed too far. There are likely to be many combinations of model parameters—whole regions of parameter space for which numerical solutions give utter nonsense. Even if we construct a model with a firm theoretical basis, we cannot blindly accept the results of our simulations. It is a fact that complex systems of the kind typically encountered in neural modeling can be extremely sensitive to the initial conditions assumed for network parameters and state information, and we must carefully test the outcome of any neural network simulation for this sensitivity.

Further, we cannot ignore the pitfalls awaiting the unwary in the area of numerical computation. Numerical truncation errors and other machine-related effects can render our most painstakingly crafted model useless. Moreover, in order to fit the differential equations of the neural net model onto a digital computer, we must usually cast them in the form of difference equations. As a result, we do not see the condition of the system at truly infinitesimal time intervals, and it sometimes takes considerable effort to know that we have not introduced either a spurious instability or a false stability that would not be there in the real system.

Nevertheless, people regularly write neural network simulations in higher programming languages such as C, Pascal, FORTRAN,

---

High Fashion Modeling

We model a physical system by a set of mathematical equations. The system can be a small cluster of atoms, a diesel engine, a society, a brain, or a galaxy; the equations can be anything from a single algebraic expression to a complex set of coupled tensor relations. These equations describe the way the parts of a system behave and the way those parts interact among themselves and with the outside world. If our equations are derived from the laws of physical, biological, or other science, we have made a physical model. If our equations are algebraic expressions that describe the external behavior of the system but have no known basis in scientific law, we have made a phenomenological or ad hoc model. Most actual models, certainly those for neural networks, fall somewhere between these extremes.

BASIC, or Lisp, and many of those programs work well in real-world applications. Mainly, however, they are used to provide proof-of-principle demonstrations for new network architectures, to test suitability of network designs for specific applications, and to carry out some types of research in neurobiology and other disciplines.

We said that writing usable simulations is time-consuming, and that we would present a way to overcome this obstacle partially. That way is through commercial simulation-software packages. These packages provide prewritten shells for the major network architectures, and a convenient user interface that allows us to select an appropriate shell and easily enter the parameters for a particular net design. These shells are just carefully debugged and tested simulation programs into which the user enters parameters describing the specific network desired. Although the expertise of the shell programmer makes a difference in the speed, stability, and accuracy of the simulation, the interface environment is arguably the most important feature of a simulation package. With a good interface, the user is guided smoothly through the design process; without one, the user might as well do his or her own programming from scratch.

The strength of commercial simulation packages is that they save time. These packages do not let us design systems without knowing

Speaking in Tongues

Simulations have been written in virtually every high-level programming language (although we doubt if many have attempted the feat in COBOL). The difference in execution speed among identical simulations written in different languages can be significant. In general, the languages offering the greatest degree of machine-level access produce the fastest simulations. For this reason, C has gained favor among commercial simulation producers and currently seems to be the language of choice for serious neural network simulation. The C language has limitations for network design, however, such as a lack of built-in matrix and vector operations, and these may cause it to lose preeminence in the future in favor of more object-oriented languages. Three possible contenders are C++ (an object-oriented version of C), ANSpec (from SAIC, San Diego), and AXON (from I INC, San Diego).

anything about the theory of neural networks. We still must know which type of network architecture is appropriate to a particular application, and we must usually tell the package how many neurodes, how many levels, and how many and what kind of interconnects to use. But they do let us design networks without explicitly coding low-level mathematical details of the model. We no longer need to write the network simulation code, and more important in terms of time saving, we need not provide the large amount of code required to make the simulation user friendly. The producer of one commercial simulation package states that 70 percent of their software code relates solely to user interface issues; we believe this estimate to be conservative. A well-written, convenient user interface is indeed more valuable than the code for the neural network model itself.

Neurocomputers

For many applications, the days of the simulation program are numbered. Neurocomputers are reshaping the way neural network

---

What's in a Name? The Sequel

Emulator and *virtual processor* are other names commonly used for neurocomputers. Both are accurate. The term *emulator* reflects the fact that the machines copy the action of true neural networks. To call them virtual processors expresses the fact that the neurodes and connection paths do not physically exist in a neurocomputer.

---

research and development is done and are making feasible applications that are too demanding for even the fastest simulations.

A neurocomputer is a dedicated, special-purpose digital computer optimized to perform efficiently the multiplications and other mathematical operations common in neural network simulations. Using high clock rates, high-speed bus structures, ROM-based control instructions, special-purpose arithmetic chips, and a generous supply of fast memory, a neurocomputer mimics the concerted action of an entire interconnected network of neurodes using one or, at most, a few microprocessors. It should be clear from this description, however, that a neurocomputer is still only simulating a parallel, analog neural network with a serial, digital computer, albeit one that is specialized and optimized for neural network simulations.

In the simplest neurocomputer, one high-speed microprocessor assumes the identity of each virtual neurode in turn, applying input signals to the network, evaluating its activity level, calculating all of its associated synapse weights, and storing these quantities in RAM memory. When every neurode in the system has been treated in this way, that is, when the entire network has been updated, the microprocessor reports the final system values to the outside world and begins the process again.

Such machines operate from ten to several thousand times faster than software-only simulations of the same networks run on general-purpose digital computers. All available neurocomputers consist of one or more hardware boards internally or externally attached to a host digital computer. In these systems, the neurocomputer acts as a coprocessor to the host computer's regular general-purpose processor and is generally controlled by a supervisory program run on the host computer. This arrangement allows efficient use of both the host systems and the neurocomputer's processors and memories, since both systems act in concert but largely independently.

The value of neurocomputers lies in two areas. The first is the size of the network they can mimic. Commercially available systems can emulate networks having several million neurodes and interconnects, and these limitations are expanding constantly. Neurocomputers are currently the only practical way to implement neural networks having more than a few hundred neurodes and a substantial number of interconnections. Their second value is operating speed. The unit of speed for a neurocomputer is interconnects per second (IPS). Systems now available are capable of well over 10 million IPS in recall mode—that is, when training is not taking place. For some applications, such systems are capable of emulating large networks in real time. (Although such speed ratings are far from the best means of evaluating a neurocomputer, they at least offer one reasonably objective comparison among models. Truly meaningful hardware ratings will have to wait for the field to become less fluid and for independent benchmarking systems to be developed.)

The necessity of maintaining arrays in memory that keep track of thousands or millions of interconnection paths and of calculating and storing an associated synaptic weight for every one of these virtual interconnects during each update cycle limits the speed of both simulations and neurocomputers. It would seem to be much better if we could use real, physical neurodes, interconnections, and synapses and do away with these computational steps. Let's look at how this is being accomplished.

Networks in Hardware

There are a number of ways in which we can expect eventually to implement fully parallel neural networks in hardware. In the remainder of this chapter, we will look at electronic integrated circuits and at optical techniques, which are likely to provide at least modest near-term successes. In the concluding chapter of the book, we will discuss more-distant possibilities.

Because of their simple interconnect geometry, crossbar associative networks are naturals for microelectronic integrated-circuit implementations. As early as 1984, researchers at Bell Laboratories, the Jet Propulsion Laboratory, MIT's Lincoln Laboratory, and other

---

Problems with Integrated-Circuit Miniaturization

A designer who attempts to build a large neural network on a single chip faces problems common to all integrated circuits. We list some of the major problems here. The first is cross talk. Closely spaced wires tend to act like little antennas and get their signals mixed together even if they are not physically connected. A second is decreased operating speed. At the very small separations found in the most densely packed integrated circuits, inductances and capacitances between the various circuit elements become so large that they greatly slow the rate of travel of electrical signals. A third is that the time spent by an electron in passing through some parts of highly miniaturized circuits is not long enough for the electron to affect the circuit. A fourth has to do with the microscopic distribution of the elements placed into the silicon to give it the desired electrical characteristics. On a macroscopic scale, these elements are randomly distributed; on a microscopic scale, however, there is no way to ensure

---

institutions constructed experimental integrated-circuit neural networks using standard silicon integrated circuit fabrication techniques. These chips had from 12 to 50 or more fully interconnected neurodes. Since that time, these and other workers have made continuing progress, and several small, integrated-circuit neural network designs are, or will soon be, commercially available.

Silicon digital integrated-circuit technology is mature, and integrated-circuit manufacturers routinely produce chips a few millimeters square containing over 100,000 components. In these chips, individual features can be as small as 1 micron (about 39 millionths of an inch), and techniques are under development that would allow these minimum feature sizes to shrink to 0.1 micron. Even with 1 micron minimum feature sizes, we might expect it to be possible to fabricate very large neural networks. So far, this is not the case, and some of those who developed the early neural network chips now

that they will be distributed evenly enough to guarantee uniform electrical properties to the silicon.

A fifth problem is electromigration. Electrons passing down the tiny conductors bump the atoms and cause them to migrate slowly toward the positive end of the wire. There are so few atoms in the tiny interconnect wires of these circuits in the first place that even a small rearrangement sometimes results in a break in the wire. Sixth, there is the problem of off-chip interconnect delays. For a given number of neurodes on each chip, the number of interchip connections required increases directly as the number of neurodes in the network being implemented. For instance, a 1-million-neurode network will require 1000 chips and 1000 sets of interconnecting wires. The speed of operation of such a system will probably be slower than if all neurodes were on the same chip because it takes time for the electrical signals to move the distance between chips. Finally, there is a serious difficulty arising from the number of pins we can physically attach to a chip. This makes it difficult to get rapid input and output for large masses of data. It also causes difficulty in building highly interconnected network structures from multiple chips.

estimate that the maximum number of neurodes that can be placed on one chip may never exceed a few thousand for fully connected networks such as crossbars. These same workers have turned their efforts to developing methods to connect many relatively small chips in parallel to construct networks having a large number of neurodes.

In order to appreciate the difficulties these workers have encountered, let's compare the process of simulating a neural network to that of producing one in hardware. In the simulations and neurocomputers discussed, neurodes, interconnects, and synapses are not real entities; activities and synaptic weights are only numerical values stored at specific locations in the computer's memory. Interconnects do not even need to be considered in these systems; the existence or nonexistence of a synaptic weight between two neurodes is tantamount to the existence or nonexistence of an interconnect. It is the computationally demanding task of updating and keeping track of a large number of neurode activities and a larger number of synapse weights that severely limits the speed of simulations and causes even the much faster neurocomputers to be only marginally useful for many applications.

In hardware implementations, however, interconnects are physical wires or circuit traces, synapses are resistors or other components, and neurodes are made of transistors and other circuit elements. Finding space for interconnects on integrated-circuit chips is not a serious problem for regular, fully connected networks. For example, a crossbar interconnect structure is laid down as two sets of straight wires at right angles. Five hundred 1-micron wires can easily be laid down in a 1-millimeter length using present day integrated-circuit techniques. This would allow 250,000 synapses to be fabricated onto a 1-millimeter square area, assuming they were designed so as to fit under the intersection area of the wires.

It would require many square millimeters, however, to fabricate the 500 neurodes associated with these interconnects and synapses. Although its construction is simple compared to a microprocessor or other traditional computing element, each neurode must sum the inputs from other neurodes, compute the appropriate input/output transfer function, and provide the power to drive as many other neurodes as it is connected to. As a result, even the simplest neurode design must contain many transistors, diodes, resistors, capacitors, and other circuit elements, all of which take up far more space than the interconnect or synapse structures of simple crossbar networks.

When they are implemented in a microelectronic integrated circuit, even the interconnects and synapses are often not the simple structures we might envision them to be. The simplest synapse is a resistor, and some crossbar designs are able to accommodate synaptic resistors in the crossbar structure with only a slight increase in area. So far, however, synapses of this kind are not modifiable, but some researchers believe that solving the modifiable synapse problem is just a matter of finding the right resistor material and learning how to control it effectively. If so, we will soon have truly plastic synapses that fit into the crossbar area.

Another class of synapses uses varying amounts of electric charge stored on integrated-circuit capacitors to represent the weights of synapses. Charge leaks from these capacitors quickly, however, and must be constantly replaced if the synaptic strength represented by the stored charge is not to be forgotten. Thus the capacitive design, as with most other modifiable synapse designs, requires a number of supporting transistors and other circuit elements, all of which take up much more space than the nonmodifiable resistive materials.

In spite of all these difficulties, great progress is being made in the effort to create networks on a chip. While the majority of the effort to date has begun with the simple crossbar network design, more and more researchers are beginning to try to build more complex networks on chips. Backpropagation is one of the prime candidates for this, and some preliminary chips have been built. In addition Syntonics, based in Portland, Oregon, has begun to build a modified ART network on a chip. The company claims the chips can be used like building blocks to create networks of usable size. The microcircuits are planned to be commercially available before the end of 1989. These chips, and others planned for commercial release in the next few months, will mark the first time a true hardware implementation is sold on the open market.

Optical Neural Networks

Almost since neural networks were conceived, people have sought to implement them using optical techniques. One reason lies in the potential speed of optical neural networks. Another arises from the interconnect and interference problems we just discussed. Let's look at the speed advantage first.

With optical fibers being used increasingly to carry telephone conversations, most of us are aware that light beams can carry information, and most of us know that the speed of light is the fastest speed possible. In air, light travels 300 million (3×10^8) meters per second, or about 1 foot every nanosecond. If we were to build an all-optical neural network with interconnect dimensions of about a foot that transmits the light through air, we might expect the one-way trip time required for a signal to pass through the system to be about a nanosecond. Even adding the time it takes for light to interact with the optical components of the system, we still might expect an optical neural network to operate eventually from one hundred to one thousand times faster than electronic neural networks. For the same reason, we would expect optical beams to provide very short travel times when used as interconnects between electrooptic neurodes.

Light beams offer other potential advantages when used as interconnects. As with the speed advantage, the merit of using light beams to carry information around a system comes from the unique properties of light. Light beams are especially useful for interconnecting parts of neural networks because in air or vacuum they can pass through each other without interacting. Thus, we can send signals among any number of neurodes through the same space without those signals getting mixed together. If we are clever and use the property of light known as polarization, we can even combine two separate light beams into one, make them travel together along the same path for some distance, and then separate them again without intermixing the information they carry.

If we wish, however, we can permanently combine the information of several beams into one. We can then spread the resulting beam, change its direction, or break it into a number of identical beams by inserting lenses, mirrors, prisms, or other optical devices into the path of the original beam. These operations are just the kinds useful in neural processing.

There are scores of optical neural network implementations, most of which perform a specific task or demonstrate one aspect of neural processing. These implementations range from all-optical with no electronic parts, to hybrid optical-electronic, or optoelectronic, designs full of devices combining optical and electronic characteristics. In both approaches, light beams, usually generated by a laser, carry the information around the system. In an all-optical approach implementation of neurodes and dynamic manipulation of light beams are accomplished using purely optical means such as holograms.

A hybrid design implements neurodes and manipulates light beams using active solid-state devices such as photodetectors and spatial light modulators (SLMs). A photodetector is an optoelectronic device that changes the information carried on a light beam into an electronic signal. An SLM usually consists of a two-dimensional array of many individual optical elements. These elements intersect a light beam and perform some operation on it. The operation on the beam might be to change its direction, add information to it (modulate it), or threshold it. An SLM can even be designed so that its elements sum the information contained in several beams. This, in combination with a thresholding capability, allows an SLM to mimic the action of an array of neurodes.

A hybrid neural network design may allow its information to be carried electronically in some portions of the system. For instance, by combining standard optical lenses with others having cylindrical shapes, we can average a number of beams together and combine them onto one photodetector. We can also do the opposite and spread the information in one beam among a number of detectors. In this way, for instance, the input-summation operation we are now familiar with can be carried out merely by focusing the outputs of many neurodes onto a single input detector associated with some other neurode. Similarly, the output of a neurode can be fanned out to many others by spreading the light from its output laser with the proper lenses.

Optical techniques offer a natural means to implement crossbar networks for two reasons: (1) the high degree of connectivity required by such networks is easily achieved optically, and (2) optical systems can directly implement vector-matrix multiplication and matrix summation. Recall that these matrix operations lie at the heart of the mathematical description of associative memories.

There have to be some hitches to this marvelous technology, and there are. Many of them boil down to materials. The devices used in both all-optical and hybrid optoelectronic systems use specially developed and processed optical materials. Optical neural network designs badly strain the capabilities of available materials, and future availability of networks with extended capabilities depends heavily on the development of new or improved nonlinear materials that are cheaper but have better characteristics—faster and larger response, wider frequency range, better spatial resolution, and higher mechanical strength, among others. Development of such materials is a slow, expensive, and by no means certain process. Research in this area, however, is driven worldwide by critical defense and industrial demands not connected with neural networks, and we may expect continuing improvements which neural network implementors can take advantage of.

In addition to the obvious materials problems, optical systems must also cope with relatively bulky and mechanically sensitive physical systems, difficulties in achieving high numerical and physical resolution in the system, and problems in adapting the weights of the SLMs. In addition, hybrid optical and electronic systems must deal with the problem of producing an efficient optical-electronic interface. All of these problems are serious issues that must be resolved before commercially practical optical or optoelectronic neurocomputers become a reality.

All-optical realizations of neural networks are thought by some to be the wave of the future. Certainly all-optical systems are capable of high speeds and may eventually prove nearly as versatile as purely electronic or optoelectronic realizations. We think, however, that the future in this case is well over ten years away.

Hybrid electronic-optical systems have not yet begun to reach their potential, and over the next 5 to 10 years, we expect optoelectronic implementations of neural networks to become increasingly successful and sophisticated. A key link in the chain leading from research plaything to commercial system is the perfection of one or more of the SLM designs now under development. In the longer term, continued improvement of these and other critical components of optoelectronic neural networks depends heavily on continued improvement of current nonlinear optical materials and development of new ones. We expect this to happen.

We have discussed the way neural networks are implemented. It is now time to take one more long look at how these implementations can be used. In the next chapter, we will look at selected examples illustrating some of the many ways neural networks can be used to solve real-world problems.

I like work; it fascinates me.
I can sit and look at it for hours.
—J. K. Jerome

18 Neural Network Applications

Throughout this book we have described a variety of neural network applications. Some of these were built as a proof-of-principle demonstration; some are commercial products. In this chapter, we want to consider several application areas we think will prove to be the most fruitful in the next few years. By this we do not intend to imply that these areas are the only ones where neural networks can be used; we are sure that the technology will reach into far more realms than anyone can possibly envision today, including some that do not exist now. In the meantime, the specific applications we address here are meant to convey a sense of the range of problems neural networks can solve.

In particular, we see four very broad categories of problems that seem ripe for neural network exploitation: expert systems, process control, robotics, and signal processing. We have chosen a single example application in each of these four areas to discuss, but there are dozens of others we might have used.

An Expert Mortgage Insurance Underwriter

An expert system is a relatively new invention, deriving from the efforts of workers in the field of AI. An expert system in its simplest form consists of an inference engine and a rule base. The rule base is a set of if-then rules: *if* (it is raining outside), *then* (be sure to take your umbrella and wear your raincoat). An expert system attempts to codify the knowledge and experience of an expert in some limited area into a collection of such rules. The inference engine acts as a sort of guide through these rules, selecting the rules appropriate to a given situation (according to the contents of the if clause) and then ensuring that the corresponding action (as detailed in the then clause) is performed. A typical inference engine reasons its way through the rule base, performing the actions specified by each rule that it fires and eventually (one hopes!) coming to the correct conclusion.

Expert systems technology has proved to be a big success because it fills an important need. Companies can ill afford to lose senior experts, but neither can they keep these people on the same job year after year. Truly competent people are bound to be promoted or move to other jobs, causing, in effect, the loss of their expertise. If at least some of that experience can be captured in expert systems, there are fewer barriers to moving the knowledgeable worker to a more important challenge. Expert systems have proved their worth in many fields, from the aerospace industry to medicine to finance. These systems have moved out of the AI laboratory and into our culture.

There are two key problems with these systems, however, that limit their usability: (1) figuring out all the proper rules to include in the rule base (the knowledge acquisition problem) and (2) maintaining the rule base once we have built the system.

When the expert system builder (usually called a knowledge engineer) begins, one of the first tasks is to write down the if-then rules that apply to a situation. This means that the knowledge engineer must consult closely and repeatedly with a human expert to ensure that the rules correctly capture expertise. When the first expert systems were built, a strange phenomenon was noticed: there appeared to be some likelihood that the experts were lying, or at least witholding their full understanding of the problem. No matter how congenial or cooperative the expert appeared to the knowledge engineer, when the rule base was compared to the expert's understanding, there would always be a reaction of, "Well, I forgot to tell you that when this indicator is in that range, the system needs to do something else." At first knowledge engineers assumed that the experts, either consciously or unconsciously, were concerned with eventually being replaced by the system and were actually sabotaging development of the expert system.

Explanation through Confabulation

There is one major drawback to using a neural network as an expert system. In any system that people must directly interact with, we nearly always want the system to be able to explain why it makes the judgments it does. In a traditional expert system, with its collection of explicit if-then rules, it is quite easy for the system to respond to such a question with a list of the rules it followed to produce its answer. This allows the user of the system to feel comfortable that the decision presented makes sense. In a neural network, we have no such rules for users who ask for an explanation. There is no logical chain of reasoning that details how the network got from the initial input to its final answer. As a result, the likelihood of the network's gaining acceptance by the people who must directly interact with it is distinctly lessened.

One proposal on how to overcome this is to combine a neural network and a traditional rule-based system. The network would be allowed to respond to each input case and produce the appropriate decision. Whenever the user asked for an explanation, the rule-based system would be provided with the input and the network's decision and allowed to reason backward from the decision to the input to produce a plausible chain of reasoning. This then would be the user's explanation. It would be as though the system behaved as people often do: reacting instinctively and then rationalizing their behavior when asked for an explanation.

As experience with these systems expanded, it came to be realized that this was not the case at all. It is simply true that people have a difficult time articulating how they solve problems. In fact, while some situations are consciously handled by explicit if-then rules, in many other situations we do not reason our way through the problem but merely react to it. Only after the fact, if asked, do we then go back and construct a chain of reasoning to justify our response. The problem with this is that the task of actually defining the appropriate if-then rules for an expert system rule base becomes excruciatingly difficult. On top of this, if there are multiple experts, it is often found that the experts themselves disagree on the rules to be applied to a given situation. (Anyone asking three tax experts for advice can attest to this phenomenon.) Reconciling these divergent opinions into a coherent and consistent set of rules can become a gargantuan task indeed.

The second problem with expert systems is that once we have built a large rule base, containing perhaps thousands of rules, we have to maintain and correct it as the system is used. Since many of the rules interact and interrelate to many other rules, the tasks of correcting errors and extending the rule base to cover new situations can be enormously difficult. This causes the maintenance of large expert systems to be expensive, time-consuming, and often uncertain.

Neural networks may offer a better way, at least where an expert system requires a rule base that is particularly difficult to generate and maintain. For problems where the solution relies as much on the judgment of the expert as it does on a specific, articulatable set of rules, a neural network is a likely candidate. Let's look at an example system to see how this might work in practice.

Nestor, Inc. is a neural network company that has specialized in developing products for the financial and insurance industries. One of its achievements is an expert system that determines whether a mortgage insurance company should accept a particular application. Nestor's network is a proprietary algorithm called RCE (reduced Coulomb energy), which we have not covered in this book. For the purposes of our discussion, however, it is not the specific kind of network used that is important but the overall design of the system. We will look at exactly how Nestor researchers Edward Collins, Sushmito Ghosh, and Christopher Scofield built their system, called the MNNLS (Multiple Neural Network Learning System).

A mortgage loan application contains an enormous amount of data. The MNNLS, however, uses only about twenty-five fields of information, separated into four distinct categories. The first category contains cultural information about the applicant—items such as the borrower's credit rating, number of children, and employment history. The second category contains financial information about the borrower, including income, debts, and how much income is nonsalary. The third category contains information on the mortgage itself, such as the amount, interest rate, and duration of the loan. Finally, the last category contains information about the property, such as the age of the property, its appraised value, and whether it is a single-family house or multiple apartment units.

The MNNLS uses a unique scheme to process this information. The system itself is a collection of nine neural networks, arranged in three layers of three networks each. Each layer is considered to be a panel of three experts in the field. One of these experts concentrates on the borrower's financial information, one concentrates on the cultural and mortgage information, and the third views all four categories of information equally.

When a mortgage application is presented to the network, the first panel of experts (the first layer of three networks) tries to decide if the application should be accepted or rejected. The three experts in this layer are polled; if all agree, the decision is made, and the next application is presented. If any of the three disagree with the others, the application is bounced to the second layer, containing its own panel of three experts. The second-layer experts are set up to concentrate on subsets of the total information, just as before. These three experts are then polled for their decisions. Again, if all agree to accept or reject the application, the decision is made; if any disagree, the application is bounced one more time to the last layer of expert networks.

The cleverness of this approach lies in its ability to process a wide range of problems. The first layer of the network can accurately handle most problems (coarse categorization), the second handles moderately hard problems, and the third layer processes the very difficult problems (fine categorization). By using this network of networks, the MNNLS can handle a much wider range of problems without sacrificing accuracy or having to use individual networks that are extremely large. Compared to human underwriters, MNNLS performed remarkably well. Nestor collected a database of 5048 total cases, of which 2597, or about 51 percent were accepted by the human underwriters, and 2451 were rejected. The cases came from a particular mortgage insurance company's records over the final four months of 1987 and from offices all over the United States. As a result, the cases included decisions from a number of individual human underwriters. When compared to the decisions actually reached by human underwriters, the MNNLS agreed about 82 percent of the time. (Up to 96 percent accuracy was obtained by insisting on complete agreement by all network experts; unfortunately this has the effect of not permitting the system to decide all cases.)

What about the cases where the system disagreed with the underwriter? Nestor scientists carefully analyzed many of the error instances. About half the time, the system would have accepted the application, but the underwriter rejected it; the rest of the time the system would have rejected the application, but the underwriter accepted it. In nearly every case, it was found that the human underwriter's decision was inconsistent with the examples used for training; the MNNLS system proved itself to be more consistent in applying the underwriting rules than the underwriters were.

The MNNLS system was more consistent in part because it effectively insists on a consensus opinion of a panel of experts. A human underwriter processing an application is a single expert working alone; it would be far too labor intensive to insist on a panel of people to process every application. Because of the clever design of the MNNLS, however, this panel of experts is literally built-in to the automated system, resulting in a higher degree of consistency and (ideally) better judgments on the mortgage insurance applications. While it will take several years for Nestor to be able to compare the MNNLS's judgment against actual mortgage performance (as opposed to the human underwriter's judgment), it seems clear that neural networks can indeed make a competent expert system.

A Process Controller That Drives the Freeway

In 1987 John Shepanski and Scott Macy of TRW in Redondo Beach, California, created a modified backpropagation network that learned to drive—and survive—on a simulated freeway. We have named their network the neurocommuter. It illustrates well the use of networks for process control, which is potentially one of the most fruitful application areas for neural networks. Before we describe the network and its action, let's examine what a typical process controller does.

Many industrial processes are no longer controlled directly by a person; rather, a process controller, usually electronic, constantly compares the actual state of the process to an ideal state for that process. We use *state* here to mean "condition"—how the process is doing. The controller determines the state of the process by reading sensors built into the processing apparatus and that constantly monitor important process variables—the temperature at a number of locations, the speed of several motors, the flow rate of a fluid, supplies of raw materials, or a host of other physical quantities. We call these monitored physical quantities the "measured variables."

In the simplest type of control, the process controller maintains each measured variable at some preset value. In a more common application, ideal values for each measured variable for each instant of time are programmed into the controller. It then forces these variables to match their preprogrammed values by continuously adjusting the value of one or more controlled variables. For instance, if the measured variable is the speed of a motor, the corresponding controlled variable might be the voltage supplied to the motor; if the measured variable is the temperature of a liquid, the corresponding controlled variable might be the current maintained in a heater immersed in the liquid.

Although the idea is simple, the practice is often decidedly not simple. First, it is not unusual for the required settings of several process parameters to depend on each other in a complex way. For instance, the correct settings of several motor speeds, several temperatures, and a flow rate may depend on the available amount of one or more raw material supplies, or worse, on some uncontrollable quality of a raw material such as its moisture content. In such cases, forcing measured variables to match preprogrammed values will not work because they cannot be known ahead of time. The system must adapt to conditions that are not predictable. It is in this and similar adaptive control situations that neural networks should make a large contribution.

Shepanski and Macy's freeway driving network is a simple example of an adaptive controller and is perfect for our purpose. Let's say that we want to use a neural network to make a robot system—call it the commuter—that will maintain a safe and reasonably constant highway speed on a moderately busy interstate highway. At the very least, our commuter would have to be able to steer and operate a throttle. It would also need to be able to establish a safe separation between its car and the one ahead, and it would need to be able to change lanes so that it could maintain an optimal speed and not be forced to stay forever behind slower traffic. Ideally the commuter would need to operate brakes, but we can assume for a minimal system that frictional forces quickly slow the vehicle when the robot commuter decreases the throttle.

In order to perform these control functions, the commuter would need to know several things about its environment; that is, it would need to be supplied with several measured variables. It would need to be able to measure the distance between its car and other cars on the road; it would need to know its own speed and either the speed or the relative speed of all cars ahead of and behind it in both lanes; it would need to know which lane it and each nearby car was in; it would need to know the angle it was traveling with respect to the road; and it would need to know the deviation of its position from the center of its driving lane. It is this minimal system that Shepanski and Macy taught to drive a simulated freeway.

Their first attempts were less than successful. When they turned the untrained commuter and one pace car loose on a simulated two-lane road with straight and curved sections, the commuter's speed oscillated wildly and it regularly ran over the pace car. By allowing a human observer to start and stop training judiciously, however, the commuter learned to keep a proper distance between itself and the pace car after about 1000 trials.

For the full freeway simulation, two new and more sophisticated training approaches were adopted; these proved to be successful. One method was used to teach the commuter to follow a road and maintain proper spacing and another to teach it when to change lanes safely. The former operations involved control of a continuous variable, and the latter involved decisions.

To teach the commuter to control the continuous variables, it was given full sensor input and allowed to react as it moved along the simulated freeway, but actual control of the simulated vehicle was left in the hands of a human operator. In this way, the network's synapse weights were trained as if it had control of the vehicle even though it did not; it could make mistakes without suffering any consequences. The human operator passed control of the vehicle to the commuter at intervals to judge its progress in acquiring the necessary skills. Shepanski and Macy taught the commuter to pass safely by telling it when to change and when not to change lanes. This binary pass/don't pass information supplied the desired output for training the network; sensor information served as the training input. By this method, they were able to use backpropagation as their supervised learning scheme.

The researchers found that the commuter took on the driving characteristics of its teacher. If it was trained by an overly cautious driver, the commuter seldom changed lanes to pass another car; it accepted the resulting lower speed as a desirable alternative to passing. If it was trained by an aggressive driver, however, the commuter passed frequently and cut off other cars as it attempted to fit its vehicle into barely adequate openings in the adjacent lane.

The network that finally emerged from this research has two blocks that are, in reality, two complete, multilayer networks in a hierarchical arrangement. The first network controls the commuter's speed and decides when a lane change is desirable. It receives speed information for the commuter's vehicle, as well as distance, lane, and relative speed information for other vehicles. The second network receives lane change decisions and such sensor input as lane number, relative vehicle orientation, road curvature, and the lateral (cross-lane) distance to other cars. It controls the steering of the commuter's vehicle.

Both networks are three-layer backpropagation networks, but they have different architectures from the ones discussed previously in the book. In these networks, the input layer is fully connected to both the middle and output layers. The designers settled on this more complex interconnection scheme and the resulting more complicated error backpropagation procedure because the resulting networks trained more quickly and reacted more smoothly than ones that used the standard interlayer connection method discussed in chapter 14.

We chose to discuss this application not because it is immediately useful as an automobile autopilot; it is not. Rather, it illustrates a number of features that must be present in more serious process control applications. First, it is adaptive. The vehicle does not follow a predetermined path but must adapt its operation to existing conditions. Second, the network utilizes a hierarchical structure. We expect that systems capable of complex control tasks will need the combination of versatility and specificity afforded by hierarchical schemes. Third, a blend of training methods was employed in preparing the network. Again, we expect that complex robots and other adaptive systems will require training in small steps and utilization of more than one training approach, both of which these researchers employed. Finally, we think that at least one of the training methods is likely to become common in such applications. It seems natural to train a network to perform a complex series of operations or a difficult task by letting it watch a human expert perform the same operation or task until it is competent to take it over. This master-apprentice approach should prove useful in applications from conduct of single manufacturing operations to control of large autonomous systems. We will also see it in the following application.

A Robotic Arm

Scenes of robot arms performing welding and other operations on automobile assembly lines tell us that AI techniques have enjoyed some measure of success in the robotics field. But robotic arms are usually programmed to carry out one specific task. Separate programs or lookup tables must be provided to dictate the detailed motion of the arm throughout its trajectory, and these programs or tables must be different for each object the arm grasps. What is needed are adaptive robotic arms that can learn to move over any pathway while carrying a variety of loads. Neural networks are beginning to provide these adaptive arms.

The problem of providing adaptive motor control has already been solved once—by nature. Fortunately, significant progress has been made by neurobiologists in the past several years in understanding the way in which the motor cortex, cerebellum, and other areas of the central nervous system interact to allow humans to perform complex motor tasks smoothly under a variety of external conditions. It is not surprising, therefore, that one of the areas in which recent neural network research has profited the most from neurobiological studies is adaptive motor control.

The seemingly simple act of reaching for and lifting a cup of coffee to our lips requires a constant stream of real-time information feedback to the brain and muscles from both internal and external sources. This means that our brains require not only constant information on, for instance, the location and velocity of every nearby object in the outside world but also an accurate, detailed model of how our own musculoskeletal system works.

Mitsuo Kawato, Kazunori Furukawa, Hiroyuki Miyamoto, and Ryoji Suzuki, of Osaka University, have developed and demonstrated a hierarchical adaptive robot arm controller based on current understanding of human motor control. The biological model on which they base their controller is shown schematically in figure 18.1, adapted from drawings by the researchers. We must understand this biological model at least superficially to appreciate the manner and degree to which these researchers implement it with neural networks.

The primary action of the model is shown in bold lines and proceeds something like this. An idea (pick up the coffee cup) is trans-

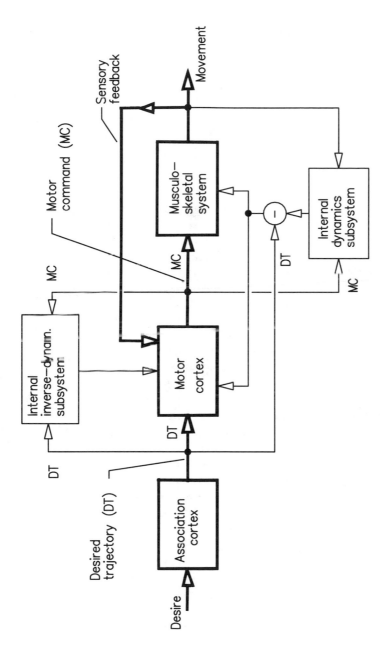

Figure 18.1. Block diagram of the robot arm system

mitted to an area of the brain, the association cortex, which translates the idea into a series of rough motion commands (move your hand out, down, and to the right toward the coffee cup). In the figure, this series of commands is labeled the "desired trajectory" (DT). When this desired trajectory information arrives at the part of the brain known as the motor cortex, it is translated into the approximate muscle forces necessary to accomplish the desired action. We have labeled the output command of the motor cortex the "motor command" (MC). This series of commands causes the muscles to start moving along a trajectory in the general direction of the cup. At this point, the motion is quite rough, as if the eyes of the reacher were closed. As the muscles move, however, input from the eyes and other sensors in the body provides sensory feedback information, which the motor cortex uses to fine-tune the motor command.

This sounds good, but in practice, it does not work very well. Motions using only this feedback scheme are jerky, slow, and subject to uncontrollable oscillations, even for unloaded arms—ones not carrying an object. The scheme often fails completely if the arm is loaded. Two other feedback paths are needed to carry out the smooth body motions characteristic of animals. The first added feedback path is the lower one through the subsystem labeled "internal dynamical subsystem." In the biological model, this box corresponds to specific areas of the central nervous system; in our robot arm version of this subsystem, we can just assume that the box represents a neural network. This subsystem (in both the biological and robot models) uses the motor command and the sensory feedback as input signals.

In the biological model, this subsystem is an adaptive network, and it has observed the corrective actions required by a great variety of specific combinations of motor commands and muscle motions of the coffee reacher for many years. It has formed, therefore, a set of opinions—a dynamic model of the motions that actually result from a given set of motor commands. This subsystem predicts the probable trajectory of the arm every time it receives a set of motor commands and sensory feedback signals. When translated into the robot arm model, the corresponding neural network subsystems output is passed through a small network whose output is the difference between this probable trajectory and the desired trajectory. This difference signal is sent to both the motor cortex and the muscles of the robot arm. Thus, the lower feedback path in the figure provides a signal that constantly updates and corrects the motor commands arriving at the robot's muscles.

The subsystem uses constant input from external cues to achieve smooth motion of the arm toward the coffee cup. Think about your own actions, however. You usually do not need to watch your hand carefully as you reach for an object; rather you normally glance at the object, perform your reach, and check the action only at critical points. In walking, even less external sensory input is used. This capability requires an internal knowledge, or model, of the way your body moves under specific circumstances. It is the second, upper, feedback loop that provides this model.

In this loop, the motor command and the desired trajectory are each provided as inputs to the subsystem labeled the "internal inverse-dynamical subsystem." Note that this subsystem does not receive any information on how the motion is going relative to the external world. Instead it learns something about the internal workings of the overall system: what desired trajectories usually produce which motor commands. Thus, the subsystem develops a knowledge of the range of possible motor commands that can result from a particular desired trajectory. It can produce outputs that help the motor cortex control the motion of the arm without direct external input. This loop provides several dividends. It grants us an ability to generalize from a familiar action to a similar one that has not been carefully learned; it allows the motor cortex to vary its commands slightly to take into account transitory internal conditions, such as motion of the body; and it lets us smoothly repeat the same trajectory when setting the coffee cup back down, even though the muscle forces required for the task differ greatly from those used when no heavy object was in our hand.

The Osaka University researchers built a hierarchical neural network system that controlled a robotic arm with three degrees of freedom. The term *three degrees of freedom* means that the location in space of the end point of the arm is completely specified by three angles. For each network shown in the figure, they used adalinelike neurons having nonlinear filters in their input lines. The general form of these networks is shown schematically in figure 18.2. Signal inputs, training inputs, and network outputs were either arm angles or motor torques as appropriate to the subsystem. The networks were similar in form to those used by Donald Specht for his vector-cardiograph network described previously. The forms of the nonlinear filters were not simple polynomials in this case but were combinations of trigonometric functions and first and second derivatives of the specifying angles chosen from the equations of motion for such an arm. For the internal inverse-dynamical subsystem, for instance, 26 nonlinear inputs were used on the 3 threshold elements controlling the three angular motions.

As a comparison, the researchers first put the arm through a series of standard motions under computer control, using only the sensory feedback path. They then connected the feedback and training inputs of the internal dynamical subsystem and allowed the arm to operate under computer control while the subsystem learned. After about an hour, the output of the internal dynamical subsystem was connected to the system and the series of standard motions repeated. The system was more accurate but still rather slow.

The inputs and output of the internal inverse-dynamical subsystem were then connected and a series of specific motor patterns run for 20 minutes each. As training proceeded, the inverse subsystem

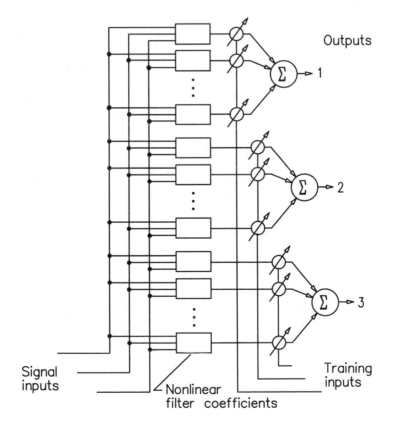

Figure 18.2 The adaline-like neurodes of the robot arm.

gradually took over as the main controller of the arm, and the operation of the arm became both smoother and more accurate. Moreover, with the inverse subsystem in place, the arm was able to perform rapidly unfamiliar motions on which it had not been trained. It was able to do this because the hierarchical network does not learn specific motions that go with specific motor commands but rather develops a general model of the dynamics of the inner workings of the robotic arm. Finally, the system was able to adapt to a limited amount of loading. More complete adaptability to load changes would require additional adaptive neurodes to develop a more comprehensive internal model of the dynamics under a wide variety of load conditions.

Although the researchers do not give the total number of neurodes and synapse weights required for the system described, it is not large. A more versatile 6-degree-of-freedom arm required only 800 synaptic weights. Thus, Kawato, Furukawa, Miyamoto, and Suzuki have demonstrated that, using a relatively small neural network, a robotic arm system can be built capable of learning general motion under varying load conditions. Unlike many other systems, their arm does not need to be told in advance the exact trajectories to follow, nor does a human operator need to understand well the mechanical properties of the robot arm being trained. As this and other similar systems are perfected, we can expect to see great strides in this domain of the field of robotics.

Sonar Signal Processing

The problem of classifying unknown radar and sonar returns is of obvious commercial and military importance, and if you have been paying attention, you know that it is one that neural networks should be good at. Paul Gorman, at the Allied Signal Aerospace Technology Center, and Terrence Sejnowski, of Johns Hopkins University, have demonstrated a small backpropagation network that performs a simple sonar-return classification task as successfully as trained human subjects.

Gorman and Sejnowski had a dual intent in their work. They clearly wanted to demonstrate the suitability of neural network technology for real-world signal classification tasks, but they also wanted to add to the store of scientific knowledge on backpropagation networks. As a result, they spent considerable energy examining the role and operation of the middle layer in their networks.

Using a fast minicomputer, they simulated backpropagation networks having varying numbers of neurodes in their middle layers. They then trained and tested these networks on standard data sets and compared the classification success of each network to that of the other networks, to a standard signal processing algorithm, and to humans trained on the same data.

Gorman and Sejnowski chose the sonar returns from two similar objects, a metal cylinder and a roughly cylindrical rock, as their test cases. Both objects were slightly under two meters in length and were positioned on a sandy ocean floor. The researchers made recordings of sonar returns from a distance of about 10 meters over essentially the entire range of possible angles between the object's long axis and the returned sonar signal, the so-called aspect angle. To obtain the data, they used a frequency-swept system in which each pulse of outgoing sonar energy was swept, or chirped, rapidly over a wide frequency range.

The researchers took the Fourier transform of the recorded time-domain signals and broke the spectrum into 60 connected frequency bins, which were used as input to the network, just as in Kohonen's phonetic typewriter. In this case, however, the identity of the Fourier frequency bin of interest varied because the frequency of the chirped sonar signal was intentionally altered while the sonar returns were being collected. As a result, Gorman and Sejnowski appropriately offset the times after onset of the sonar return signal at which each frequency bin was collected.

Armed with a set of vectors representing 208 unambiguous return signals—111 cylinder and 97 rock—they began training their networks. For the training and test sets, they used 104 vectors selected to be statistically similar. Actually two kinds of training/test sets were selected: one to mimic the random distribution of aspect angles that might be encountered operationally, and another in which at least five examples from each aspect angle were included in each set. The performance of their network using either kind of training/test set was impressive. We report first the performance of those networks that were trained and tested using the randomly selected data. These networks would be expected to show the poorer classification capability of the two.

They used networks having 0, 2, 3, 6, 12, and 24 middle neurodes. All of the networks had 60 input neurodes, one for each frequency bin, and two output neurodes, one for rock and one for cylinder. As each network trained, Gorman and Sejnowski continuously plotted its success rate in classifying the training data. By the end of 300 training passes, the frequency of correct classification of the training set patterns was virtually stable for all of the networks. Two-layer networks with no middle layer initially trained faster than networks with middle layers but quickly began to saturate. Such networks averaged only about a 90 percent correct classification rate on training data. Networks having 2, 3, 6, and 12 middle-layer neurodes initially trained more slowly than two-layer networks but quickly outperformed their two-layer cousins. By the end of 300 passes, the network with two middle neurodes was able to classify correctly its training vector 96.5 percent of the time; those with 3, 6, and 12 were successful 98.8, 99.7, and 99.8 percent of the time, respectively. The network with 24 middle units showed no material improvement over one with 12 in these or subsequent tests.

On the test set, these same networks showed lower performance, as we would expect. The fully trained two-layer network correctly classified only 77.1 percent of the test set. The three-layer networks with 2, 3, 6, and 12 middle neurodes correctly identified 81.9, 82.0, 83.5, and 84.7 percent of the patterns, respectively.

The networks trained and tested using data sets chosen to have a good balance of examples from each aspect angle and that had 0, 2, 3, 6, and 12 middle neurodes identified 73.1, 85.7, 87.6, 89.3, and 90.4 percent of the test patterns correctly, respectively. With the exception of the two-layered network, these identification rates are four to six percentage points better than the corresponding networks discussed previously.

How do these results compare to those expected from other systems? The answer is gratifying to a neural network enthusiast. A popular signal processing algorithm, the nearest neighbor classifier, identified 82.7 percent of the patterns correctly. This number is lower than the highest values of either of the neural networks, 84.7 and 90.4 percent. In fact, both kinds of networks performed in the range expected for a theoretically optimal identifier. For the data used, that range was estimated to be 82.7 to 91.4 percent.

The researchers also compared the performance of the networks with that of humans trained on the same data. The humans were not trained on the frequency-domain waveforms. Rather, 100 of the original time-domain echo patterns from which the frequency-domain training and test sets had been constructed were selected at random. The frequency of each waveform was then electronically translated from the ultrasonic to the audio range and was used to train the human subjects. Another 100 similarly selected and treated waveforms from the original set of 208 were used to test the subjects. The trained human subjects identified 88 to 97 percent of the test patterns correctly. To probe into possible differences in the way the humans and networks went about classifying the sonar returns, Gorman and Sejnowski asked the subjects to identify the features that they knowingly used to identify each type of pattern. The subjects seemed frequently to use the attack, or onset time, of the cylinder waveform and the decay or falloff time of the rock waveform as major aids in identifying the patterns. The researchers found that a trained network used these same cues. Let's talk more about the researchers' investigations into the self-organization of the middle layers of their networks.

Gorman and Sejnowski spent considerable energy investigating the way in which the middle layers of their networks self-organized during training. The results of their investigation of the middle-layer strategies are both fascinating and potentially useful in designing more complex networks. They chose a network for detailed investigation that had three neurodes in its middle layer. This network had identified all but one of the patterns in the test set correctly. When they probed the way in which the middle layer of this network self-organized, they discovered that it had developed a definite strategy.

The basic method the network developed was to classify everything as a cylinder unless there was good evidence that it was a rock. This is understandable since the particular rock involved was roughly characterizable as a lumpy cylinder. The evidence that a return was actually from a rock took the form of a narrow-band feature, the shape of which did not depend on aspect angle. The frequency at which the narrow-band feature was centered did depend on aspect angle, however. The network divided the frequency spectrum spanned by the data into thirds and assigned the job of recognition of the narrow band feature in each of the three frequency ranges to one of its three neurodes. These spectral feature detectors served a dual purpose. If any one of the neurodes sensed the presence of the narrow-band feature, the return was probably from a rock; if none of them did, the return was probably from a cylinder. The network handled the few special cases not covered by this strategy by memorizing the locations of the peaks and valleys in the spectra of the troublesome returns. It handled only eight in this way.

Lest this cursory analysis mislead us into concluding that the network merely constructed an efficient set of spectral feature detectors appropriate to the data, Gorman and Sejnowski are quick to point out that this is not the case. What the network did was much more involved. It more nearly constructed a general model of rock-ness and cylinderness than a set of feature detectors by which it could distinguish between a rock and a cylinder. This observation is important. A system that constructs a model of its environment is of more use than one that simply develops an ability to recognize discrete features of that environment, and one that does both is even more useful. Fortunately there are indications that many neural network designs are capable of working on both levels simultaneously.

These applications are drawn from just a few of the fascinating problems that are currently being attacked by neural network researchers. There are hundreds of other problems under investigation as potential neural network applications. There are a number of applications under commercial development as well for problems ranging from chemical process control to the inspection of airline baggage for explosives and drugs. Several of these systems promise to be commercially competitive and successful products. In the next chapter we will offer some personal opinions on the near future of neural network technology and applications.

Consider nothing, before it comes to pass, as impossible.
— Cicero

19   A Look Ahead

This chapter is aptly titled "A Look Ahead," because this is where we dust off our crystal ball and try to envision how the development of neural networks might progress. We will stick out our necks a bit and talk about our vision of the future of this technology. Yet at the same time, it is important that we do so cautiously; neural network researchers have vivid recollections of the colorful hyperbole that attended the public awareness of artificial intelligence and the corresponding disappointment when practical realities did not live up to high-flown expectations. The resulting backlash has tarnished the luster of AI to those that matter most: industry, government, and research organizations. We would like to avoid such a backlash for neural networks by not making promises we cannot fulfill.

What is a reasonable set of expectations for this technology? What can it do in the months and years ahead? An occupational hazard of predicting the future is being wrong, and often very wrong. What's more, history has shown that even a well-informed technology forecaster is as likely to underestimate as to overestimate the impact of a technology or the time scale on which it will come into use. Nevertheless, we will press boldly onward and guess how the field will evolve over the next few years.

Let's consider the field from three separate perspectives and try to predict where each of these will be in the future: the development of neural network implementations of any variety or technology, the development of new neural network theory and paradigms, and the development of practical, marketable applications of neural networks and their influence in the marketplace.

Implementations Development

Hardware systems that truly implement neural networks are essential to the long-term development of this technology. Neural networks are not like conventional digital computers, and any implementation of them on such computers is, in a sense, merely an imitation. We have seen that neural networks are inherently both parallel and analog, so there is no existing commercially available hardware that implements them in a direct fashion. We therefore will briefly consider the development of software simulations, neurocomputer emulators, and true hardware implementations.

It seems evident that just as simulations have become better, faster, more user friendly, and more flexible (and we think this trend will continue), neurocomputers will also become faster, more powerful, cheaper and easier to use. It is likely that the current generation of software simulations has a limited lifetime, perhaps only a few more years. We think they will eventually become unable to compete with such faster-cheaper-easier neurocomputers. Although this is a likely consequence of our expanding technological base, it is not inevitable.

A new technology is like a sprouting seed. It is not enough that the seed merely sprouts; many more seeds sprout than develop into mature plants. Rather, a seed must come to life at the right time and in the right environment, and it must receive proper nourishment if it is to survive to maturity. As this book is being written, the field of neural networks is akin to a seed that has barely sprouted, and its survival is by no means certain.

Whether a new technology is successful depends on a number of things, and the history of technology is full of useful, even important ideas that never caught on. Some were introduced too early or failed because of expectations that were too high for the technology's performance. Others were too expensive or could not do needed jobs any better than existing technologies. Yet others were introduced at an inauspicious time—for instance, when there was an economic or intellectual blight on the land or no pressing military or economic impetus. Still other useful and good technologies have foundered because people just did not want them at the time. The picture telephone of the 1950s and the ambitious mass transport networks planned in the 1970s are examples. Thus, the reasons for failure of a technology may be political, technological, cultural, or economic and do not necessarily have anything at all to do with its intrinsic potential.

What does this have to say about the development of neurocomputers? The development and availability of neurocomputers are intimately tied to their expected sales volumes. Sales, on the other hand, are dependent on available funding from government and private sources. And such funding is, in turn, dependent on a confused mix of world events, election outcomes, economic conditions, competing technologies, and the individual philosophies of those who provide research and development funding. If we are to believe neural network folklore, the disastrous drop in funding for neural network research that occurred after publication of Minsky and Papert's book *Perceptrons* in the 1960s provides a prime example of how the progress of a technology depends on seemingly random events.

Yet was it such a straw that really broke neural networks' back? We think not. Instead it seems to us that the first sprouting of this technology occurred in an environment too barren for growth. Neural networks need large and powerful computers for proper simulation and investigation. In the early 1960s the available tools were too feeble for proper nourishment of the field. Computers were too small, too expensive, too hard to use, too memory and processor limited, and the idea of a graphical interface was still only a dream. Without such tools, it is difficult to imagine how the technology could have developed and matured. With the wide availability and growing power of today's workstations and personal computers, many problems may never leave the realm of software simulation. Certainly for problems of a few hundreds of neurodes in size, current digital computers are easily powerful enough for applications development. And many potential uses for neural networks can be achieved with just such limited-size networks.

On the other hand, some neurocomputer boards available today are many times faster than even the fastest workstations; one commercial board has been benchmarked in 1988 (by a company other than the manufacturer) as being 35 times faster than a 20 megahertz 80386/80387 Sun workstation, one of the most powerful workstations on the market. The current version of this neurocomputer board is even faster. The speed of this neurocomputer is such, in fact, that it is second only to a supercomputer for neural network emulations (among single-processor systems). In addition to the sheer raw speed of the neurocomputer, it has the advantage of adding enormous amounts of memory, up to 12 megabytes, to be used to store the network's weights and states. Most personal computers and workstations do not have such memory capacity, and thus the size of the network they can simulate is correspondingly reduced. In addition, they sometimes have problems in dealing with memory arrays that are extremely large, particularly with the microprocessors used in IBM-PC systems, which have a segmented memory architecture. Neural network simulations, especially those for backpropagation networks, tend to require a number of such large arrays. So we think that even with the speed and power of today's workstations, there will be a market niche for neurocomputer boards for some time to come.

Neurocomputer hardware systems may face increasing competition from parallel computer systems. We do not think that today's parallel computers are likely to cut too much into the near-term neurocomputer market; however, if and when cheap general-purpose parallel computers become available, present neurocomputer designs will no longer provide a substantial advantage. In saying this we are also assuming that user-friendly operating systems, compilers, and languages will be available for these hypothetical parallel computers. Why would such a development affect neurocomputers? It may be possible to use simulations run on parallel computers to perform real-time applications; this could even cause stand-alone neurocomputers to disappear for a while, only to return in a new form when the needs of neural network technology again begin to outstrip the speed or size of general-purpose computers of their day. Certainly whether or not there are parallel neurocomputers available, the appearance of cheap and efficient parallel computers will once again make computer simulations of neural networks a prime implementation method.

What about neurocomputers implemented in the form of microelectronic systems? Many researchers believe that available chip manufacturing technologies and techniques can continue to provide ever-smaller and more complex electronic packages, perhaps as long as to the end of this century. During this time, we might expect to see chip circuit-element densities increase to perhaps a hundred times current levels. While this may not necessarily translate directly into a hundredfold increase in neural network chip implementation sizes, we should still expect to see significant increases in the size of networks we can implement microelectronically. It seems certain that microelectronic implementations of neural networks are only beginning; the 1990s will see a proliferation of commercial neural network chips. While most, we suspect, will be designed to accomplish a specific application or task, many general-purpose chips or chip sets with fully modifiable synapses will also become available in this period.

Progress is being made in producing neural network chips for some rather sophisticated networks. In particular, Syntonics has introduced its version of an adaptive resonance network during 1989; this is one of the first commercially available neural network chips. We expect other network models, particularly backpropagation networks, to become available almost immediately as well. While none of these chips will be able to build particularly large networks, the prospect is there for true hardware implementations. And we reemphasize that many applications will be solvable with networks built from such small-scale chips.

Over the next few years we also expect optical and optoelectronic implementations of neural networks to become available. The key obstacle for optoelectronic systems noted in chapter 17—the need for faster, larger, and more efficient spatial light modulators—now seems on the way to being overcome. Before the turn of the century, we should see a number of practical all-optical neural network implementations as well. These will all be of networks of a few thousand neurodes or fewer, however. It will probably be considerably longer before systems are available that have the many thousands or millions of neurodes and interconnections necessary to implement very large neural networks.

Weird Science

Among the more arcane possibilities for future neural network implementations are molecular circuits. Researchers in molecular-level implementations of computing regularly meet to share and discuss the latest developments. Hoped-for methods range from etching atom-sized channels in semiconductors to the use of waves induced in carefully engineered configurations of organic molecules. Most of these attempts never leave the laboratory, but some day one will, and we will then see the beginning of a new era in the miniaturization of computing hardware and of microelectronic circuits of all types.

A few years ago, molecular implementations of neural networks received a gift. Workers at the IBM Research Laboratory in Zurich,

Switzerland, developed a type of microscope capable of resolving individual atoms on the surface of a conducting material. This surface-tunneling microscope, and more recent instruments capable of performing similar feats on insulating and organic materials, may help us develop a new era in electronic fabrication in which, in principle, atoms can be individually placed on a material. Fabrication techniques based on the mature versions of these techniques may indeed mark the beginning of the long-awaited era of molecular-level electronic miniaturization.

Another potential revolution is the possibility of literally growing the networks we need. Success in manipulating living things at the molecular level has begun to grow explosively. Recombinant DNA technology and other emerging biological techniques promise to allow us eventually to grow whatever neural configuration we need for a given application. Although researchers in Japan and the United States are beginning to work with this technique, don't hold your breath until C3-PO appears to serve guests in your living room or to translate and provide protocol instruction for you as you travel to exotic lands. The level of sophistication required to produce anything capable of even the simplest applications is way off.

The ethical and legal problems arising when we begin to grow intelligent networks may seem insurmountable from this distance. Such concerns have not traditionally been one of the stumbling blocks to the development of new technologies, however, and the ultimate hierarchical neural network—the one we might expect to exist in a robot of the year 2100—will almost certainly be partially or totally biological in nature. Isaac Asimov's robots, with their positronic brains, may well come to pass but not, we think, in this generation.

Neural Network Theory

A neural network is only as effective at performing a task as the limitations of its paradigm allow it to be. All network paradigms have limitations; we have explored many of these in this book. Backpropagation networks are slow to learn and become unacceptably slow as the network gets larger. Competitive filter networks require finicky training regimens and careful preprocessing of the data. Adaptive resonance networks are complex and unproved and need careful adjustment for effective use. Counterpropagation networks have the drawbacks of any scheme based on competitive filter learning and also lack accuracy in their mappings. We could go on, but the point is that we have not yet discovered the perfect network paradigm that will solve all problems easily and effectively. Probably, in fact, such an all-purpose paradigm does not exist. When we look at the organization of the brain, we realize that it is not a featureless blob but rather has specific substructures that perform specialized tasks. It is likely, therefore, that we will have to develop a similar array of neural network architectures to perform the variety of tasks required for highly sophisticated applications.

The learning laws described in this book were chosen to represent particular classes of such rules. Within each class (hebbian, differential hebbian, competitive filter, outstar, drive reinforcement, backpropagation, and so forth), there is room for many variations, and some of these may indeed replace the classical version of each paradigm. A learning rule ripe for such evolutionary change is backpropagation. Considering the popularity of this network and the number of people using it, it will not be at all surprising if major improvements and extensions appear quickly. One such extension is the one developed by Samad, and briefly described in chapter 14. Other possibilities are presented at nearly every neural network conference or meeting and just as frequently in the literature. The workhorse of the field is likely to remain backpropagation for the next few years; however, more and more people are developing variations and improvements to it so that backpropagation by the mid-1990s will likely bear little resemblance to the learning model we call by that name today.

Networks based on differential learning laws have also shown a similar degree of activity lately and also seem likely to generate frequent and diverse variations over the next months and years. These efforts to extend and enhance existing learning paradigms and architectures are prodded not by fundamental or basic research activities but by the needs of application developers. Already there are applications that demand weight changes proportional to the time rate of change of a neurode's activation. It is not difficult to imagine that other applications will require still other differential laws. Some of them may have characteristics that make them useful in a broad range of applications.

We see two concurrent processes that promise to enhance the development of network models. Each is exciting in its own right, and each resembles not so much a revolution as an evolution in our understanding. The first is the appearance of networks that combine currently known networks in clever and exciting new ways. An excellent example is the counterpropagation network described in chapter 15. Combining competitive filter learning with outstar learning offers much in the way of potential usefulness.

The second evolutionary force is one in which a large number of complete networks are combined in both vertical and horizontal hierarchical structures. Such complex structures are much more similar to the structure of our brains than uniform architectures and offer the possibility of combining several types of sensory input. This allows such systems to perform feats of processing, control, and machine intelligence not remotely possible with individual networks.

Where are new learning paradigms likely to arise? The most promising architectures today are those directly based on biological structures: adaptive resonance networks and competitive filter networks. A number of research groups are working on such direct biological analogs that have effective, if quite limited designs. Researchers are also looking at network algorithms that mimic the evolutionary learning of a species rather than that of individual organisms; this has already given rise to neural networks based on the mathematics of genetics. We feel that the best new paradigms will almost certainly come from the ranks of those who are exploring neural networks from these neurobiological and evolutionary perspectives, perhaps in conjunction with others who can provide a solid mathematical basis for the work.

In the past, theoretical frameworks for understanding neural networks have been developed by researchers trained in the mathematics and metaphors of some other field of study. By metaphor in this context, we mean not only the imagery and vocabulary used to represent ideas in a discipline but also the collection of necessary but generally unexamined assumptions shared by workers in the discipline. Theoretical treatments of neural networks cast in the mathematics and metaphors of signal processing, experimental psychology, neurobiology, statistical mechanics, nonlinear dynamics, computer science, and other fields exist. Probably none of these adopted metaphors provides the ideal perspective in which a general theory of neural networks can be expressed. We are now, however, beginning the third generation of scientists and engineers trained in this technology, and it is out of this, or the next, generation that we expect a consolidating theory will most likely be developed. After that, neural networks will begin to develop its own metaphors and mathematics, and the job of understanding and extending network theory will become easier.

When will the new learning systems come? The answer to that question is entirely speculative; however, we feel sure that by the early 1990s at least one major new paradigm will have been introduced, as well as a large number of significant variations to the tried-and-true backpropagation network.

Applications

The reason most of us care about neural networks is our expectation of what they may be able to do for us in the real world. Neural networks have been developed for a limited number of commercial applications. In chapter 18 and throughout the rest of this book we have explored various applications that researchers have already produced. What does the future hold?

In the long term, we can expect neural networks to be used for applications ranging from the grand and glorious, such as vision and speech systems, to the mundane and pragmatic, such as noise filters and quality control systems. A true vision system, sufficient for a simple robot to maneuver successfully in unknown and unstructured environments, is probably five years off; a more limited version will be practical much sooner. There is already a robot system that melds vision with robot arm motion control to learn eye-hand coordination. This system can be expected to be extended over the next years to produce intensely sophisticated robotic systems.

Speech is, in some ways, a more difficult problem because of its inherent temporal nature and because of the vast amount of language and context understanding required, but the Kohonen voice typewriter and other laboratory systems appear to be making enormous strides toward becoming commercial systems. Continuous, speaker-independent speech systems with nearly unrestricted vocabularies are likely to be another two to five years in development before they are commercially available; however, limited vocabulary systems will be on the market sooner.

What about other application problems? To some extent the availability of practical commercial systems depends on the availability of neural network hardware or at least on high-quality neuro-computers. However, commercial systems for the development of quality control, inspection, and testing systems for industry are very close to being practical now, for limited applications. (One such, a commercial system that "sniffs" airline baggage for explosives, is already on the market.) The biggest need is for a slight improvement in hardware, which will be commercially available soon. In addition, applications in security and process control systems for many industries that are being performed with small neural networks today. Other networks appear in automobiles that are on the market now, and this application realm is expanding rapidly. We should also mention the bounty of potential applications in the field of medicine, particularly in such areas as patient-monitors and instrumentation, as well as direct patient support equipment for the handicapped. And there already are neural network financial expert systems, as well as systems that can understand handwriting. The possible applications for neural networks are nearly unlimited, and their presence in the marketplace is likely to grow enormously.

A Final Word

It is not likely that you will wake up tomorrow morning to find that neural networks have revolutionized your life. It is not even likely that this will have happened six months from now, or a year from now, or even five years from now. Neural network technology is still a tiny, fragile seedling, struggling to survive in a capricious world. We have already seen one similar seedling falter and die. Will the same thing happen this time? We think not, but there is no crystal ball that gives a clear-cut answer. Certainly neural network research and development offers the excitement of a quest, the possibility of dramatic success—and the possibility of disastrous failure. There seem today to be many youthful souls who, no matter what their physical age, possess the requisite adventurous spirit to try to succeed at the difficult goal of making a naturally intelligent artificial system. They may succeed, or they may fail. In either event, we will certainly be the richer for trying. If all we accomplish with our efforts is to have a better understanding and appreciation of the marvelous complexity of our own brains, the journey may well be worth the price. In any event, the quest will be exciting and interesting.

New technologies have a way of changing us as well as the world around us. James Burke said it best when he pointed out that when we change the way we perceive the universe, it is as though the universe itself has changed. By modifying our perceptions of intelligent systems and by generating tools with capabilities and sophistication unmatched in today's world, we may well be generating a new universe to explore and cope with. It will be challenging and difficult and exasperating and scary, but, most of all, it will be fun.

Glossary

accretive associative memory

An associative memory that responds to unfamiliar data by returning the nearest stored data item.

activation function

The function that determines the level of excitement or activity of a neurode for a given input stimulus.

activity

The total level of activity of a neural network or of some portion of the network (such as the activity of a single layer of neurodes). Activity is measured by the value of the activation function of each of the neurodes in the network or layer.

adaline

Acronym for <u>ada</u>ptive <u>line</u>ar element, one of the oldest adaptive filter networks, developed by Bernard Widrow and Ted Hoff of Stanford in 1960.

adaptive

Anything that is able to be modified during operation, generally used to refer to synaptic weights in a neural network. An adaptive weight is one that changes (learns) during training or operation; a nonadaptive weight has a fixed value.

adaptive filter network

A neural network that acts as a filtering system to classify input patterns into categories.

adaptive resonance theory

A learning system introduced by Stephen Grossberg and Gail Carpenter that is truly self-organizing and serves as one of our best models to date of many psychological learning phenomena.

AI

Acronym for **artificial intelligence**.

algebraic sum

The mathematical value computed by adding a series of scalar terms.

algorithm

A recipe or method of solving a particular problem. Usually this consists of a finite number of specific steps involved in the solution.

AM

Acronym for **associative memory**.

analog

Any continuously variable quantity, as opposed, for instance, to binary or discrete quantities.

Glossary

analog computer

A computing device that operates directly on real numbers rather than binary numbers; more specifically, an electronic computer that solves mathematical equations using special-purpose amplifiers to perform specific mathematical operations. By appropriately connecting such *operational amplifiers (op amps)* together, many equations can be solved.

analytic function

Any functional relationship that can be described by a specific, known equation.

annealing

See *simulated annealing*.

architecture

The specific way neurodes are connected together to make a neural network. See also *computer architecture*.

array (of numbers)

A collection of numbers with a specific order. The order of the array elements can be linear, or it can have a higher dimensionality.

ART network

A neural network built following the principles of adaptive resonance theory.

ART 1

Acronym for adaptive resonance theory 1, the first version of adaptive resonance that could process only binary input patterns.

ART 2

Acronym for adaptive resonance theory 2, the second version of adaptive resonance that can process gray-scale input data patterns.

artificial intelligence

A discipline that attempts to mimic the cognitive and symbolic skills of humans using digital computers.

artificial neural system

Another term for neural network, which distinguishes between biological and nonbiological neural systems.

ASCII code

A common means of coding characters as 7- or 8-bit binary numbers, used in most computers today. Each character is represented by a specific binary number, for example, "A" is coded by "0100 0001" in binary or 65 in decimal; "a" is coded by "0110 0001" in binary or 97 in decimal.

associative memory

A memory system that stores information by associating or correlating it with other stored information.

attentional signal

A specific signal to a neurode or network used to instruct the neurode to treat an input stimulus in a special way. Often used as a cue for training.

autoassociative memory

An associative memory in which a stored data item is associated or correlated with itself.

automaton (automata)

A device that can carry out simple or complex tasks with little supervision; a robot.

autonomous learning

Learning characterized by trial and error, with no teacher assistance, that occurs selectively—only important information is learned; see also *unsupervised learning; self-organization.*

avalanche

See *avalanche network.*

avalanche network

A network using a series of outstar structures for learning or execution of patterns, especially spatiotemporal patterns.

axon

The output of a biological neuron, over which signals are sent to other neurons.

axon collateral

One of many branches of an axon.

backpropagation

See *generalized delta rule.*

BAM

Acronym for *bidirectional associative memory.*

basin of attraction

An area of the energy surface of a network in which all network states will converge to a particular network state that represents some item of stored information. Similar in concept to an energy well in physics.

bidirectional associative memory

A crossbar or correlation matrix associative memory where the activation resonates between the two layers of neurodes until a stable state is reached.

binary

Having only two possible values. In neural network technology, the value pairs (0,1) and (1, −1) are common.

binary number system

A counting system in which numbers are represented as a sequence of binary digits, each having only the possible values of 0 or 1. For example, the decimal numbers 1, 2, 3, 4, 5 are represented by the binary numbers 1, 10, 11, 100, 101, respectively.

bipolarization

The process by which a binary vector made up of 1s and 0s is converted to a vector made up of 1s and −1s. Each 0 in the original binary vector is converted to a −1; the original 1s are unchanged.

bit

A binary digit; usually represented as either a 0 or a 1.

Boltzmann machine

A distributed parallel processing algorithm developed by Geoffrey Hinton and Terrence Sejnowski based on statistical mechanics that uses simulated annealing to find stable solution states to problems. This system attempted to overcome some of the recall problems of crossbar networks.

border neurode (of an outstar)

One of the collection of neurodes that receive the output of an outstar neurode.

bottom-up

Signals proceeding from the input layer toward higher levels of a system; used especially in reference to adaptive resonance networks. See also *top-down*.

bus

A data transmission path used by or within a computer; it can refer to a collection of parallel signal lines or an individual signal line.

byte

A unit of binary data; normally it refers to eight binary digits, or eight bits.

CAM

A *content addressable memory*.

CAN

Acronym for *crossbar associative network*.

cell membrane equation

Another name for the *shunting equation,* which defines a more complex version of *outstar learning.*

central nervous system

That part of the nervous system of animals comprising the brain and the spinal cord.

clocked system

An electronic system in that all operations occur in lockstep, paced by a high-frequency oscillator, or "clock."

CNS

Acronym for central nervous system.

coarse-grained architecture

A parallel computer architecture characterized by having few processors or by breaking problems into large blocks for solution.

cognitive functions

The human functions of reasoning and inference.

cognitive tasks

Tasks requiring the use of cognitive functions for performance.

competitive filter associative memory

A self-organizing system developed extensively by Teuvo Kohonen with the property of modeling the *probability distribution function* of the input data set.

competitive learning

A learning system in that neurodes compete with each other for the right to adjust their weights.

computer architecture

The way the components of a computer are connected.

connection weight

The strength of a synaptic connection to a neurode.

connectionism

A term often applied to the use or study of neural networks.

connectionist architecture

A parallel computer architecture that uses many processors, each of which performs a simple computation and has a small amount of memory; each computing node is connected to many other nodes.

connectivity

A measure of the relative or absolute number of connections among the nodes of a parallel computer or among the neurodes of a neural network.

content addressability

That feature of a memory system that enables it to determine the storage location of data based on the contents of the data being stored.

content addressable memory

One that has the trait of content addressability.

coprocessor

A processor in a computing system that works alongside the main processor to enhance system operation.

correlation matrix

A matrix formed by taking the outer product of two column vectors.

counterpropagation network

A hierarchical network with the middle layer using Kohonen learning and the output layer(s) using outstars. The name is derived from the fact that a fully implemented network accepts input and generates output from both sides of the hierarchy, allowing the activation to counterflow through the network.

crossbar network

A neural network with the physical connectivity of a telephone crossbar switch, where each of two layers of neurodes is fully interconnected to each other.

CUPS

See *IPS*.

data compression

A process by that data of a certain size (number of bits) are reduced to a fewer number of bits. Ideally the important information encoded by the original data will still be recoverable from the compressed version.

data domain

The form in which data are cast for transmission or processing. Data domains include the digital-discrete-analog distinctions, as well as others, such as mechanical-chemical-electrical.

dead vectors

In a Kohonen network or counterpropagation network, these are weight vectors that point to a portion of the hypersphere that contains no input pattern vectors. These vectors are constrained by Kohonen learning rules from ever becoming the "winning" neurode; thus they form no part of the resulting probability distribution model.

delta rule

Original training rule that modifies the weights of a neurode by adding a "delta vector" to the current weight. This is the same as the Widrow-Hoff training rule or the LMS training rule used in the adaline. The term may also be used for the *generalized delta rule.*

dendrite

One of the postsynaptic filamentary arms of a neuron used to collect input signals.

derivative

A mathematical relationship that defines the rate of change of a function at any point along the function's curve. It also has the value of the slope of the function's curve at every point along the function.

differential hebbian learning

A version of hebbian learning that assumes that learning occurs in the recipient neurode's synapses only when there is a change in that neurode's activity at the same time as there is a change in the stimulating neurode's activity. Compare to *neohebbian learning* and *hebbian learning.*

digital computer

A computer that performs its fundamental operations using binary numbers.

direction (of a vector)

The second component of a vector, that indicates where the arrow points, the first component being the magnitude of the vector. For example, the direction of an object's velocity vector is the direction in that the object is moving, say east. See *magnitude.*

distributed memory

A memory system that stores information throughout the system rather than in a single identifiable address.

distributed processing

A term often used to refer to processing with neural networks; may also be used to reference standard parallel computer systems.

dot product

A scalar multiplication of two vectors. It can be computed as the sum of the products of their corresponding elements or as the product of their magnitudes times the cosine of the angle between them. Geometrically it corresponds to the length of the projection of one vector on the other.

drive-reinforcement theory

A variation on *differential hebbian learning* that considers not just the current changes in activity in the stimulating and receiving neurodes but all the cumulative changes in each over some significant time period.

DRT

Acronym for *drive reinforcement theory.*

emulator

See *neurocomputer.*

energy surface

A mathematical property of neural networks that corresponds to the energy wells of physics. The concept is useful in understanding the behavior of many networks.

ENIAC

One of the first digital computers, built in the 1940s, it was based on the decimal number system instead of the binary number system used in today's computers.

excitation

Leading to an increased activation within a neurode.

excitatory (synapse)

A synapse that, when stimulated by an input signal, causes an increased activation in its attached neurode.

exclusive OR

A binary function that returns 1 if one, but not both, of its two binary inputs is a 1; otherwise the function returns 0.

expert system

A system specifically designed to display a high degree of knowledge about a specific, limited subject. Usually these are capable of making inferences or decisions based on that knowledge and are normally implemented as a collection of if–then or production rules.

exponential decay

A mathematical function with an incremental loss in value proportional to the function's current value at each increment. Such a function rapidly decays from its initial value to near-zero but can never actually reach exactly zero.

fail soft

The smooth degradation of performance of a system as individual components of the system fail; synonymous with "graceful degradation."

fan-out layer

A layer that receives an input pattern and then, by virtue of its interconnections, presents the entire input pattern to each neurode in the subsequent layer.

fast Fourier transform (FFT)

One of a set of algorithms that efficiently perform a *Fourier transform* on a digital computer.

fault-tolerant

Has the property of being *fail soft*.

feed-forward network

A network in that the signal pathway goes only one way—from the input layer to the output layer.

feedback

The process whereby part of the output signal of a circuit echoes back to the input of the circuit, usually after some filtering operation.

feedback competition

A means of implementing competition among the neurodes of a network. The output pattern is echoed back to the input layer after thresholding or some other filtering process. See also *lateral inhibition*.

firmware

Computer instructions contained in a hardware electronic chip, such as a read-only memory.

Fourier transform

A form of spectral analysis in which the relative amount of each frequency contained in a time-domain signal is plotted versus that frequency.

frequency domain

The signal domain in which a signal is presented as a function of frequency. See also *time domain*.

fully interconnected

A neural network or layer that has the output of every neurode in one layer serving as an input signal to every neurode in the other layer, and vice versa. Sometimes called "fully connected."

Glossary

gain

(1) in electronics, the ratio of the value of the output to the value of the input of a system, similar in concept to a volume control on a radio or television; (2) in ART networks, a term describing the ability of a particular subsystem to affect the operation of its target layer.

generalized delta rule

A modification to the original delta rule used by backpropagation networks; sometimes referred to simply as the "delta rule."

geotopic map

A topology-preserving map corresponding to the physical structure, or geography, of some area or location.

gestalt

A pattern so unified that its properties as a whole pattern cannot be derived from the properties of its parts.

giga-

Prefix meaning U.S. billion; 10^9.

global

A signal or feature that is sent to all neurodes or subsystems of a layer or system.

graceful degradation

See *fail soft*.

graded learning

Learning systems that provide performance "grades" as feedback rather than specific error values; they do not require knowledge of the specific answer for a given input pattern, only the ability to rank the network's performance.

grandmother cell

An output neurode that acts as the sole recognizer of a particular input pattern; also called "grandmother node."

gray-scale

A range of possible discrete (noncontinuous) values for each element of the input vector to a neural network.

hardware

Systems composed of actual electronic, optical, or other devices and circuits.

hashing algorithm

A scheme of determining the location to store data in a database. The data to be stored are processed by a "hash function" that does nothing more than convert the value of the data to a numerical address. This address is the location at which the data will be stored in the database. The hash function generally has the property that nonidentical data will nearly always produce unique addresses.

hebbian learning

A training rule in which learning takes place in a synapse only if both of its associated neurons are active at the same time.

heteroassociative memory

An associative memory in that stored data items are associated or correlated with other, different data items.

hidden units (layer)

See *middle units*.

hierarchical network

A network consisting of at least three distinct layers of neurodes. In networks with more than three layers, each succeeding layer often represents successively higher levels of processing.

Hopfield networks

Named after John Hopfield of Caltech, this is another name for any one of several designs for *crossbar networks*.

hyper-

A prefix to indicate that the geometrical form following may be of any dimensionality, including two dimensions, three dimensions, or any higher dimensions. See *hypercube; hyperplane; hypersphere*.

hypercube (computer)

A connection scheme for parallel processing in which, for an n-dimensional hypercube, any node in the system can communicate with any other node in at most n steps.

hyperplane

A generalized n-dimensional construct equivalent to a plane in three-dimensional space. A straight line is a one-dimensional hyperplane in 2D space; a plane is the two-dimensional hyperplane in 3D space; etc.

hypersphere

A generalized n-dimensional construct equivalent to a sphere in three-dimensional space. A circle is a two-dimensional hypersphere.

inheritance

A characteristic of a language or database that ensures that specific data items include the properties of any groups containing the data items. Thus, an instance of pet cat named "Delilah," a member of group "cat," inherits the characteristics "furry," "warm-blooded," etc.

inhibition

Leading to decreased activation in the nodes.

inhibitory (synapse)

A synapse that, when stimulated by an input signal, causes a decreased activation in its attached neurode.

input transfer function

See *activation function.*

input vector

The pattern presented to the input neurodes of a network.

interconnect

One of the pathways over which neurodes communicate in a neural network.

interneuron

A neuron structure along the axon of a primary neuron that distributes the primary neuron's activity to other neurons.

interpolative associative memory

An associative memory that responds to unfamiliar data inputs by producing a blended or interpolated response of the nearest stored data patterns.

involuntary (temporal pattern recall)

Recollection of a temporal pattern sequence that, once started, cannot be changed or stopped.

IPS

Acronym for interconnect updates per second. This is becoming a standard unit of measure for the operational speed of a neural network implementation and refers to the speed at that synaptic weights can be updated. Sometimes referred to as CUPS ("connection operations per second").

Kohonen self-organizing network

See *competitive filter associative memory.*

Kolmogorov's theorem

A mathematical theorem proving that any real mapping can be exactly performed by a three-layer neural network of limited size.

lateral inhibition

A way of introducing competition among the neurodes of a network layer, characterized by a specific pattern of lateral, or intralayer, interconnections.

learning law

A rule for updating the synaptic weights of a neural network during training.

linear

In reference to a function or other mathematical relationship, any mathematical relationship that can be described as a constant times one element, possibly with the addition of another constant. A linear relationship can be expressed with the elements raised to the first power, and with no cross-terms. For example, $y = (4x + 10)/2.4$ is linear; $y = (4x^2 + 10)/2.4$ and $xy = 1$ are not.

linearly separable

As applied to a two-category classification problem, it means that all examples of the two categories ("A" and "not A") can be separated by a single straight hyperplane.

Lisp

A high level computer language particularly suited to symbolic and list processing; often used in artificial intelligence programming.

LMS rule

The least mean squared training rule, or the delta rule.

long-term memory

Memory that persists over extended periods of time; memory associated with learning. See also *short-term memory*.

madaline

Acronym for multilayered adalines; an array of adaline adaptive filter elements.

magnitude (of a vector)

The first component of a vector corresponding to the length of the vector; for example, the magnitude of an object's velocity vector is the object's speed. See *direction*.

mapping

An association of one collection of patterns or numbers with another collection of patterns or numbers. A mathematical function $y = f(x)$ is a mapping from the legal x values to their corresponding y functional values.

matrix
> A two-dimensional array of scalar elements organized into rows and columns, with all rows and all columns the same size. If the row size is the same as the column size, it is a square matrix.

meatware
> A slang term referring to biological neural systems used in neural experiments. See also *wetware*.

memory system
> A system that can store and recall information on demand.

middle units
> Neurodes or nodes with no direct connection to either the input or output of the network; sometimes called *hidden units*.

monotonically increasing function
> A function with the property that its value at larger values of its variable is always larger than the function's value at smaller variable values; such a function's graph always appears to slope upward to the right.

motor functions
> Functions of a biological organism relating to muscle movement; when used in conjunction with robotic systems, it refers to functions controlling movements of the robot's physical system, including locomotion, and hand or arm movement.

MRII
> Acronym for madaline rule II which is an adjustment principle for the madaline. Under this system, the change made on the madaline elements is always that which minimally disturbs the system.

multipass network
> A hierarchical network where the network activity flows from the input layer to the output layer, and then back through the network at least once before a stable state is reached. An example is the backpropagation network during training.

multiprocessor
> A parallel processor.

neohebbian learning
> A mathematical form of *hebbian learning* developed by Stephen Grossberg and Michael Cohen of Boston University.

NETtalk

A neural network system that learned to reproduced phonemes to pronounce English-language words accurately
from text.

netware

Software designed for use with neurocomputers or simulations of neural networks. Nonneural network usage may
refer to systems used to supervise local-area networks of
personal computers.

network paradigm

In this book, the features of a neural network solution that
make it different from other neural networks, typically including the connection scheme, the transfer function, and the
learning law of the network. The specific sizes of the network layers are not distinguishing features.

neural network

(1) A type of data processing system whose physical architecture is inspired by the structure of biological neural
systems. (2) One of many networks composed of neurons,
dendrites, axons, synapses, and other biological structures
making up the neural systems of living beings.

neurocomputer

A dedicated, special-purpose digital computer designed to
efficiently perform the mathematical operations common in
neural network simulations.

neurode

The element of an artificial neural network that corresponds
to the neuron of biological networks; also known as *processing element*.

neuron

A biological neural cell.

node

(1) An individual processor and associated computing and
memory chips in a parallel computer; (2) a functional grouping of neurodes that acts as a single unit within one layer of
a network.

nonlinear device

A device for which the value of the output is not a constant
multiple of the value of the input.

nonspecific

Global; the term is usually found in descriptions of *adaptive
resonance networks*.

on center–off surround

Another name for *lateral inhibition*.

op amp

A shorthand term for *operational amplifier*.

operational amplifier

An electronic amplifier specially constructed to perform a mathematical operation such as addition, subtraction, multiplication, integration, or differentiation.

optical computers

Computers that perform their mathematical functions by the manipulation of beams of light. If the computers perform some processing by optical means and some by electronic means, they are called optoelectronic or hybrid optical computers.

orthogonal

A characteristic of vectors in which they have no geometric projection upon each other. In normal Euclidean space, this is equivalent to being perpendicular to each other.

oscillator

A system with output that varies regularly over a limited range. A pendulum is an example of an oscillator; a binary oscillator vibrates rhythmically between two specific values.

output function

The function describing the relationship between the output of a neurode and its internal activation level.

output transfer function

See *output function*.

outstar avalanche

A type of neural network that is capable of performing a temporal series of recall operations. See *avalanche network*.

padaline

Contraction of "polynomial adaline," Don Specht's variation on the adaline that uses a polynomial surface to categorize input patterns. Also called "polynomial discriminant method" or "PDM."

parallel distributed processing

Another term for computing with neural networks.

parallel processor

A digital processor design that operates on several parts of a problem simultaneously.

parity

A means of determining if errors occurred during transmission. There are many varieties of parity; a common one is to count the number of 1-bits in each block of binary data and to add an extra "parity bit," which is 1 if the count was even and 0 if the count was odd. The receiving party can then count the 1-bits in the received data and decide if the block arrived without error. Simple parity can detect only single-bit errors, not multiple-bit errors.

PDP

Acronym for *parallel distributed processing.*

PE

Acronym for *processing element.*

Perceptrons

Book by Marvin Minsky in 1969 that proved single-layer neural networks could not solve anything except linearly separable problems. The title also refers to a very early neural network developed by Frank Rosenblatt, that had the first training algorithm.

pixel

The smallest unit of information in a picture or pattern, for example, a single dot on a CRT screen. Derived from "picture element."

plastic

Adaptive, capable of modification.

postprocessing

Treatment of a signal to extract additional information after it has been processed by a signal processing system.

postprocessor

Postprocessing hardware or software.

postsynaptic

Pertaining to the input signal arriving at the neurode or neuron after it has been modified or weighted by the synapse; compare to *presynaptic.*

preprocessing

Treatment of a signal to prepare it for processing by a signal processing system, for example, normalization or Fourier transformation of the signal.

preprocessor

Preprocessing hardware or software. Used to convert raw input signals into a form acceptable to a neural network or other processing system.

Glossary

presynaptic
> Pertaining to a signal after it leaves its source, but before it is modified or weighted by a synapse. Compare to *postsynaptic*.

probability distribution function
> A functional relationship that correlates a particular input pattern with its likelihood of appearing in the input data set; see *competitive filter associative memory; Kohonen self-organizing system*.

processing element
> A neurode.

processing node
> In a parallel computer, an individual architectural element that acts as a data processor; unlike a neurode, the parallel computer's processing nodes may contain memory, coprocessors, and other highly complex circuit elements, as well as the local processor itself.

Prolog
> A computer programming language especially suited for logical analysis and reasoning problems; derived from "Programming with Logic." Prolog is commonly used for solving artificial intelligence problems, particularly in Europe and the Far East.

RAM
> Acronym for random access memory.

random access memory
> As generally used, integrated circuits in which information can be stored and retrieved in any order. The working memory of digital computers is composed of such chips. Compare to *content addressable memory*.

randomization
> The process by which a collection of vectors is randomly oriented about the unit hypersphere or about some portion of the unit hypersphere.

read-only memory
> A memory chip in that the contents are frozen so that they can be retrieved but not modified, generally used to supply permanent programming instructions for high-speed access.

real-time
> Refers to events taking place concurrently with the operation of a system. A real-time system is one that can operate (ac-

cept and process input data) concurrently with the actual events and thus keep up with events as they happen.

reset

In a neural network, the process of shutting off and keeping off all currently active nodes in a system without interfering with the ability of inactive nodes to become active.

resonance

When used in reference to a neural network's activity, it refers to a state of the network such that activation flowing between layers of the network is self-sustaining and generates no changes to the activity patterns of any of the layers involved. The network has thus reached a stable state, where no activity changes occur.

robust

A system that has one or both of the following attributes: (1) it can continue to operate reasonably well even with the loss of function of a portion of the system, or (2) it can successfully generate the correct output, even when the input is incomplete or garbled.

ROM

Acronym for read-only memory.

scalar

A quantity that consists simply of a numerical size; a constant. (Compare *vector* and *matrix*.)

self-organization

The process by which a neural network learns about its input data without the aid of an external tutor. Self-organizing systems do not need to be told the correct response to a particular input pattern; rather, they determine their own responses to the input. See also *autonomous systems*.

self-organizing system

A neural network that trains without being provided with the correct answer and that physically orders its connections during training in such a way that the resulting physical structure of the network models some aspect of the training data's organization.

short-term memory

The short time interval during which a signal exists in a biological or artificial neural system before it decays or causes learning to occur.

Glossary

shunting equation
> A more complex form of outstar learning than the one developed in this book. Also called "cell membrane equations."

simulated annealing
> The process of slowly lowering the amount of random noise introduced into the weights and/or input signals of a network as training progresses.

simulation program
> A software program that directs a digital computer to mimic the operation of a neural network.

single-pass network
> A hierarchical network where the activation flows from input layer to output layer only. (Compare to *multipass network*.) An example is the *counterpropagation network*.

software
> The stored program that dictates the operation of a digital computer.

sparse coding
> A method of encoding data so that the resulting patterns have many fewer 1-bits than 0-bits. This technique is useful in improving the storage capacity of *crossbar networks*.

spatiotemporal pattern
> A pattern characterized by changes in both space and time; a time-dependent spatial pattern.

spectral analysis
> See *Fourier transform*.

spin glass
> A material with the magnetic fields of the atoms pointing in random directions even though the atoms may be ordered. The mathematics of spin glasses is similar to the mathematics of *crossbar networks*.

spurious minima
> Extra, unwanted depressions in the energy surface of a network that cause incorrect responses to input stimuli.

state
> A particular collection of weights and activations of a single neurode or within a neural network.

statistical mechanics
> The branch of physics dealing with the statistics of large collections of atoms or other simple physical entities.

stored program
> See *software*.

summed input

The weighted, algebraic sum of the individual postsynaptic input signals.

symbolic processing

Data processing that primarily involves the manipulation of symbols rather than numbers.

synapse

(1) In biology, the junction between an axon collateral and a dendrite; (2) in neural networks, the junction at an interconnect's end that joins the output of one neurode (or a signal from the environment) to the input of another neurode.

system clock

A high-frequency binary *oscillator* that paces the operation of a digital computer and keeps every part of the system synchronized with every other part.

test set

A collection of data patterns different from the training set but similar to it used to judge the effectiveness of a network's training.

threshold

The activation level that the neurode must attain before its output rises above zero.

threshold function

The mathematical function enforcing the threshold.

time domain

The signal domain in which the signal is presented as a function of time. See *frequency domain; Fourier transform.*

toggle

A neural structure that has the property of reset; also called "dipoles." Toggles are the basic unit of the storage and input layers in *ART 1 networks.*

tonotopic map

A topology-preserving map that corresponds to an ascending or descending ordered set of frequency inputs.

top-down

Signals proceeding from higher (later) levels in the network to lower (earlier) levels in the network. See also *bottom-up.*

topology

The mathematical study of geometrical shapes and their properties.

topology-preserving map

> A network organized in such a fashion that its physical structure models some aspect of the topology of the input data patterns. The topology might be a sequence of frequencies in an auditory system (*tonotopic map*), or the physical organization of a particular area (*geotopic map*), or some other feature of the data patterns. See also *competitive filter associative memory; self-organizing system.*

training set

> A collection of data typical of that which a neural network will see in operation, and that is used to train the network.

transfer function

> A mathematical function that relates the input or some state of a system to the output or other state of the system. In a neurode, the transfer function includes the combined effects of the input function, the activation function, and the output function.

transpose (a matrix)

> The process by which a matrix of size $(a \times b)$ is changed to one of size $(b \times a)$. Each row becomes the corresponding column of the transposed matrix; the first row is the first column of the transpose, the second row is the second column of the transpose, and so on.

Traveling Salesman Problem

> A classic problem in computer science. It is an optimization problem: what is the optimal path for a salesman to take if he must visit a number of cities of varying distances and paths with the constraint that he must not visit any city more than once? This simple statement of the problem conceals its profound importance to such industries as airlines, long distance telephone companies, and delivery services.

TSP

> Acronym for *Traveling Salesman Problem.*

unidirectional counterpropagation network

> A variation of the counterpropagation network that accepts input data only from one side of the network and responses from the other side of the network. See also *counterpropagation network.*

uniprocessor

> A serial digital processor.

unsupervised learning

> Learning that occurs without the system being provided with the correct answers. Also called "unsupervised training." See *autonomous learning; self organization.*

vector

> A quantity that consists of a magnitude and a direction. A vector is usually represented by an arrow with its tail at the origin of the coordinate system. The length of the arrow represents the magnitude of the vector and the direction the arrow points represents the vector's direction. Vectors are often broken down into their component magnitudes along each of the coordinate system axes. This is commonly expressed as a column or row matrix where each matrix element is the magnitude along one of these axes. (See also *vector sum; magnitude; direction*)

vector quantization

> A process that replaces a probability distribution model of an input data set with a smaller, proportional representation of vectors that represent input data features.

vector sum

> The vector quantity computed by adding two vectors together. Two vectors, A and B, are added by drawing B with its tail at the arrow end of A (instead of at the origin of the coordinate system). The result vector, A+B, is drawn from A's tail to B's arrow. See also *vector.*

vectorcardiograph

> A particular kind of electrocardiograph that takes heart activity information simultaneously along three perpendicular directions.

vertex

> In a geometrical figure, a corner. Each corner of a cube, for example, is a vertex. A sphere has no vertices (or, rather, an infinite number of them).

vigilance

> The characteristic of autonomous systems by which they learn more or less detail in a particular associative category.

virtual

> Effective but not real. The image in a mirror can be a virtual image that can be seen, but its apparent location does not correspond to actual rays of light in that location.

virtual processor

In a neurocomputer, the effective processor simulating a neurode in a neural network. Because one or a few physical processors mimic many neurodes, the neurodes are only virtual neurodes; they are effectively there, but there is no physical device corresponding to a single neurode.

VLSI

Acronym for very large scale integration; the process of manufacturing integrated circuits with several hundred thousand components on each chip.

voluntary (temporal pattern recall)

Recall of a time-series of patterns that is under the control of the recalling system, so that the time series can be modified or stopped at will.

von Neumann architecture

The architecture used in virtually all serial digital computers today, characterized by the use of the binary number system, a stored program of instructions, a single processor, a system clock, and a separate memory.

weight (synaptic)

A measure of the amount a synapse affects the signal passing through it; also called "synaptic strength."

weight vector

The vector that has components corresponding to the weights on the interconnects of a neurode.

weighted sum

Computed by multiplying the value of each input signal by its corresponding weight and then algebraically adding the resulting terms together. Mathematically this is equivalent to computing the dot product of the weight vector and the input vector.

wetware

Neural systems in living beings.

Widrow-Hoff training rule

The original *delta rule,* or the *LMS rule.*

XOR

Abbreviation for *exclusive OR* function.

Index

Index

Index

Index